The NEW ENCYCLOPEDIA *of* SOU

D0562199

VOLUME 1 : RELIGION

Volumes to appear in

The New Encyclopedia of Southern Culture

are:

Agriculture and Industry	*Law and Politics*
Architecture	*Literature*
Art	*Media*
Education	*Music*
Environment	*Myth, Manners, and Memory*
Ethnicity	*Race*
Folklife	*Recreation*
Foodways	*Religion*
Gender	*Science and Medicine*
Geography	*Social Class*
History	*Urbanization*
Language	*Violence*

The NEW

ENCYCLOPEDIA *of* SOUTHERN CULTURE

CHARLES REAGAN WILSON General Editor

JAMES G. THOMAS JR. Managing Editor

ANN J. ABADIE Associate Editor

VOLUME 1

Religion

SAMUEL S. HILL Volume Editor

Sponsored by

THE CENTER FOR THE STUDY OF SOUTHERN CULTURE

at the University of Mississippi

THE UNIVERSITY OF NORTH CAROLINA PRESS

Chapel Hill

This book was published with the
assistance of the Anniversary Endowment Fund
of the University of North Carolina Press.
Designed by Richard Hendel
Set in Minion types by Tseng Information Systems, Inc.
Manufactured in the United States of America
The paper in this book meets the guidelines for permanence and
durability of the Committee on Production Guidelines for Book
Longevity of the Council on Library Resources.

Library of Congress Cataloging-in-Publication Data

The new encyclopedia of Southern culture / Charles Reagan
Wilson, general editor ; James G. Thomas Jr., managing editor ;
Ann J. Abadie, associate editor.

p. cm.

Rev. ed. of: Encyclopedia of Southern culture. 1991.

"Sponsored by The Center for the Study of Southern Culture at
the University of Mississippi."

Includes bibliographical references and index.

Contents: — v. 1. Religion.

ISBN-13: 978-0-8078-3003-1 (cloth : v. 1 : alk. paper)

ISBN-10: 0-8078-3003-8 (cloth : v. 1 : alk. paper)

ISBN-13: 978-0-8078-5674-1 (pbk. : v. 1 : alk. paper)

ISBN-10: 0-8087-5674-6 (pbk. : v. 1 : alk. paper)

1. Southern States — Civilization — Encyclopedias. 2. Southern
States — Encyclopedias. I. Wilson, Charles Reagan. II. Thomas,
James G. III. Abadie, Ann J. IV. University of Mississippi.
Center for the Study of Southern Culture.
V. Encyclopedia of Southern culture.

F209.N47 2006

975.003 — dc22

2005024807

The *Encyclopedia of Southern Culture*, sponsored by the Center for
the Study of Southern Culture at the University of Mississippi, was
published by the University of North Carolina Press in 1989.

cloth   10 09 08 07 06   5 4 3 2 1

paper   10 09 08 07 06   5 4 3 2 1

Tell about the South. What it's like there.

What do they do there. Why do they live there.

Why do they live at all.

WILLIAM FAULKNER

Absalom, Absalom!

CONTENTS

In 1989, years of planning and hard work came to fruition when the University of North Carolina Press joined the Center for the Study of Southern Culture at the University of Mississippi to publish the *Encyclopedia of Southern Culture*. While all those involved in writing, reviewing, editing, and producing the volume believed it would be received as a vital contribution to our understanding of the American South, no one could have anticipated fully the widespread acclaim it would receive from reviewers and other commentators. But the *Encyclopedia* was indeed celebrated, not only by scholars but also by popular audiences with a deep, abiding interest in the region. At a time when some people talked of the "vanishing South," the book helped remind a national audience that the region was alive and well, and it has continued to shape national perceptions of the South through the work of its many users — journalists, scholars, teachers, students, and general readers.

As the introduction to the *Encyclopedia* noted, its conceptualization and organization reflected a cultural approach to the South. It highlighted such issues as the core zones and margins of southern culture, the boundaries where "the South" overlapped with other cultures, the role of history in contemporary culture, and the centrality of regional consciousness, symbolism, and mythology. By 1989 scholars had moved beyond the idea of cultures as real, tangible entities, viewing them instead as abstractions. The *Encyclopedia*'s editors and contributors thus included a full range of social indicators, trait groupings, literary concepts, and historical evidence typically used in regional studies, carefully working to address the distinctive and characteristic traits that made the American South a particular place. The introduction to the *Encyclopedia* concluded that the fundamental uniqueness of southern culture was reflected in the volume's composite portrait of the South. We asked contributors to consider aspects that were unique to the region but also those that suggested its internal diversity. The volume was not a reference book of southern history, which explained something of the design of entries. There were fewer essays on colonial and antebellum history than on the postbellum and modern periods, befitting our conception of the volume as one trying not only to chart the cultural landscape of the South but also to illuminate the contemporary era.

When C. Vann Woodward reviewed the *Encyclopedia* in the *New York Review of Books*, he concluded his review by noting "the continued liveliness of interest in the South and its seeming inexhaustibility as a field of study." Research on the South, he wrote, furnishes "proof of the value of the *Encyclopedia* as a scholarly undertaking as well as suggesting future needs for revision or supplement to keep up with ongoing scholarship." The decade and a half since the publication of the *Encyclopedia of Southern Culture* have certainly suggested that Woodward was correct. The American South has undergone significant changes that make for a different context for the study of the region. The South has undergone social, economic, political, intellectual, and literary transformations, creating the need for a new edition of the *Encyclopedia* that will remain relevant to a changing region. Globalization has become a major issue, seen in the South through the appearance of Japanese automobile factories, Hispanic workers who have immigrated from Latin America or Cuba, and a new prominence for Asian and Middle Eastern religions that were hardly present in the 1980s South. The African American return migration to the South, which started in the 1970s, dramatically increased in the 1990s, as countless books simultaneously appeared asserting powerfully the claims of African Americans as formative influences on southern culture. Politically, southerners from both parties have played crucial leadership roles in national politics, and the Republican Party has dominated a near-solid South in national elections. Meanwhile, new forms of music, like hip-hop, have emerged with distinct southern expressions, and the term "dirty South" has taken on new musical meanings not thought of in 1989. New genres of writing by creative southerners, such as gay and lesbian literature and "white trash" writing, extend the southern literary tradition.

Meanwhile, as Woodward foresaw, scholars have continued their engagement with the history and culture of the South since the publication of the *Encyclopedia*, raising new scholarly issues and opening new areas of study. Historians have moved beyond their earlier preoccupation with social history to write new cultural history as well. They have used the categories of race, social class, and gender to illuminate the diversity of the South, rather than a unified "mind of the South." Previously underexplored areas within the field of southern historical studies, such as the colonial era, are now seen as formative periods of the region's character, with the South's positioning within a larger Atlantic world a productive new area of study. Cultural memory has become a major topic in the exploration of how the social construction of "the South" benefited some social groups and exploited others. Scholars in many disciplines have made the southern identity a major topic, and they have used a variety of methodologies to suggest what that identity has meant to different social groups. Literary critics have adapted cultural theories to the South and have raised the issue of postsouthern literature to a major category of concern as well as exploring the links between the literature of the American South and that of the Caribbean. Anthropologists have used different theoretical formulations from literary critics, providing models for their fieldwork in southern communities. In the past 30 years anthropologists have set increasing numbers of their ethnographic studies in the South, with many of them now exploring topics specifically linked to southern cultural issues. Scholars now place the Native American story, from prehistory to the contemporary era, as a central part of southern history. Comparative and interdisciplinary approaches to the South have encouraged scholars to look at such issues as the borders and boundaries of the South, specific places and spaces with distinct identities within the American South, and the global and transnational Souths, linking the American South with many formerly colonial societies around the world.

The first edition of the *Encyclopedia of Southern Culture* anticipated many of these approaches and indeed stimulated the growth of Southern Studies as a distinct interdisciplinary field. The Center for the Study of Southern Culture has worked for more than a quarter century to encourage research and teaching about the American South. Its academic programs have produced graduates who have gone on to write interdisciplinary studies of the South, while others have staffed the cultural institutions of the region and in turn encouraged those institutions to document and present the South's culture to broad public audiences. The center's conferences and publications have continued its long tradition of promoting understanding of the history, literature, and music of the South, with new initiatives focused on southern foodways, the future of the South, and the global Souths, expressing the center's mission to bring the best current scholarship to broad public audiences. Its documentary studies projects build oral and visual archives, and the New Directions in Southern Studies book series, published by the University of North Carolina Press, offers an important venue for innovative scholarship.

Since the *Encyclopedia of Southern Culture* appeared, the field of Southern Studies has dramatically developed, with an extensive network now of academic and research institutions whose projects focus specifically on the interdisciplinary study of the South. The Center for the Study of the American South at the University of North Carolina at Chapel Hill, led by Director Harry Watson and Associate Director and *Encyclopedia* coeditor William Ferris, publishes the lively journal *Southern Cultures* and is now at the organizational center of many other Southern Studies projects. The Institute for Southern Studies at the University of South Carolina, the Southern Intellectual History Circle, the Society for the Study of Southern Literature, the Southern Studies Forum of the European American Studies Association, the new Deep South Regional Humanities Center at Tulane University, and the South Atlantic Humanities Center (at the Virginia Foundation for the Humanities, the University of Virginia, and Virginia Polytechnic Institute and State University) express the recent expansion of interest in regional study.

Observers of the American South have had much to absorb, given the rapid pace of recent change. The institutional framework for studying the South is broader and deeper than ever, yet the relationship between the older verities of regional study and new realities remains unclear. Given the extent of changes in the American South and in Southern Studies since the publication of the *Encyclopedia of Southern Culture*, the need for a new edition of that work is clear. Therefore, the Center for the Study of Southern Culture has once again joined the University of North Carolina Press to produce *The New Encyclopedia of Southern Culture*. As readers of the original edition will quickly see, *The New Encyclopedia* follows many of the scholarly principles and editorial conventions established in the original, but with one key difference; rather than being published in a single hardback volume, *The New Encyclopedia* is presented in a series of shorter individual volumes that build on the 24 original subject categories used in the *Encyclopedia* and adapt them to new scholarly developments. Some earlier *Encyclopedia* categories have been reconceptualized in light of new academic interests. For example, the subject section originally titled "Women's Life" is reconceived as a new volume, *Gender*, and the original "Black Life" section is more broadly interpreted as a volume on race. These changes reflect new analytical concerns that place the study of women and blacks in broader cultural systems, reflecting the emergence of, among other topics, the study of male culture and of whiteness. Both volumes draw as well from the rich recent scholarship on women's life and black life. In addition, topics with some thematic coherence are combined in a volume, such as *Law and Politics* and *Agriculture and Industry*. One new topic, *Foodways*, is the basis of a separate volume, reflecting its new prominence in the interdisciplinary study of southern culture.

Numerous individual topical volumes together make up *The New Encyclopedia of Southern Culture* and extend the reach of the reference work to wider audiences. This approach should enhance the use of the *Encyclopedia* in academic courses and is intended to be convenient for readers with more focused interests within the larger context of southern culture. Readers will have handy access to one-volume, authoritative, and comprehensive scholarly treatments of the major areas of southern culture.

We have been fortunate that, in nearly all cases, subject consultants who offered crucial direction in shaping the topical sections for the original edition have agreed to join us in this new endeavor as volume editors. When new volume editors have been added, we have again looked for respected figures who can provide not only their own expertise but also strong networks of scholars to help develop relevant lists of topics and to serve as contributors in their areas. The reputations of all our volume editors as leading scholars in their areas encouraged the contributions of other scholars and added to *The New Encyclopedia*'s authority as a reference work.

The New Encyclopedia of Southern Culture builds on the strengths of articles in the original edition in several ways. For many existing articles, original authors agreed to update their contributions with new interpretations and theoretical perspectives, current statistics, new bibliographies, or simple factual developments that needed to be included. If the original contributor was unable to update an article, the editorial staff added new material or sent it to another scholar for assessment. In some cases, the general editor and volume editors selected a new contributor if an article seemed particularly dated and new work indicated the need for a fresh perspective. And importantly, where new developments have warranted treatment of topics not addressed in the original edition, volume editors have commissioned entirely new essays and articles that are published here for the first time.

The American South embodies a powerful historical and mythical presence, both a complex environmental and geographic landscape and a place of the imagination. Changes in the region's contemporary socioeconomic realities and new developments in scholarship have been incorporated in the conceptualization and approach of *The New Encyclopedia of Southern Culture*. Anthropologist Clifford Geertz has spoken of culture as context, and this encyclopedia looks at the American South as a complex place that has served as the context for cultural expression. This volume provides information and perspective on the diversity of cultures in a geographic and imaginative place with a long history and distinctive character.

The *Encyclopedia of Southern Culture* was produced through major grants from the Program for Research Tools and Reference Works of the National Endowment for the Humanities, the Ford Foundation, the Atlantic-Richfield Foundation, and the Mary Doyle Trust. We are grateful as well to the individual donors to the Center for the Study of Southern Culture who have directly or indirectly supported work on *The New Encyclopedia of Southern Culture*. We thank the volume editors for their ideas in reimagining their subjects and the contributors of articles for their work in extending the usefulness of the book in new ways. We acknowledge the support and contributions of the faculty and staff at the Center for the Study of Southern Culture. Finally, we want especially to honor the work of William Ferris and Mary Hart on the *Encyclopedia of Southern Culture*. Bill, the founding director of the Center for the Study of Southern Culture, was coeditor, and his good work recruiting authors, editing text, selecting images, and publicizing the volume among a wide network of people was, of course, invaluable. Despite the many changes in the new encyclopedia, Bill's influence remains. Mary "Sue" Hart was also an invaluable member of the original encyclopedia team, bringing the careful and precise eye of the librarian, and an iconoclastic spirit, to our work.

INTRODUCTION

Scholars have long recognized religion as a key factor in the culture of the American South. Since the early 19th century, evangelical Protestant groups have dominated the region's religious life. Baptists, Methodists, Presbyterians at times, Pentecostal and holiness groups—all have fully or tangentially shared much theology, ritual, and social attitude. Differences in religious behavior and belief among rich and poor, black and white, urban and rural, and men and women have also been notable in defining religion's role in southern life. Although the nation as a whole was historically more diverse than the South in its religious demography and practice, the region can indeed be seen as pluralistic in the presence of Roman Catholics and Jews, if in smaller numbers than elsewhere in the nation. The image of the Bible Belt is a deeply entrenched one that shapes national understanding, and sometimes misunderstanding, of the South.

The *Religion* section of the *Encyclopedia of Southern Culture* charted the religious landscape of the region. The overview essay provided a historical narrative and also analyzed distinctive liturgical forms and theological beliefs that anchored an interdenominational Protestant tradition. Thematic articles explored major expressions of religious influence in the South, ways of understanding its defining features, and diverse points of entry into religious life within a regional context. Topical entries gave factual information for select religious figures, leading denominations and religious organizations, and concepts important to the region's religious development.

Since the *Encyclopedia*'s publication in 1989, change has been palpable in the American South, including in its spiritual life. Immigration has brought Roman Catholics from Hispanic traditions in numbers that have made that religion of growing prominence in the South. Not only are new Catholic churches appearing in the once solid Protestant South, but Protestantism itself is embracing change through new evangelistic, missionary, and humanitarian efforts to assist newcomers. Immigrants from the Middle East have given Islam a southern branch, and Asian religions are present in areas of the South that have experienced rapid recent economic development. Even migrants from other parts of the United States have brought a diversity of faiths that are expanding the context for religious life in the region. The *Religion* volume of *The New Encyclopedia of Southern Culture* has responded to a changing South through new entries, among others, on Asian religions, Latino religion, New Age religion, Islam, and religious diversity. Exciting recent scholarly work led the editors to commission entries on Native American religion, social activism, urban religion, country churches, spirituality, and sports and religion. In addition, when appropriate, contributors revised their original articles to take changes into account, or the editors sought new essays altogether on such topics as politics and religion, a topic that has taken on dramatic configurations with the significance of the South's religions in national elections.

The NEW ENCYCLOPEDIA *of* SOUTHERN CULTURE

VOLUME 1 : RELIGION

RELIGION

The South's religious life is distinctive in ways that parallel the region's general distinctiveness. Its fervently religious people are frequently described as "born again," their religion as "fundamentalist." There is some accuracy in the use of these terms. But even they refer to complex concepts. Moreover, they do not do justice to the diversity of the South, which includes the religion of white people, the religion of black people, and the expanding varieties of each.

Students of religious movements always do well to ask about the intentions of the religious people themselves. What do they believe? What has powerful meaning for them? What happens to them when they attend religious services? What are they seeking to express when they worship and when they support religious causes?

As is well known, Protestant Christianity is the South's dominant religious form. Focus on baptism and the Lord's Supper, the two Protestant sacraments, or "ordinances" as they are often called in the South, affords insight into the dynamics of regional faith. Why baptism is such a persistent and public issue tells a great deal about the religious history of the region. It also discloses much about the interaction of religion and culture there. Similarly, such topics as the character of church services, their tone and emphasis, the style of church architecture, and the activity that takes place there suggest what the people believe and how their faith is expressed.

Perspectives such as these yield understanding of the humanistic dimensions of the South's religious life. They point to the metaphors in which the message is couched, the mythos on which it is founded, and the value system that prompts characteristic behavior. They are integrated in the general regional culture, in history and in the present, yet they have a life of their own and are simply by-products of economic, political, or social forces.

Distinctiveness of Southern Religion. Three features stand out in making the religion of the South different from the patterns that prevail elsewhere. (1) The forms that are common in the region are relatively homogeneous. The range of popular options has been historically quite narrow. (2) The South is the only society in Christendom in which the evangelical family of Christians is dominant. Evangelicalism's dominance is decisive in making the South the "religious region" that it is and in marking off the South from patterns, practices, and perspectives prevalent in other parts of America. (3) A set of four common convictions occupies a normative southern religious position. Movements and denominations in the South are judged for authenticity in the popular mind by how well they support these beliefs: (a) the Bible is the sole reference point of belief and practice; (b) direct and dynamic access to the Lord is open to all; (c) morality is defined primarily in individualistic and interpersonal terms; and (d) worship is informal, loose structuring and spontaneity being preferred over prescription.

The permeation of religion throughout the southern population continues to puzzle observers imbued with the "modern mind" and a secularist outlook. To a remarkable degree for a modern Western culture, the South adheres to traditional Christianity. It believes in a supernaturalism reminiscent of medieval Europe. Religion continues to be treated as a vital concern. A majority of southerners accept orthodox teachings. And many who are not church members believe they should submit to conversion and expect that someday they will. Traditional faith remains the popular form; its hold on the hearts and minds of people is quite firm.

The identification of Christianity with the "old-time religion" makes believing difficult for other southerners, however. To a sizable and growing segment of the region's population, the South's traditional religion seems outdated and untenable. Many of these southerners have not abandoned the faith, however; rather, they are unable to respond to it through the typical regional forms. This condition bears out the truth of Flannery O'Connor's description of the South as "Christ-haunted." The old-fashioned faith is integral to the regional way of life. Even many who resist the traditional formulations cannot give up religion or get away from it. They are so deeply indoctrinated in the orthodox faith that they cannot articulate alternative formulations of it, much as they wish they could.

Few characterizations of the South are more acute than the recognition that it has been a limited-options culture. Historically that has been true, especially in the 75 years following the Civil War, when national economic development largely bypassed the region and the society hardened its practice of racial segregation. In hardly any other aspect has the limitation of choices been more pronounced than in religion. Southerners' range of options with respect to personal faith has been narrow. Roman Catholicism's place in the society has been minor in both size and influence. Such classical Protestant churches as the Episcopal and Lutheran have been viewed as suited to certain classes, families, and tastes in the former case and to people of German stock in the latter. Other denominations such as Moravians and the Brethren have been seen as "ethnic."

Pulpit of Rose Hill Baptist Church, Vicksburg, Miss., 1974
(William Ferris Collection, Southern Folklife Collection, Wilson Library,
University of North Carolina at Chapel Hill)

It is only a partial exaggeration to classify the remaining Protestant options as variations on a theme. From Presbyterian to Pentecostal, from Churches of Christ to Holiness, in black churches and white, there is an insistent preoccupation with the "four common convictions"—the Bible as authority, direct access to the Holy Spirit, traditional morality, and informal worship.

Notable differences in style, teaching, and emphasis differentiate the Presbyterian churches from the Assemblies of God, the Southern Baptists from the United Methodists, the Disciples of Christ from their historical kin in the Churches of Christ, black Methodists from white Methodists, the southern Congregationalists from the independent Baptist congregations. But, all things considered, the impact of a single coherent way of understanding Christianity is extensive and tenacious in the South.

Protestantism can be classified into four major families—liturgical, classical (or Reformation), evangelical, and radical. In the South, the evangelical family predominates. Even Presbyterianism, which falls within the classical category, takes on features of evangelicalism. Radical Protestantism—Mennonite, Amish, Quaker—has left its stamp on regional forms but has had very little acceptance in the South. At the same time convictions about the possibility and necessity of biblical primitivism have contributed to the popularity of restorationist thought. Prominent among Churches of Christ and Landmark Baptists (some of them members of Southern Baptist churches) especially, restorationism seeks to duplicate church life exactly as it was in New Testament times.

Other families of Protestantism do exist in the South. The Presbyterian presence represents the classical Protestant heritage, even though evangelical influence has modified it somewhat. Radical Protestantism's absence must surprise those who expect to find all kinds of conservatism in the South. A few Mennonite congregations can be found here and there, but even fewer Amish and no Hutterite. The Episcopal Church represents the liturgical family throughout the region. The Lutheran tradition, partly liturgical by classification, is present in select small areas, sometimes in strength. Episcopalianism's influence has always exceeded its size. It has served as home for certain kinds of regional traditionalists and as an alternative for people dissatisfied with evangelicalism.

Nevertheless, the dominance of the evangelical family is striking. The hold of the four common convictions concerning Bible, Spirit, morality, and worship dramatizes this point. To cite negative examples of their normative standing: the Episcopal Church is judged deficient because it practices liturgical worship; similarly, the Presbyterian Church departs from the norm, owing to its understated adherence to the direct access of each Christian to the power of the Holy Spirit.

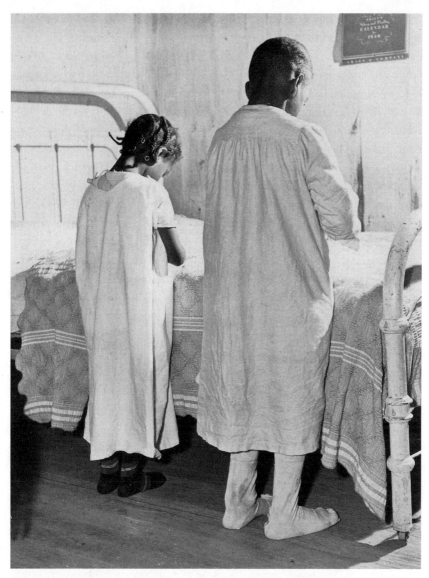

Children saying their prayers, Greene County, Ga., 1941 (Jack Delano, photographer, Library of Congress [LC-USF-34-46523-D], Washington, D.C.)

The Black Church. The faith of black Christians in the South is both very similar to that of white Christians and quite distinctive from it. Nearly all of what has been discussed about "southern religion" applies to both racial groups in the region. Recent research has shown how co-implicated white religion and black religion were in the antebellum period. At one level, the same denominational traditions, the Methodist and the Baptist especially but also the Presbyterian, the Episcopal, and the Roman Catholic, have served both groups. The evangelical approach has been particularly effective in its appeal to blacks. When white Christians sought to evangelize black people (most of whom were slaves), blacks responded in great numbers and with enthusiasm, especially after 1790. The extent of that responsiveness reinforced the white commitment to evangelism because (1) it attracted a black following and (2) in church services where whites and blacks worshipped together the black presence contributed to the music, the theology, and the overall vibrancy of the gathering. Aware of the evangelical faith's power in the daily lives of blacks and in their separate religious services, white Christians had strong incentives to promote it. Also, their own views of evangelicalism were enriched, and somewhat modified, by the participation of blacks in it. The significant differences in the forms of evangelism between the two races came to the fore once blacks had formed independent congregations and denominations in the months and years following the end of the Civil War. To a degree unrivaled by the theology of the white church, the black churches balanced a passion for both personal evangelism and social ministries.

Rituals. In notable ways, the role of the two central rituals of historical Christianity, baptism and the Lord's Supper, reveals the South as a distinctive religious setting. These sacraments, or "ordinances," hold a significant place in regional life and are viewed differently in the southern setting than typically in other Christian venues. For example, baptism outranks Communion in importance. Communion often has a limited importance and place. To be sure, it is observed in all churches. Nevertheless, on a value scale honored by millions of southern Protestants, especially those most vocal about the positions of these sacraments, baptism has primacy.

During most of the colonial period white southerners were practicing Anglicans, nominal Anglicans, or nothing. As we have noted, few slaves embraced Christianity in any form before the 1790s. An outburst of enthusiastic faith, evangelical in theology and revivalistic in method, altered the denominational profile. The movement developed from Presbyterian beginnings in the 1740s into a "great" awakening in Baptist hands during the 1750s. Soon thereafter Methodist-leaning Anglicans took up the same cause, with the result that there were "Methodists" before the Methodist Church was officially organized in 1784.

The southern evangelicals acted on the conviction that faith is a relationship one claims in a very personal way. The individual is not born into it, edu-

River baptism in rural Kentucky (Photographic Archives, University of Louisville [Kentucky])

cated into it, or even gradually nurtured into it. Instead, one experiences God's presence and saving power directly, intimately, sometimes in dramatic fashion. Thus each life is divided into two periods, life before and after a person receives the gift of salvation. The transition becomes central. Entry into this new condition is life's greatest need and most decisive event.

Baptism understood as a rite of initiation is thus essential. Passage from nominal to genuine practice, from being lost to being saved, from knowing intellectually to experiencing with the heart, becomes a pivotal event. It does not follow, however, that all denominations using revivalism as the technique for introducing people to personal faith have practiced "believer's baptism." Evangelical Presbyterians and Methodists juxtaposed their views of the "new birth" with several other Christian teachings—the family as a covenantal unit, the doctrine of election, and an organic connection between entry and what followed it in a person's spiritual growth. The revivalistic Baptists were more single-minded. Even so, entry, passage, the division of life into a before and after, came to the fore as a fundamental feature in the southern religious tradition. It was soon to hold an even more prominent position.

The Great Revival on the Kentucky-Tennessee frontier between 1799 and 1805 reinforced and enlarged the role of *entry* into the Christian life. That event assumed primacy and acquired a ritualistic character. One could know, indeed must know, when the passage from death to life occurred. So signal an event ought to be symbolized by an outward sign. The Bible-devout Christians did not have to look far to find one. Indeed, as they read in their Bibles, the Lord had intended all along that only people making this transition were subjects for baptism—as the Baptist people had insisted from their English origins, dating from about 1610. And as they reproduced the pattern as it existed in the time of Christ, they followed the idea to its logical conclusion, namely, to perform the rite by submerging the new Christian in water, baptism by immersion. Of the three earliest denominations to be both evangelical and revivalistic, only the Baptists insisted on the straight logic of the position. To their minds, only those personally assured of regeneration in a conscious, willful experience should be baptized; also, proper baptism was by immersion. Presbyterians and Methodists set conversions in a wider context, understanding several doctrines dialectically rather than hierarchically and seeing entry as having organic continuity with what went before in a person's life and with what was to follow.

Soon the restorationist movement began to develop and take hold. These "Christians" or "Disciples of Christ," those of the Stone-Campbell tradition, were identifiably on the scene by 1830. For them, too, entry into the Christian life was of critical significance. They sought the restoration of New Testament practices in every detail and as a test of faith. Proceeding from somewhat different perspectives, Baptists and "Christians" both seized on the "rite of initiation" as the distinguishing doctrine in biblical Christianity. The act of entering the saving relationship with Christ and the state of being a Christian claimed first place. Baptism, the badge of entry, thus acquired a dominating significance in the region. It is no wonder that so many denominational squabbles have occurred over the mode of baptism.

At no other time and place in the history of Christendom has baptism been elevated to such eminence—and Communion so deemphasized. Popular southern religion's treatment of the two classic Protestant sacraments adds up to a basic regional distinctiveness, highlighting a unique history. In viewing the place of baptism and the Lord's Supper, one sees the genuine continuity in religious patterns dating from the period 1800–1850. (By contrast, the "North" began to be metamorphosed socially, culturally, and religiously in the 1830s.) Understanding this singular arrangement underscores that the South created its distinctive path in the historical career of the church.

That the sacraments, their nature and their place, can tell so much about the social history of a region is astonishing. Conventional wisdom would raise doubts that anything so "sacred" could make such a "secular" impact. But their impact has been great. Yet one must take pains not to stretch the truth. For many southern Protestants, Episcopalians and Presbyterians among the larger denominations and Congregationalists and Moravians among the smaller, baptism is not so dominant. Moreover, it is administered to infants by "sprinkling." In addition, Methodists stand as a special case. Some evangelical-revivalistic blood courses through Methodist veins. But the fact of entry, the moment of entry, and the mode of entry do not define Methodist sensibility and practice. That is due to the breadth of its teachings and concerns as well as to the strength of the worship component in its heritage. Within that denomination Communion is granted a large place vis-à-vis baptism.

Communion, the Holy Communion, the Eucharist, or the Lord's Supper — all terms used to refer to taking the bread and the fruit of the vine in celebration of Christ's suffering — is the foremost rite within traditional Christianity. Historically, it has been considered the central act in worship by most branches of the church. Thus worship defines Christian living, and Communion is the primary expression of worship.

In the popular religion of southern whites, worship ranks below evangelism and concern with moral uprightness. Converting lost souls, which entails training laypeople to engage in that ministry, is the first priority. Not far behind is instruction in and practice of Christian ethical standards. The act of worshipping God, prizing patience and mystery as it does, comes after. In fact, much of the focus in "church services" is on converting the lost, urging members to become involved in soul winning, and denouncing unrighteous living. Worship as an end in itself, as itself the "work of the people of God," is much less important.

It is not surprising that among Baptists, Pentecostals, Holiness people, and other highly evangelistic groups the Lord's Supper is observed because it is considered a commandment to be obeyed, but it is usually observed quarterly and marks a departure from the congregation's ordinary rhythm. Whereas exhortation is fast paced and bent on results, Communion is deliberate and done for its own sake. It simply follows a different cadence. Moreover, a ritual (such as the Lord's Supper) takes some time, makes no person or group or people the primary object (the minister's role being rather minor and passive), and cannot be used for purposes other than its own. It is not the occasion for exhorting or for the preacher to pursue a direction of his own choosing. The service of the Lord's Supper controls; it is inevitably liturgical. The cadence is radically different from the "preaching service," in which everything moves with vigor and rises to a crescendo in the sermon and the altar call or "invitation" that follows.

The instrumental nature of many white church services and of whites' preference for evangelism over worship offers an interesting comparison with church services of black evangelicals in the South. There is nothing instrumental about black services. The "preaching service," "worship," "going to church" are ends in themselves for the South's black Christians. The gathering is a joyous one, a vital event in the course of the week. Singing is spirited, much of the music coming from black Christian experience. The congregation actively participates in singing, responds to prayers and the sermon with vocal expressions, contributes its offering to plates that may be passed more than once, and accepts assignments in the choir or in the usher force. The preacher proclaims God's Word for the comfort, challenge, and reassurance of the people. The congregation joins its utterances with the preacher's in a rhythmic call-and-response. A sermon that does not elicit its vocal participation is regarded as a failure. For the preacher's part, a congregation that does not give back its encouragement and testimony is indifferent.

To sum up, what happens in a black church — whatever the denomination — on Sunday or during a revival meeting is the central activity of the church. The service does not focus exclusively on individuals in need of conversion (although they may be led to make that decision). It is an act of worship by all the people present. They praise God for daily blessing and for the forgiveness of sins. They pray to God for strength and courage, for healing, and for the power of the Holy Spirit. The other activities of the congregation, support for mission causes or colleges or appeals for help for those in need, may be mentioned, but they are incidental to the singing, praying, testifying, and preaching that are the reasons for the service.

Communion rates well below baptism in the evangelical-revivalistic religion that pervades the American South. Preoccupation with introducing people to faith and the church has proved to be a legacy with staying power. A worship-related, self-contained action, which Communion is, will always have a place but does not quite fit. Nowhere else in Christendom, to repeat, does the ceremony around Christ's final meal with his disciples occupy such a small place. Its rhythm is simply different from that of evangelism. What a momentous season it was when when southern churches ceased alternating worship services and evangelistic services and turned nearly all into the latter.

The two ordinances are correlated in another way: the affinity between the deemphasis on Communion and the insistence that only conscious, decision-making candidates are suited to baptism. Clearly the stress in this understanding of religion falls on each persona's part in the process, on everyone being an active agent. Terms such as the following are in common usage — decide, follow, commit, yield, surrender, give, sacrifice. That is the lexicon of evangelism and believer's baptism (under the conditions of revivalism). It is not the language of Communion. In the Lord's Supper one acknowledges that everything is done for him or her, affirming that grace is raw grace. The rite (and maybe even the elements themselves) suffuses the communicant. Something laden with mystery confronts the dynamic of each person's existence. Its impact cannot be measured. It is not likely to generate immediate activity. Instead its essence is more liquid. Receiving renders one quiet, submissive, reflective, consoled, and nourished. A people conditioned to operate in the active voice does not readily shift into that sort of disposition. There is far more affinity between the raw grace of infant baptism and the receptive posture of Communion. (A simple glance at their historical symbiosis would seem to confirm such an interpretation.)

Religion and the Senses. Which senses (or faculties) are most prominent in the evangelical-revivalistic nature of southern religion? What are the roles of seeing and tasting, for example? From a different perspective, what kinds of sense-based achievements emanate from religion of this kind? Standing in the Protestant and Puritan traditions, popular southern religion maximizes hearing and speaking. The term "Word of God" referring to the Bible is not taken metaphorically. Words are sacred, an utterly reliable guide to reality. Thus, speaking and hearing enable one to participate in reality in the most effective way. Tasting, touching, and smelling are simply not considered as potential means of divine revelation. Rites involving bread and wine (regularly grape juice, for the past century or so) are deemphasized. The visual sense likewise is not highly cultivated because it too is not regarded as a potential link between the divine and creation. Art and architecture accordingly do not flow from religious sensibilities. Southern religion rarely generates art, whether paintings or sculpture. One exception is baptistery wall depictions of the river Jordan. Architecture is mostly functional, although surprisingly good forms, classic and modern, sometimes appear in Baptist, Assemblies of God, Seventh-day Adventist, and other settings.

Speaking and hearing, then, are the senses brought alive by southern religion. It has been remarked that Protestants hear entirely too much, more than they can possibly put into practice. Be that as it may, the Word, words, sermons, exhortations, testimonies, soul-winning conversations, and the like are endemic to this religious style. Relating to the Almighty through seeing, tasting, and smelling—whatever might be specific forms of such responses—is foreign to this sensibility.

References to the oral and auditory senses suggest music. Singing has a vital place in southern Christianity. The expression of faith through this medium, especially as joy for sin's forgiveness and God's daily blessings, is a regular, natural, and indispensable part of church services, revival meetings, church socials, youth gatherings, and even Sunday school assemblies. Music has to do with the ear and the voice; that makes it a neat fit in the setting of a voice/ear religion.

In a large number of Baptist churches, the music is of diverse sorts, ranging from classical hymnody to gospel songs to choruses and spirituals. In the rest of the denominations that make up popular regional religion, classical hymnody generally disappears. Musical forms include everything from quieter, semiformal gospel songs (or popular-style hymns such as "How Great Thou Art") to simpler choruses. With church services more inclined to the revivalistic and less to worship, musical tastes are predictable. Thus, "living it up," "let's really sing, all together now," and "pulling out all the stops" are representative expressions used by the person leading the singing to arouse the congregation to robust participation.

A glance inside the auditorium—a term far more apt than "sanctuary" when listening is primary and conduct is informal—is revealing. The choir is seated behind and above the rostrum on which the pulpit stands. Its members are facing the congregation and are in the direct vision of most or all of it. The minister of music or song leader typically directs the choir in its special numbers, having turned around from facing the congregation when leading it in the singing of the hymns. In most popular churches of any size, each song is called out by name and number by the "song leader," who directs from the rostrum.

The positioning and these actions afford clues to the understanding of worship prevalent in the popular southern religious tradition. It is not altar-centered. Everything centers on the stand where the Holy Bible rests and from behind which the preacher declares its message. Additionally, in the visual line of the pulpit people seated in the congregation may see the choir and the music director. That central area in the front of the "auditorium" is the focus of attention, by theological intention. The reason for the Word, the words, the congregational and choral music, and the entire event of gathering is the improved spiritual condition of the people in the congregation. They do not move to the special area raised in the front of the building, as happens in the liturgical traditions; rather, the message of truth and inspiration is projected to them from there.

When this conception of the theological architecture is put into practice, the preacher becomes an exhorter or a persuader, whose aim is to convince members of the error of their ways, to point them to the path of spiritual treasures, such as conversion, power for living, perhaps the gift of tongues, or to rally their support for causes, typically evangelistic in purpose. This approach generates direct response. It takes shape as personal accountability to the Lord— for the salvation of your own soul or as the mandate of dedicated service at his bidding. Closely related is the call to personal responsibility, to follow his commandments concerning your own righteousness and what he wills you to do for others. With the individuals present pressured to respond in active ways, set liturgical forms could hardly be expected to have wide usage in church services. Subtlety and belief that religious growth occurs best at a gradual rate are not features of this approach. Instead, the pace is energetic, the mood urgent, and the manner of approach straightforward.

Seriousness of Southern Religion. The mode of much popular southern religion is rooted in the view that religious issues are enormously significant. The God who has given everything requires a total commitment in return. To fail to heed his commandments, to spurn the pardon he offers to lost humankind is grievous indeed. So to behave in that way makes no sense and misses the mark; moreover, it entails the direst consequences. A religious animation of this kind instills a keen attitude of guilt, the knowledge that one has defied, disobeyed, and rejected an all-loving and all-requiring God.

Millions of the southern religious are open, even vulnerable, to the message, delivered so forthrightly, that they have fallen short and must conform their lives to God's will. On the positive side, they respond to the appeal of loyalties and causes. They really hear urgings to support their church and its projects. Accordingly, impressive percentages are involved in the organizational life of the congregation, often attending three or more activities per week. Their generosity with money matches their dedication of time. Many tithe, giving 10 percent of the family's gross income. Concern for the work of the church, evangelistic and mission programs, and charitable institutions run deep and stimulate much giving.

Some scholars have argued that religious guilt is a natural by-product of the white southerner's treatment of black people. The convincing demonstration of that interpretation is fraught with problems. Guilt is surely much appealed to in southern religious life, and the fundamental injustice of slavery and seg-

Religious sign on roadside, north of Carthage, Miss., 1985 (Tom Rankin, photographer)

regation is equally evident. How they correlate, however, remains a matter of interpretation.

One is struck by the strength revivalistic evangelicalism attained during the period of slavery's tightest hold and of that ideology's rapid growth during the Jim Crow era, when segregation reached its zenith. However, it would take a thoroughly cynical interpretation to attribute southern religiosity *solely* to guilt. Guilt can be, after all, a constructive and appropriate reaction to a religious understanding that divine love should bear the fruits of grateful obedience. Evidence abounds that many of the southern faithful have drunk from a wellspring of joy and gratitude for deliverance, rather than being driven by fear accompanying visions of an eternal hell.

Black religious attitudes concerning guilt have been somewhat different from white attitudes. Through the age of slavery, the experience of dramatic conversion rooted in the acknowledgment of each sinner's guilt was as much a part of black faith as of white. But the roles of guilt and responsibility shifted somewhat once southern black Christians had their own churches. Everything came to be seen in communal terms, including personal salvation and ethics. Being a part of the worshipping congregation and seeing the needs of others in the (segregated) black community diffused and redirected the previously more individualistic orientation. Guilt, pardon, and gratitude continue to be elements in black religious practice, but the evangelism-based program of many white churches has been significantly recast.

Church life of the sort that is informal, direct, urgent, and evangelistic remains standard for a great many southern whites. Almost everywhere else in America such an approach to Christianity is viewed by the majority as somewhat strange, a form of faith limited to a single issue, or even extremist. Southern products of this kind of religion may be referred to indiscriminately as "born-again" Christians. That ascription, rarely understood in most communities, is what a great many southerners think all Christians, if serious, are. What is mainline in the South is peripheral elsewhere.

To repeat, four common convictions distinguish serious religion in the eyes of the rank-and-file southern religious: (1) the Bible as the sole reference point; (2) direct and intimate access to the Lord; (3) Christian morality defined in the terms of individualistic and interpersonal ethics; (4) informal, spontaneous patterns for worship. The Baptist-like approach scores high on all four tests and is the most popular form of southern religious life. Catholicism, to take the opposite example, fails on all four counts and is hence judged deviant. The American South perpetuates a distinctive type of religion. Although it is different from forms of Christianity found elsewhere only in degree, the degree is decisive. The evangelical form has wielded normative influence on many expressions of Christian faith. When this condition is added to the historical linkage between church life and regional culture, the South is seen as a distinctive religious region on the American map.

A great many disruptions of the historical regional culture have occurred since the end of the Second World War, especially within the past 40 years or so, much of it keyed by the civil rights movement and the revised public policy that issued from it. The effects of all that change have left their imprint on the South's culturally at-home religious life, of course. Urbanization is one major factor contributing to the significant change; the in-migration of thousands of people from other parts of the country — and more than a few from other continents — is another. The presence of an enhanced prosperity and the South's achievement of a vital role in the national economy reflect a dramatic alteration. The racial desegregation of the society could hardly be more important on any listing of forces for change. Secularization, the lessening of the religious factor in determining a person's beliefs and motives for action, has crept into the lives of many citizens still attending church regularly who are hardly aware of its impact. Others practice a new freedom to admit that their outlook on living has shifted from a decisive concern with religious commitment to its dilution through recognition of additional norms and values.

At the same time, conservative religious forces have appeared on the scene. From other regional perspectives, perhaps, southern forms are thought to be incapable of moving any farther to the right. Yet historically the predominant white denominations, the Baptist, Methodist, and Presbyterian, have generally embraced openness and a measure of self-criticism. The last two have enjoyed a cooperative relationship with their "northern" coreligionists for many decades. And of course there has been a national Methodist Church since 1939. "Mainline" American Presbyterians merged into a single body in 1983, concluding decades of gestures toward unification. The Southern Baptist Convention has maintained its separateness from its founding in 1845. Suggestive as that fact is, we need to note that there has been a general practice of open inquiry and respect for diversity within its constituency. This huge body has been more isolationist and self-referential than it has been hostile to other Christians or to human culture.

Major shifts have been occurring since the 1970s. These parallel developments in American culture at large. This means that for a long time, when left to their own, southern denominations pursued a kind of free and open, and indigenous, course of behavior. Recently, the Southern Baptists (emphatically in the convention's central leadership) have taken a hard-line stance against compromised doctrinal positions in favor of a uniform theology and ecclesiology, for example, on matters relating to the role of women in the family and in the church. This particular rectification, though, is only the most celebrated and controversial among several concerns all of which spell a preoccupation with the authority of the Bible, its infallibility and inerrancy. This insistence on uniformity is a new thing for the Southern Baptists.

Those Methodists disturbed by the laxness and indiscriminate embracing of positions judged unfaithful have formed submovements within the one national church. They engage issues with vigor and persistence, seeking to spread their orthodox views, but rarely with the attitude of desiring to "excommunicate" those who practice error or to form a new denomination. Presbyterians, true to their Calvinist tradition, care greatly about theology. In 1973 a minority within the southern church withdrew to form the Presbyterian Church of America (PCA). Now considerably expanded in size and influence, the PCA holds the line on doctrinal matters ranging from sexual issues to fellowship with other Christian bodies. Thus the transformed Southern Baptist Convention and the PCA exemplify the conservative drift in the South's religious life with respect to the historically prominent, pace-setting bodies.

All of that is news, but certainly not the only bold-type headline stories of the conservative direction of southern church life over the past 30 years. Two conditions are new: the first is fundamentalism's surge to popularity and its gaining social acceptance; the second is the rise of an evangelicalism that used to be confined largely to the lower socioeconomic classes and was therefore not treated as a live option by the leadership classes or a serious social movement.

Despite much popular tendency to refer to a southern religion as fundamentalist, fundamentalism has been a minor and tangential part of the regional tradition. Defined precisely, it is a form of evangelical Protestantism that lives by correct belief, by a requisite acceptance of certain doctrines, related serially, not organically, most having to do with the authority of the Bible and the exact nature of the person and work of Christ. Historical fundamentalism has had some representation in the South but always was a predominantly "northern" phenomenon. With deep conviction it has stood outside the prevailing culture, refusing to become involved with "worldliness"; indeed, it has been hostile to participation in politics and most social movements. Keeping itself unstained by worldly entanglements through an unyielding devotion to purity has been its stock-in-trade. Thus, when Jerry Falwell and those of like mind founded the Moral Majority and comparable efforts, they modified traditional fundamentalism. With surprising speed they became a major social and political force. The Christian Right generally has been making its mark in the South, religiously and politically. From many a pulpit, its message of saving this Christian nation from forsaking its God-given mission through compromise, liberalism, and all forms of relativism is being heard. This is a new development in the region on any large scale. Yet we must be clear that the recently emerged Southern Baptist and Presbyterian conditions referred to earlier reflect something of the fundamentalist program. They too insist on correct belief—which is not the same as "sound doctrine"—and they too are aggressive in reclaiming the national public life from the degradation into which it has fallen. But they never have been hostile to culture; indeed, Baptists and Presbyterians have been "movers and shakers" in the formation and governing of the culture.

In another instance of recent change, forms of evangelicalism that have become popular and influential used to be largely confined to the province of the "sects." In these manifestations, Protestant Christianity is warm, highly expressive through gospel music, personal testimony, and congregational fellowship. The people hear the "full gospel" message, are wrapped in the love of fellow believers, and are impelled verbally to share the good news and actively to serve others in their needs. Once associated mostly with Pentecostal, Holiness, and Adventist sects, this cause continues to enjoy the support of those communities of faith, which themselves have grown greatly and won social acceptance. No less important, their styles and programs have been adopted by other churches; indeed, many of the megachurches along the highways and streets of towns and cities are precisely this kind of evangelical. More than a few of them are not denominationally affiliated, and some of them are so large and successful as to be virtual denominations in their own right. For many thousands of these dedicated folk, the restraints that have kept traditional southern Baptist and Methodist evangelicals from such expressiveness and informality have been relaxed in favor of joyful and articulate celebration in praise of God in a community of believers where "belonging" is a stated goal and an accomplished fact.

While the center-to-right Protestant heritage in its distinctively southern forms has been widely influential and, arguably, normative for the cultural life of regional religion, other religious groups have long been present. Roman Catholicism continues to be strong where it has always been, in certain parts of Texas, Louisiana, and Kentucky, notably, with its presence much more broadly distributed since large-scale in-migration has affected cities and towns. The Jewish presence dates from colonial times, assuring that Jews would make up a significant sector of leadership in Savannah, Charleston, Norfolk, Richmond, Baltimore, and other places. Atlanta became a national center of Jewish life following the Civil War. Jewish population is spread throughout the region, still much more in urban centers than in small towns or in rural areas. The sprawl of the nation's capital through northern Virginia and southern Maryland has changed all demographic conditions, with similar developments in central and south Florida and the massive expansion of Texas cities.

Finally we note the Hindu temples, Buddhist centers, and Muslim mosques that have become a feature of the landscape. Large cities may contain several of these nontraditional religious houses. Meditation centers and retreat houses have sprung up here and there, sometimes holding attraction for Christians who are drawn to meditative practices. The once religiously homogeneous South is less and less that way, notwithstanding the staying, and adaptive, power of evangelical Protestantism. Demographically and culturally the American South grows steadily more like the rest of the nation in its interaction with global civilization.

SAMUEL S. HILL
University of Florida

David T. Bailey, *Shadow on the Church: Southwestern Evangelical Religion and the Issue of Slavery, 1783–1860* (1985); Kenneth K. Bailey, *Southern White Protestantism in the Twentieth Century* (1964); Tod A. Baker, Robert P. Steed, and Laurence W. Moreland, eds., *Religion and Politics in the South: Mass and Elite Perspectives* (1983); John B. Boles, *The Great Revival, 1787–1805: The Origins of the Southern Evangelical Mind* (1972), *Maryland Historical Magazine* (December 1982); Dickson D. Bruce Jr., *And They All Sang Hallelujah: Plain-Folk Camp-Meeting Religion, 1800–1845* (1974); Will Campbell, *Brother to a Dragonfly* (1977); John R. Earle, Dean D. Knudsen, and Donald W. Shriver Jr., *Spindles and Spires* (1975); J. Wayne Flynt, *Alabama Baptists: Southern Baptists in the Heart of Dixie* (1998); Sylvia R. Frey and Betty Wood, *Come Shouting to Zion: African American Protestantism in the American South and British Caribbean to 1830* (1998); Jean E. Friedman, *The Enclosed Garden: Women and Community in the Evangelical South, 1830–1900* (1985); William R. Glass, *Strangers in Zion: Fundamentalists in the South, 1900–1950* (2001); David Harrell, *All Things Are Possible: The Healing and Charismatic Revivals in Modern America* (1976), ed., *Varieties of Southern Evangelicalism* (1981); Paul Harvey, *Freedom's Coming: Religious Culture and the Shaping of the South from the Civil War through the Civil Rights Era* (2005), *Redeeming the South: Religious Cultures and Racial Identities among Southern Baptists, 1865–1925* (1997); Christine Leigh Heyrman, *Southern Cross: The Beginnings of the Bible Belt* (1997); Evelyn Brooks Higginbotham, *Righteous Discontent: The Women's Movement in the Black Baptist Church, 1880–1920* (1993); Samuel S. Hill, ed., *Encyclopedia of Religion in the South* (1984), *The South and the North in American Religion* (1980), *Southern Churches in Crisis* (1966); E. Brooks Holifield, *The Gentlemen Theologians: American Theology in Southern Culture, 1795–1860* (1978); C. Eric Lincoln, ed., *The Black Experience in Religion: A Book of Readings* (1974);

Anne C. Loveland, *Southern Evangelicals and the Social Order, 1800–1860* (1980); Charles Marsh, *God's Long Summer: Stories of Faith and Civil Rights* (1997); Donald Mathews, *Religion in the Old South* (1977); Randall M. Miller, Harry S. Stout, and Charles Reagan Wilson, eds., *Religion and the American Civil War* (1998); Robert Moats Miller, *Southern Humanities Review* (Summer 1967); William E. Montgomery, *Under Their Own Vine and Fig Tree: The African American Church in the South, 1865–1900* (1993); Laurence W. Moreland, Tod A. Baker, and Robert P. Steed, eds., *Contemporary Southern Political Attitudes and Behavior: Studies and Essays* (1982); Ted Ownby, *Subduing Satan: Religion, Recreation, and Manhood in the Rural South, 1865–1920* (1990); Albert J. Raboteau, *Slave Religion: The "Invisible Institution" in the Antebellum South* (1978); Beth Barton Schweiger, *The Gospel Working Up: Progress and the Pulpit in Nineteenth-Century Virginia* (2000); Beth Barton Schweiger and Donald G. Mathews, eds., *Religion in the American South: Protestants and Others in History and Culture* (2004); Samuel C. Shepard Jr., *Avenue of Faith: Shaping the Urban Religious Culture of Richmond, Virginia, 1900–1929* (2003); Mitchell Snay, *The Gospel of Disunion: Religion and Separatism in the Antebellum South* (1993); Daniel Stowell, *Rebuilding Zion: The Religious Reconstruction of the South, 1863–1877* (1998); Grant Wacker, *Heaven Below: Early Pentecostals and American Culture* (2001); Charles Reagan Wilson, *Baptized in Blood: The Religion of the Lost Cause, 1865–1920* (1980), ed., *Religion in the South* (1985), *Judgment and Grace in Dixie: Southern Faiths from Faulkner to Elvis* (1995); Norman Yance, *Religion Southern Style: Southern Baptists and Society in Historical Perspective* (1978).

Appalachian Religion

Many Appalachian people have clung to their religious traditions as they have to other beliefs. This devotion has troubled other American Christians, and so mainline denominations sent great numbers of missionaries into the region. Some missionaries felt that the mountaineers had to be saved from themselves and their culture, as well as for God. Many mountain people joined the mission churches, but others went on worshipping as their forebears had.

Deborah McCauley, in *Appalachian Mountain Religion: A History* (1995), has questioned the missionary intrusion into the region and has made a convincing argument that the Appalachian religion is an authentic counterstream to modern, mainstream Protestantism. She contrasts the mountain church's emphasis on grace and the Holy Spirit with the mainstream preoccupation with social action and "highly aggressive evangelical interpretations of the role of freewill . . . and souls 'won' or 'saved.'"

Appalachia has most of the denominations one would find elsewhere in America, especially in the larger towns, but it also has many subdenominations, some of which are locally autonomous. Theologically, these smaller churches range from the strongly Calvinistic Primitive Baptists to Pentecostal-Holiness churches that represent the doctrinal opposite of Calvinism.

The disagreements between the Calvinists and the freewill, or Arminian, groups were part of frontier life. The Methodists brought the first ideas heralding human perfectibility and universal atonement, in contrast to the Calvinist belief that the human condition offered bleak hope of earthly improvement and that a limited number of people would be saved. Many, therefore, listened eagerly to the Methodist gospel offering a possibility of salvation for all, as well as hope for the improvement of human nature. A great debate over old and new doctrines came out of the Second Great Awakening in the early 1800s. Many Presbyterians and Baptists had joined the Methodists in the frontier revival, thus setting themselves against their Calvinistic brothers and sisters. Many introduced Arminian ideas into their formerly Calvinist churches, bringing a multitude of doctrinal splits.

In North Carolina, Virginia, and Kentucky, Baptists attempted to unite the opposing groups under the name United Baptists, seeking to rewrite articles of faith to include rather than to exclude. They debated the questions of predestination, mission efforts, Sunday schools, and seminary education of ministers. The Old School or Primitive Baptists maintained that God knew his purposes and would bring into his fold all those he had elected, that the Bible itself is sufficient for all religious instruction, and that God calls preachers and reveals to them the necessary spiritual knowledge. The freewill side, mainly Separate Baptists, believed in the efficacy of revival preaching, Sunday schools, missionary effort, and seminaries. There was no bringing all of them together, and the split was irrevocable by the 1840s. The Primitive Baptists are still the most Calvinistic, although a few in the Uplands reject the concept of hell and believe in universal salvation. Some United Baptists moved back toward Calvinism, although many joined with the Separatist strain and eventually became American Baptists or Southern Baptists. Some also became Regular or Old Regular Baptists, who are now found primarily in the Appalachian region. They represent a position somewhere between the Primitive and Freewill Baptists, holding to some Calvinistic tenets but maintaining that God never predestined anyone to hell and that only those who do not heed the Word of God will be lost. There are many Freewill or Missionary Baptist churches in Appalachia along with the Southern Baptist congregations that are affiliated with both state and national conventions. Some, however, are locally autonomous. The Southern Baptist Church has more members than any other in the region, except in West Virginia, where Methodists are predominant.

The Presbyterian Church was divided over the same issues that separated the Baptists. The "New Light" wing moved toward Arminianism; the "Old Light" remained Calvinists. The Cumberland Presbyterian Church was formed in 1810, separating from Kentucky's Transylvania Presbytery after the latter censured the Cumberland church for ordaining ministers who did not have seminary training and raising questions about damnation of infants and limited atonement. In part it was a split between well-to-do Presbyterians and poorer Kentucky and Tennessee farmers.

The Christian church movement also grew out of the Presbyterian doctrinal debates, led by Barton Stone and Thomas and Alexander Campbell, who were bent on returning the church to New Testament Christianity and to unity, peace, and purity. They differed with their former Presbyterian brothers and sisters over doctrine, rejecting infant baptism but placing a much greater emphasis on baptism of believers and the sacrament than other groups and raising questions about substitutionary atonement and the Trinity. The Stoneites (calling themselves simply Christians) and Campbellites (Disciples of Christ) came together in Lexington, Ky., in 1832 to form the Disciples of Christ. Some followers disagreed with the Disciples over such issues as central government, mission programs, and musical instruments in the church and formed the Church of Christ (with instrumental and noninstrumental divisions). In the 20th century, other churches broke away from the Disciples to form independent Christian churches.

The Pentecostal-Holiness movement had its beginnings in Appalachia with the work of Methodist preacher Richard G. Spurling in Monroe County, Tenn., starting in 1886. Spurling thought that the churches had become enmeshed in creeds, rituals, legalisms, and philosophy to the extent that the Bible was less important. He also wanted to go back to Wesley's idea of holiness. With a few converts, Spurling formed the Christian Union. The movement spread into North Carolina, where it linked with Baptists who were intrigued by the idea of perfection. A revival in Cherokee County, N.C., attracted large numbers of people and spread into other states. A convert, American Bible Society sales-man A. J. Tomlinson, helped to evangelize western North Carolina, east Tennes-see, and north Georgia. By 1926 some 25 Pentecostal churches were in the area. As general overseer, Tomlinson moved the church headquarters to Cleveland, Tenn., where it became the Church of God. Tomlinson later fell into disagree-ment with his governing board, and the church split. In a legal battle over which was the true Church of God, the court ruled against Tomlinson and ordered that his new church be renamed. It became the Church of God of Prophecy. Another Appalachian Pentecostal body is the Church of God Mountain Assem-bly, with headquarters in Jellico, Tenn. In addition, other Pentecostal-Holiness groups, such as the Church of God, Anderson, Ind., the Assemblies of God, and the Church of the Nazarene, have congregations in Appalachia. The region also has many locally autonomous churches that call themselves Holiness or Pente-costal.

There are many Lutheran, Brethren, and Mennonite churches in the areas settled by Germans, such as parts of Virginia, West Virginia, North Carolina, and Tennessee, with mission churches elsewhere. Some Mennonite groups have more recently bought farms and formed communities in Kentucky. In addition, there are Episcopal and Catholic churches, but their doctrine in Appalachia is not different from what it is elsewhere. Also there are Jewish synagogues in the larger towns of the area, and in recent years Middle Easterners, Asians, and others have settled in the region and formed worship groups.

The earlier divisions among Christians were over Calvinism versus Armini-anism. Modern misunderstandings are still rooted in these older disagreements about the human condition and the nature of God. Another conflict is be-tween the social gospel and the old practices of preaching and worshipping. Mission workers have often accused Appalachian Christians of being too con-cerned with personal salvation and not having a sense of social conscience. These Christians have countered that their critics do social work rather than spiritual work. Some Appalachian churches have discouraged activities that do not relate directly to worship. However, as individuals and as members of non-church groups, many of these Christians have been involved in important secular issues.

Some mainline Christians have not recognized the importance of the non-mainline churches to beleaguered people, as a source of strength and reassurance of their worth, as havens from and strongholds against a troubled world and an economic system that has usually worked against them. No single description sufficiently explains the churches of the southern mountains. Appalachia is not homogeneous, and neither are its churches.

LOYAL JONES
Berea College

Howard Dorgan, *Giving Glory to God in Appalachia: Worship Practices of Six Baptist Subdenominations* (1987); Clifford A. Grammich Jr., *Local Baptists, Local Politics: Churches and Communities in the Middle and Uplands South* (1999); Loyal Jones, *Faith and Meaning in the Southern Uplands* (1999); Deborah V. McCauley, *Appalachian Mountain Religion: A History* (1995); Elder John Sparks, *The Roots of Appalachian Christianity: The Life and Legacy of Elder Shubal Stearns* (2001).

Architecture, Church

The earliest southern churches, Roman Catholic missions, dotted the east coast from Florida to Virginia beginning in the 16th century. Although none of these is extant, Roman Catholic missions and chapels built in the 18th century in Texas survive in such places as San Antonio, El Paso, and Goliad. These buildings reflect the then-current styles of Spain, including the elaborate stone carving at San Jose mission, San Antonio, and the Moorish details at St. Francis Espada in San Antonio. The Roman Catholic parish churches of Louisiana, on the other hand, reflect 18th- and 19th-century French classical styles.

The earliest Anglican churches of Virginia reflect a nostalgia for English Gothic (Jamestown, 1627; St. Luke's, Smithfield, 1681). By the end of the 17th century widespread experimentation in building for Anglican worship became evident and continued in the next century. Existing buildings scattered throughout the Tidewater region of Virginia and Maryland mirror a willingness to seek new forms and arrangements for Anglican worship. The Anglican churches of St. Michael's and St. Philip's in Charleston, S.C., reflected English sophistication, but in backcountry South Carolina a variety of influences prevailed, including the traditions of the West Indies and Huguenot builders. St. James, Goose Creek (1711), is a marvelous baroque building arranged around a central pulpit and altar table.

The 18th century saw the arrival of other groups whose buildings, whether

Thorncrown Chapel, Eureka Springs, Ark., opened in 1980
(Arkansas Department of Parks and Tourism)

Presbyterian, Methodist, or Baptist, took exterior forms that were rather domestic in appearance. These usually had balconies on three sides and a dominant pulpit raised high on the fourth. Congregationalists built distinctive structures at Midway, Ga., and Lutherans at Jerusalem, Ga. After the Revolution, new buildings were oriented so that a short side faced the road; a tower and, occasionally, a portico were sometimes added. High pulpits and horseshoe-shaped balconies continued to characterize the interiors throughout most of the 19th century.

Like the rest of the nation, the South was overrun by stylistic revivals in the 19th century. Greek Revival buildings appeared in the 1830s and continued to be popular in neoclassical forms among Methodists and Baptists up through the 1920s. The Gothic Revival appeared a decade later and found expression in such early examples as the Chapel of the Cross, Chapel Hill, N.C. This style flourished off and on until World War II, reaching its apex in the Duke Chapel at Duke University. There were two Gothic revivals—a rather primitive one in the 1840s and a more academic one in the early 20th century. The latter found favor among Methodists and Presbyterians especially. The work of Gothicist Ralph Adams Cram is represented by Trinity United Methodist, Durham, N.C. In the late 19th century the neo-Romanesque styles pioneered by H. H. Richardson gave way in time to eclectic combinations of various styles.

An important factor in 19th-century church architecture was the widespread development of Sunday schools. These led to the addition of classrooms and meeting halls so that today many church plants tend to rival the worship space in size. The scale of buildings increased in time, and by the 20th century, worship space was frequently referred to as the "auditorium."

Changes in the worship space occurred. In many churches, choirs were introduced in the 19th century, necessitating a new liturgical space for them. Revivalism popularized a platform instead of the older tub pulpit. On the platform appeared a desk pulpit plus chairs for preacher, guest preacher, and song leader. A small table for the Lord's Supper stood lower down, and, for Baptists and Disciples, a baptismal pool was often built into the wall above the pulpit and hidden by a curtain. The popular Akron Plan—which was designed by an Ohio Methodist Sunday school superintendent to allow easy movement between the congregational worship area and surrounding classrooms—fitted pulpit and choir into a corner of a square building and surrounded them on three sides by semicircular seating. Overflow seating was provided by moving partitions.

The 20th century increased the variety of options. Baptists tended to build a Greek-temple form in the early years but then favored brick Georgian Revival buildings, more reminiscent of New England than the South. Methodists and Presbyterians went through a Gothic phase in the 1920s but since World War II have favored a whole spectrum of styles. Increasingly the altar table receives the same emphasis as the pulpit.

Modern architecture appeared slowly in the South. Frank Lloyd Wright pioneered with the chapel at Florida Southern College, Lakeland. More recent monuments have been Paul Rudolph's chapels at Tuskegee Institute and the Bishop William R. Cannon Chapel at Emory University. Thorncrown Chapel, designed by Fay Jones, opened in a remote area of the Ozark Mountains, near Eureka Springs, in 1981.

Roman Catholics and Protestants alike have found contemporary architecture congenial, especially in Florida and such urban centers as Dallas and Houston. Lutheran churches with little connection to Old South traditions have especially embraced modern styles. Important examples of innovative contemporary architecture are St. Richard's Roman Catholic, Jackson, Miss.; First Baptist, Austin, Tex.; St. Michael's and All Angels Episcopal, Dallas; and Temple Emmanuel (Jewish), Dallas.

Much of the church architecture of the South is a vernacular architecture, built without the aid of an architect. Countless roadside chapels dot hills and valleys, reflecting local building traditions more than formal architectural skill. The churches of black congregations tend to resemble the white churches in each area. The typical country church is a wooden structure, painted white, often with pointed windows and a small tower. The pulpit dominates the one-room interior, which is usually filled with pews. A cemetery surrounds the building, and often there is a space in a grove of trees for homecomings and meals on the grounds. Occasional camp meeting grounds have space for outdoor sessions or provide wooden tabernacles. Such buildings have provided the setting for the South's vital folk religion for generations.

Recent years have seen the advent of a number of megachurches belonging to a number of denominations or independent of any. These usually consist of large auditoriums devoid of Christian symbols. Some mimic Georgian architecture, but many have moved to a more functional style.

JAMES F. WHITE
University of Notre Dame

Robert C. Broderick, *Historic Churches of the United States* (1958); Charles M. Brooks, *Texas Missions: Their Romance and Architecture* (1936); Elmer T. Clark, *An Album of Methodist History* (1952); Stephen Dorsey, *Early English Churches in America, 1607–1807* (1952); Carl Julien and Daniel W. Hollis, *Look to the Rock: One Hundred Ante-bellum Presbyterian Churches in the South* (1961); Jeanne Kilde, *When*

Church Became Theater (2002); Kenneth Murray, *Appalachia* (October–November 1974); James Patrick, *Winterthur Portfolio* (Summer 1980); James F. White, *Protestant Worship and Church Architecture: Theological and Historical Considerations* (1964); Peter W. Williams, *Houses of God* (1997).

Asian Religions

In 1965 Congress passed the Immigration and Nationality Act, which liberalized codes regarding quotas on Asian immigrants. This law eventually affected the entire country, but in the South, a region known for its religious homogeneity and cultural provincialism, the growing numbers of Asian religious groups stand out as striking anomalies. The emergence of these groups also coincided with economic, legal, and industrial gains in the South since World War II. Between the Civil War and the 1960s, southern states were always among those with the lowest immigrant population. With the incremental transformation of an agriculturally based economy to one of diversified industries, and with the radical changes in civil rights, the South eventually offered itself as a more open and opportune place for the newcomer.

Almost 40 years after the Immigration and Nationality Act, Asian communities have emerged as a decisive presence within the South. In metropolitan areas, small towns, and rural areas, immigrants from India, Southeast Asia (Cambodia, Laos, Vietnam, Thailand, and Sri Lanka), Taiwan, Hong Kong, and Japan have begun to play a role in the reshaping of southern culture. The majority of Asians live in urban and suburban areas. Consequently, most temples and centers are found in and near large cities or in areas easily accessible by an interstate highway. But one also finds Asian families living in the remote hamlets of the Carolina Piedmont, in fishing villages along the Gulf Coast, and near the lonely crossroads of Delta farms, devoutly practicing the traditions of their ancestors. Among Indian immigrants are found Hindus (the largest group), Muslims, Jains, and Sikhs. The majority of immigrants from Southeast Asia and the Pacific Rim are Buddhists, who represent diverse ethnic, regional, and sectarian backgrounds. Increasingly, then, discussions about the relation of religion to southern identity must take into account the impact of emergent Asian religious communities.

For many Asian families, religion has played a pivotal role in developing strategies of adaptation for living in the South. They have found themselves in a culture strongly shaped by evangelical Christianity, with the rather commonplace expectation of belonging to a religious body. Consequently, Asians have sometimes become more self-consciously "Hindu" and "Buddhist" than before their arrival. The growth in Asian religions has also influenced the creation of numerous interfaith groups dedicated to promoting religious understanding, such as Partners in Dialogue in Columbia, S.C., and Faiths Together in Houston. In the wake of 11 September 2001, such groups played a key role in prompting the critical reflection on issues of violence and religious stereotyping. In the fall of 2003, Memphis hosted the Festival of Faiths, an interreligious event, which featured a lecture by Arun Gandhi, the grandson of Mohandas Gandhi.

Hinduism and Buddhism have been introduced in America through both conversion and immigration. Convert Hinduism usually stressed the work of a guru, whose audience was made up primarily of non-Asian converts. Examples in the South include the Meher Baba Clinic in Mrytle Beach, S.C.; the Yogaville Ashram in central Virginia; and the ISKCON (International Society for Krishna Consciousness) centers in Atlanta, New Orleans, and West Virginia. Convert Buddhism has emphasized meditation and a philosophy of self-help. Meditations centers and groups composed of a non-Asian majority are now scattered throughout the South, such as the Shambhala Meditation Center of Asheville, N.C., and Padmasambhava Buddhist Center in Longwood, Fla. These centers have often functioned as a support group for Asian Buddhists as they settle into new communities. A good example is the Delta Insight Group in Memphis, Tenn., which was founded by a Rhodes College professor of religion. In response to the recent influx of Asian Buddhists, the group formed an organization named Dharma Memphis, which emphasizes "meditation and individual spiritual development" but also seeks to offer "a community structure" for Buddhists of all backgrounds.

In comparison with convert forms of Asian religions, ethnic or immigrant forms give greater emphasis to ritual and domestic matters. Attention to ritual has required provision for the role of religious authorities. Hindu groups support Brahmin priests, and Buddhist groups support monks and nuns, who perform temple and home or family rites. Along with the attention to ritual, ethnic forms are more family centered. Temples are founded through a genuine need for common places of worship but also as resource centers for the religious instruction of children, nurturing family values, and promoting cultural identity.

In the South, Hinduism is the most widespread religious tradition among ethnic Indians, with about 60 temples or centers. Every state of the old Confederacy, as well as Kentucky, Oklahoma, and West Virginia, hosts at least one. Georgia alone has at least seven, most in the Atlanta area. The founding of temples followed a common pattern. Hindu devotional practice centers on the family and home, and many Hindus keep an altar dedicated to a particular deity. Newly formed Hindu groups would first meet in homes and then later in rented church, school, and business spaces. As numbers and resources grew, members would then devote themselves to temple building. However, for many families, especially those in more isolated areas, home worship has remained the focus of their piety.

Hinduism has always allowed for a plurality of belief systems. In the South, this remains the case. At the same time, Hindus have accented the monotheistic nature of their faith: the multiple forms of deity point to one reality — Brahman. The monotheistic perspective corresponds to the intentional ecumenical character of Hinduism — as it is practiced in the South, as well as in the rest of America. Thus, one finds in numerous temples, such as the Vedic Center in Greenville, S.C., a kind of parity given to the forms of deity represented in the altar: no one form of God dominates. Even in temples that emphasize a particular form, such as the Sri Meenakshi temple in Houston, which in 1977 was dedicated to the Goddess Meenakshi, or the Hindu Temple of Atlanta, which in 1992 was dedicated to Venkatesvara (Vishnu), one finds an inclusive approach. Temple theology and practice transcend ethnic, regional, caste, and sectarian lines. In matters of theology and worship, Hindus in the United States are more determined to acknowledge what draws them together than what divides them. This ecumenical approach has also informed the foray into developing educational institutions, as expressed in the mission statement of the Hindu University of America. Incorporated in 1989 in Orlando, Fla., the school does not identify itself with any one sectarian group but "aims to promote the catholicity of Hinduism."

The importance of India as sacred geography and its relevance to Hindu identity remain important. To some extent, the planting of temples has become one way of replicating that sacred geography. The temple represents a sacred space; in one sense it is a microcosm that closes the gap between America and India. The temple also validates the present location, signaling a kind of being at home, a special relation between place and community. For many Hindus in America, the Sri Venkatesvara Temple in Pittsburgh, Penn., has been a major pilgrimage destination. But among Hindus in the Southeast one increasingly hears mentioned in the same breath the Hindu Temple of Atlanta. For many first-generation children, a trip to Atlanta represents their "India experience."

Generally speaking, American Hindus appoint temple priests who are trained in India and come from Brahmin families. At the Hindu Temple in Atlanta, for instance, seven priests and their families reside on the compound. Many temple communities in America lack the means to support a resident Brahmin priest and must find innovative ways to carry out the ritual duties. At both the Vedic Center in Greenville and the Hindu Society in Spartanburg, S.C., lay families share the responsibility of performing evening prayers. Both communities, however, have often solicited the services of a computer scientist with a Brahmin family background. After arriving in upstate South Carolina in the early 1970s to work with a major textile company, he responded to local Hindu families' request for his services. Largely self-trained, he has supervised major ritual events at both the Greenville and Spartanburg temples and, like a modern-day "circuit rider," has traveled throughout the state performing domestic *puja* ("prayer"), house consecrations, weddings, and funeral rites.

In the South, Buddhist groups appear more varied than Hindu groups. For instance, Swaminarayan Hindus in Houston and Sai Baba Devotees in Atlanta may acknowledge more commonality between them than would Laotian Buddhists in Spartanburg and Zen converts in nearby Greenville. Buddhist diversity in part has to do with the adaptability and resiliency of Buddhist teachings and practice. From its beginning, 2,500 year ago, the religion presented a missionary vision that stressed preaching the Dharma ("Truth" or "Law"). The religion originated in India but would eventually take root throughout Southeast Asia, China, Japan, and Tibet. The various traditions that developed in those lands are now spread throughout the South—from the Theravada embraced by Cambodian farmworkers to the Soka Gakkai groups organized on military bases, from the Chan/Pure Land shrines set up by Vietnamese merchants to the Vajrayana centers run by Tibetan monks.

Buddhist sites probably outnumber Hindu sites. One reason is that there are more Buddhist convert sites, such as the Delta Insight Group. A recent booklet on North Carolina centers listed about 20 sites of convert Buddhism in North Carolina alone. Meditation groups or centers inspired by, and in some cases representing authorized lineages of, Rinzai Zen, Soto Zen, Vipassana, and Tibetan forms are found throughout Dixie. Jack Kerouac has been counted as an early example of Buddhism in the South. In the mid-1950s, he lived in Rocky Mount, N.C., taking up meditation and writing portions of *Dharma Bums*. Nowadays, one can expect to see meditation centers wherever there is a sizable community of artists, professors, and intellectuals.

Higher education has played a critical role in exposing southerners to Buddhism. Among Buddhist traditions, the Tibetan has received major support, even though few ethnic Tibetans actually live in the South. In the 1970s, the University of Virginia received an extensive library of Tibetan Buddhist literature, eventually developing a major program in Tibetan philosophy and practice. Charlottesville is the home for the Jefferson Tibetan Society, founded in 1981, which seeks "to provide instruction in traditional Tibetan Buddhist religion, language, and philosophy to the public in general and to members in particular, and to provide a suitable setting for the practice of this religious culture."

In the late 1990s, Emory University in Atlanta established the Dresung Loseling Institute, also dedicated to the study of Tibetan Buddhist teachings and practice. And, in the spring of 2002, in commemoration of its 200th anniversary, the University of South Carolina sponsored a program in which Tibetan monks created a sand mandala in a campus building. Once they completed the mandala, they destroyed it, collected the colored sand, and then deposited it in the Congaree River as a blessing for the region.

Immigrant Southeast Asians have been the primary carriers of ethnic Buddhism throughout the South. During the 1970s, many Vietnamese and Cambodians settled in towns along the Gulf Coast and in the Carolina Piedmont. Vietnamese brought a Mahayana mix of Pure Land and Chan (Zen), while Cambodians introduced Theravadan Buddhism. In the past decade, a steady immigration of Cambodians, Thais, Laotians, and Sri Lankans throughout the South has helped make Theravadan the most widespread form of ethnic Buddhism. For instance, upstate South Carolina is now home to four Theravadan temples: two Cambodian temples located among the peach orchards of Spartanburg County, a Laotian temple in the city of Spartanburg, and a Sri Lankan temple in a small town outside Greenville. The monks and nuns who live at these locations combine a regimen of study and meditation with service to a growing lay community, consecrating homes and businesses, teaching classes, and performing funeral and ancestral rites.

One can expect to find Jain families in major metropolitan areas, such as Atlanta, Charlotte, Memphis, Houston, and Tulsa, as well as in smaller cities like Augusta, Ga., and Greenville, S.C. Throughout the South, there are about a dozen Jain temples or centers. Southern Jain families belong to Hindu temples, where they may sponsor Jain festivals and workshops on Jain practice. It is commonly the case that Jains participate in Hindu festivals and pan-Indian events. Indeed, there is a tendency in America for Jains to be absorbed into Hinduism. One example of this assimilation can be seen in many Hindu temples with significant Jain membership, such as the temples in Augusta and Greenville, which include within the altar space an image of Mahavira, the founder of Jainism. Though this pattern of assimilation is common among Jains who live near Hindu temples, it remains less so among Jains living in small towns or rural areas, such as the Jain Society of middle Tennessee, which continues to meet in a church.

Jains regard Mahavira as the 24th Thirthankara ("Ford-Maker"), the last in a series of seers who showed human beings the path to spiritual liberation. Mahavira emphasized the practice of *ahimsa*, "nonviolence," toward animals as well as human beings, which became the fundamental tenet of the Jain tradition. The most important Jain festival has become the observance of Mahavira's birthday, which takes place in the spring. It often involves a drama that reenacts the importance of *ahimsa*, hymns and recitations, and a special *puja* before the image of Mahavira. It concludes with a communal meal called a *mahaprasad*, "great food offering," which is always vegetarian. Like Hindus and Buddhists in the South, Jains have depended on the work of "circuit riders" for providing religious services. The Jain Society of central Florida, which was founded in 1981, actually supports a home for resident nuns who, from time to time, travel to other centers throughout the South to lead workshops on doctrine and practice. It remains the case, however, that southern Jains often rely on services of Hindu priests.

At first glance, the Jain practice of *ahimsa* may appear to have little relevance in the South, where hunting and fishing are respected pastimes and eating barbecue is almost a sacred feast. But this is not the case. Mahatma Gandhi, who came from a part of India where the Jain community thrived, applied *ahimsa* in his opposition to British colonial rule. Gandhi's idea of nonviolent civil disobedience, in turn, inspired Martin Luther King Jr. and the civil rights movement. Thus, it appears fitting that Arun Gandhi established the M. K. Gandhi Institute on Nonviolence in Memphis, the city of King's assassination.

In the 19th century, Sikhs were among the first Asian Indian immigrants migrating to America, with most settling in California to work as farmers. Today Sikhs remain most active on the West Coast and in New York. But in the past two decades Sikh groups in the South have been on the rise. Texas probably has the largest number of Sikhs, with established *Gurdwaras* ("temples") in Austin, Dallas, and Houston. Burgeoning Sikh communities exist now in south Florida; in Atlanta and Augusta, Ga.; in Columbia, S.C.; in Durham and Charlotte, N.C.; and in New Orleans. Southern Sikhs have worked primarily in medical, business, research, and engineering professions.

Sikhism is one of the newest world religions, founded in the 15th century in the Punjab region of northern India. Its founder, Guru Nanak, preached the unity of God and the harmony of religions. Nanak's followers eventually compiled his writings and those of successive leaders to form a body of sacred Scripture called the Adi Granth Sahib. Like many of their neighbors in the South, Sikhs meet at their Gurdwara for worship on Sundays. Worship always involves reciting verses from Scripture. Services usually conclude with a common meal that takes place in a room in the temple called the Langar Hall. The most important festival dates for Sikhs in the South are the autumn celebration of Guru

Nanak's birthday and the spring festival that commemorates the founding of Khalsa, a fraternal order whose members wear blue turbans. Sunday worship and the calendar of festivals have provided special opportunities for social networking. For instance, the Charlotte, Columbia, and Augusta Sikhs frequently worship together.

In the days following 11 September 2001, throughout America many turban-wearing Sikhs, who were mistaken for Muslims, became the target of reprisals from angry mobs. Thus, Gurdwara communities have since taken a more active role in educating the public about Sikh beliefs and practice and in promoting the message of peace and religious unity. For instance, the Singa Sabha Gurdwara in Austin, Tex., has sponsored seminars on the Sikh religion and public showings of the film documentary *Mistaken Identity*. In 2003 the Atlanta Gurdwara inaugurated its first Festival of Peace. Sikh leaders will be active in interfaith groups wherever they are found.

At the beginning of the 21st century, emergent Asian communities have contributed to the complexity of "southern religion" or "southern culture." In 2003 an Indian convert to Catholicism ran for governor of Louisiana; a Buddhist organization organized a southern tour of a Buddha relic; and, in a case strangely reminiscent of Southern Baptist battles over Scripture, an Emory professor has created controversy among regional Hindus over a critical study of Ganesha myths. These episodes hardly signal another epitaph on Dixie; rather, they attest to its unsung gift to absorb and change. Jains with Georgia accents, Buddhist temples with dogwood instead of lotus blossom seals, sweet potatoes placed on domestic shrines, and Hare Krishna singing at Mardi Gras evoke a more complex image of the South. Today that place gives birth to new multicultural identities, as expressed by the Atlanta Indian on National Public Radio, who, by paraphrasing an old saying, called himself "Indian by birth, American by choice, and Southern by the grace of God." Evangelical Christianity may yet continue to be the dominant form of religiosity, but its role in shaping southern culture will increasingly be negotiated with other faiths.

SAM BRITT
Furman University

Diana L. Eck, *A New Religious America* (2001); John Y. Fenton, *Transplanting Religious Traditions: Asian Indians in America* (1988); Thomas A. Tweed and Stephen Prothero, *Asian Religions in America: A Documentary History* (1999); Raymond Brady Williams, *Religions of Immigrants from India and Pakistan: New Threads in the American Tapestry* (1988).

Black Religion

The religious life of the majority of black southerners originated in both traditional African religions and Anglo-Protestant evangelicalism. The influence of Africa was more muted in the United States than in Latin America, where African-derived theology and ritual were institutionalized in the communities of Brazilian candomblé, Haitian voodoo, and Cuban Santeria. Nevertheless, in the United States, as in Latin America, slaves did transmit to their descendants styles of worship, funeral customs, magical ritual, and medicinal practice based on the religious systems of West and Central African societies.

Although some slaves in Maryland and Louisiana were baptized as Catholics, most had no contact with Catholicism and were first converted to Christianity in large numbers under the preaching of Baptist and Methodist revivalists in the late 18th century. The attractiveness of the evangelical revivals for slaves was due to several factors: the emotional behavior of revivalists encouraged the type of religious ecstasy similar to the danced religions of Africa; the antislavery stance taken by some Baptists and Methodists encouraged slaves to identify evangelicalism with emancipation; blacks actively participated in evangelical meetings and cofounded churches with white evangelicals; evangelical churches licensed black men to preach.

By the 1780s pioneer black preachers had already begun to minister to their own people in the South, and as time went on, black congregations, mainly Baptist in denomination, increased in size and in number, despite occasional harassment and proscription by the authorities. However, the majority of slaves in the antebellum South attended church, if at all, with whites.

Institutional church life did not exhaust the religion of the slaves. An "invisible institution" of secret and often forbidden religious meetings thrived in the slave quarters. Here slaves countered the slaveholding gospel of the master class with their own version of Christianity in which slavery and slaveholding stood condemned by God. Slaves took the biblical story of Exodus and applied it to their own history, asserting that they, like the children of Israel, would be liberated from bondage. In the experience of conversion individual slaves affirmed their personal dignity and self-worth. In the ministry, black men exercised authority and achieved status nowhere else available to them. Melding African and Western European traditions, the slaves created a religion of great vitality.

Complementing Christianity in the quarters was conjure, a sophisticated combination of African herbal medicine and magic. Based on the belief that illness and misfortune have personal as well as impersonal causes, conjure offered frequently successful therapy for the mental and physical ills of generations of

Church of God in Christ, Clarksdale, Miss., 1968
(William R. Ferris Collection, Southern Folklife Collection,
Wilson Library, University of North Carolina at Chapel Hill)

African Americans and simultaneously served as a system for venting social tension and resolving conflict.

The Civil War, emancipation, and Reconstruction wrought an institutional transformation of black churches in the South. Northern denominations—black as well as white—sent aid to the freedmen and missionaries to educate and bring them to church. Freedmen, eager to learn to read and write, flocked to schools set up by the American Missionary Association and other freedmen's aid societies. These freedmen's schools laid the foundation for major black colleges and universities such as Fisk, Morehouse, Dillard, and others. Eager to exercise autonomy, freedmen swarmed out of white churches and organized their own. Some affiliated with black denominations of northern origin; others formed their own southern associations.

Black ministers actively campaigned in Reconstruction politics and in some cases were elected to positions of influence and power. Richard H. Cain, for example, was elected to the U.S. House of Representatives from North Carolina and Hiram R. Revels to the Senate from Mississippi. With the failure of Reconstruction and the disfranchisement of black southerners, the church once again became the sole forum for black politics, as well as the economic, social, and educational center of black communities across the South.

By the end of the century, black church membership stood at an astounding 2.7 million out of a population of 8.3 million. Most numerous were the Baptists, who succeeded in 1895 in creating a National Baptist Convention, followed numerically by the black Methodists, as institutionalized in the African Methodist Episcopal (AME) Church and the African Methodist Episcopal Zion Church, both founded in the North early in the century, and the Colored Methodist Episcopal Church, formed by an amicable withdrawal from the Methodist Episcopal Church, South, in 1870.

Though too poor to mount a full-fledged missionary campaign, the black churches turned to evangelization of Africa as a challenge to African American Christian identity. The first black missionaries, David George and George Liele, had sailed during the Revolution, George to Nova Scotia and then to Sierra Leone, Liele to Jamaica. Daniel Coker followed in 1820 and Lott Carey and Colin Teague in 1821. But in the 1870s and 1880s the mission to Africa seemed all the more urgent. As race relations worsened, as lynching mounted in frequency, as racism was legislated in Jim Crow statutes, emigration appeared to black clergy like Henry McNeal Turner the only solution. Others saw the redemption of Africa as the divinely appointed destiny of black Americans, God's plan for drawing good out of the evil of slavery and oppression.

Connections between southern black churches and northern ones developed as blacks from the South migrated or escaped north and as northern missionaries came to the South after the Civil War. Several southern blacks assumed positions of leadership in northern churches. Josiah Bishop, a Baptist preacher from Virginia, became pastor of the Abyssinian Baptist Church in New York, and Daniel Alexander Payne and Morris Brown, both of Charleston, became bishops of the AME Church. Beginning in the 1890s and increasing after the turn of the century, rural southern blacks migrated in larger and larger numbers to the cities of the North. Frequently their ministers traveled with them and transplanted, often in storefront or house churches, congregations from the South.

In the cities, southern as well as northern, black migrants encountered new religious options that attracted some adherents from the traditional churches. Catholicism, through the influence of parochial schools, began attracting significant numbers of blacks in the 20th century. Black Muslims and Jews developed new religioracial identities for African Americans disillusioned with Christianity. The Holiness and Pentecostal churches stressed the experiential and ecstatic dimensions of worship while preaching the necessity of sanctification and the blessings of the Spirit. They also facilitated the development of gospel music by allowing the use of instruments and secular tunes in church services.

Though urbanization and secularization led to criticism of black religion as accommodationist and compensatory, the church remained the most important and effective public institution in southern black life. The religious culture of the black folk was celebrated by intellectuals like W. E. B. DuBois and James Weldon Johnson, who acclaimed the artistry of the slave spirituals and black preaching.

In the late 1950s and 1960s the civil rights movement drew heavily on the institutional and ethical resources of the black churches across the South. Martin Luther King Jr. brought to the attention of the nation and the world the moral tradition of black religion. Today, black religion is more pluralistic than ever. Most African Americans continue to worship in predominantly black denominations, although they also form identifiable caucuses within biracial denominations. Black liberation theology associated with southern-born writers like James Cone and Pauli Murray has been an influence on some of the faithful for decades. Roman Catholics and Muslims include significant communities of African Americans in the South. Black religious leaders and laypeople continue to work for racial justice and to cooperate in racial reconciliation efforts in the South. Churches remain important political organizing sites and encourage political participation among their members. Although the church is no longer the only institution that blacks control, it still exerts considerable power in black communities.

ALBERT J. RABOTEAU
Princeton University

Hans A. Baer, *The Black Spiritual Movement: A Religious Response to Racism* (1984); Yvonne Chireau, *Black Magic: Dimensions of the Supernatural in African American Religion* (2000); James Cone, *For My People: Black Theology and the Black Church* (1984); W. E. B. DuBois, *The Souls of Black Folk* (1903); Sylvia R. Frey and Betty Wood, *Come Shouting to Zion: African American Protestantism in the American South and British Caribbean to 1830* (1998); Samuel S. Hill, ed., *Religion in the Southern States: A Historical Study* (1983); C. Eric Lincoln, ed., *The Black Experience in Religion* (1974); Donald G. Mathews, *Religion in the Old South* (1977); William E. Montgomery, *Under Their Own Vine and Fig Tree: The African American Church in the South, 1865–1900* (1993); Albert J. Raboteau, *Canaan Land: A Religious History of African Americans* (1999), *Slave Religion: The "Invisible Institution" in the Antebellum South* (1978); Clarence Walker, *A Rock in a Weary Land: The African Methodist Episcopal Church during the Civil War and Reconstruction* (1982); James M. Washington, *Frustrated Fellowship: The Black Baptist Quest for Social Power* (1986); Joseph R. Washington, *Black Religion: The Negro and Christianity in the United States* (1964).

Broadcasting, Religious

Religious broadcasting is as old as broadcasting itself. The first wireless voice transmission was an informal religious broadcast. Beamed from Brant Rock, Mass., on Christmas Eve of 1906 to ships within a several-hundred-mile radius, the program content consisted of Bible readings, a violin solo of "O Holy Night," and a vocal recording of Handel's "Largo."

When the first regularly scheduled radio programming began at station KDKA in Pittsburgh, regularly scheduled religious programs commenced within two months. Radio broadcasting exploded in the 1920s so that by early 1925 there were more than 600 stations on the air. Just over 10 percent were owned by churches or religious organizations.

In every city and town in the country with a radio station there were preachers who wanted to broadcast. And many did. But as is still true today, for every mainline church that wanted to broadcast its Sunday worship services, there were a dozen evangelicals trying to get on the air. The current feud between the evangelical and fundamentalist syndicated broadcasters, on the one hand, and the liberal denominations affiliated with the National Council of Churches, on the other, also dates from the early years of broadcasting.

"Pastor's Study," direct from the study of Dr. Thomas J. Powers (Charles Reagan Wilson Collection, Center for the Study of Southern Culture, University of Mississippi)

The first religious telecast took place on Easter Sunday, 1940. This was the beginning of two decades of growth that would see television transformed from a laboratory experiment to a consumer commodity that was available in 90 percent of American households.

Bishop Fulton Sheen, who was the first speaker on *The Catholic Hour* presented by NBC in 1930, became the first superstar of religious broadcasting. Bishop Sheen's program, *Life Is Worth Living*, which began in 1952, remains the only regularly scheduled religious program on a network with a commercial sponsor. With an impeccable delivery, a twinkle in his eye, and an angel to clean his blackboard, Sheen attracted millions of viewers.

Sheen's success in television probably was the single most important factor in persuading evangelicals that television — far more than radio — was the medium best suited to their purposes. Television could bring back the evangelistic face-to-face meeting in which a powerful and charismatic preacher could sway audiences and enlist followers.

A few evangelical/fundamentalist preachers saw "televangelism," then, as their great opportunity to spread the gospel, but getting on television proved to be even more difficult than getting on the radio. Airtime for television was a much scarcer resource than was radio airtime. Mainline Protestants and Catholics cooperated with Jews and Southern Baptists in sharing the scarce resource of free network time.

For many years evangelicals and fundamentalists believed there was a conspiracy to keep them off the air. Broadcasting stations, under the Communications Act of 1934, are not common carriers and, hence, are not obliged to sell time just because someone wants to buy it. As radio stations grew prosperous, many adopted policies of refusing to sell time for religion and giving it only to ecumenical groups. Most television broadcasters followed the same policy.

But evangelists and fundamentalists were persuaded early that the airways, both radio and television, were a special gift from God that made possible the fulfillment of the great commission to spread the gospel to every living creature. They persisted. When radio and television stations refused to deal them in on the sharing of free public service time, they offered to buy time. When refused, they offered to pay more. Gradually, station owners recognized that they were passing up a very lucrative market. Little by little, the evangelicals inched their way onto the airwaves.

The cash the evangelists use to pay for airtime is raised through audience solicitations. Many styles and gimmicks have been developed to persuade viewers to contribute to radio and television broadcasts, and they work. By the early 1980s the total revenues from religious broadcasting in the United States were estimated at $1 billion.

Technological developments contributed significantly to the expansion of religious television. The first important development was the introduction of videotapes. Lower costs and speed of production made possible wide distribution of the same program for broadcast on the same day all across the country. The number of syndicated programs (those appearing on five or more stations) increased gradually during the 1960s. A big jump occurred during the first half of the 1970s, when the number of syndicated programs advanced from 38 in 1970 to 66 in 1975. After leveling off for the remainder of the 1970s, program development increased sharply in the early 1980s to nearly 100 syndicated programs.

Satellite broadcasting promoted the expansion of syndicated programs in the early 1980s. Three religious networks, Christian Broadcasting, PTL, and Trinity Broadcasting, began broadcasting 24 hours a day, seven days a week around the turn of the decade. Initially, they carried almost exclusively religious programs. None had the capacity to produce more than a few hours of programming daily. Hence, they were in the market for programs. For a while almost anyone who could produce a videotaped program could send it to one of these new networks and be accepted for satellite broadcast. Audiences were very small, but the broadcasts provided good exposure. And once they got on the air via satellite, many evangelists decided to go the syndication route. The quality of many of these programs was not very good, but other technological innovations significantly lowered production costs and made possible the production of technically respectable programs at a cost many preachers could afford.

Audience size, as measured by Arbitron, increased from under 10 million viewers in 1970 to over 22 million by the middle of the decade. Audience size stabilized during the second half of the 1970s and did not appear to expand much during the first half of the 1980s. Religious broadcasters dispute Arbitron and Neilsen ratings, claiming that neither organization has developed adequate methods to accurately measure broadcasts received via satellite on cable channels. There is some evidence to support their position, including various Gallup polls asking people about their viewing of religious programs.

Audience size is clearly much smaller than the claims of many individual "televangelists." Jerry Falwell, for example, has claimed as many as 50 million viewers, but Arbitron and Neilsen have consistently measured the audience for his *Old-Time Gospel Hour* at well under 2 million. Still, the total audience is a sizable minority of the American population. Together with the religious recording and publishing industries, televangelism has forged a new counterculture in America.

Like the youth counterculture of the 1960s, the religious counterculture is hardly monolithic. When Martin Luther King Jr. led civil rights activists on a march in 1965 from Selma to Montgomery, Ala., Jerry Falwell boldly castigated clergy for involvement in political protest. "Preachers are not called to be politicians," he claimed, "but to be soul winners." By 1976 he had changed his mind, and in 1979 he founded the Moral Majority, a conservative political organization.

In 1980 religious broadcasters were divided over whether it was proper for them to engage in partisan political activity. With the encouragement of Ronald Reagan, who addressed their professional organization, the National Religious Broadcasters, each year during his first term as president, a sizable proportion of radio and television broadcasters by 1984 were on the political bandwagon. D. James Kennedy, for example, who is pastor of the Coral Ridge Presbyterian Church in Fort Lauderdale, Fla., and host of a weekly television show, *The Coral Ridge Hour*, embraced in the mid-1980s a conservative "culture wars" agenda on abortion, school prayer, creation science, and television violence. Bill Clinton's presidency led him to increasingly support conservative candidates, which was the case with other televangelists as well.

The amount of religious broadcasting available varies by region and metropolitan area of the country. The major televangelists claim that they are popular in all regions of the country and that they attract the young and the old, males and females, the educated and the uneducated, the rich and the poor to view their electronic churches. In one sense these claims are true. Their programs are broadcast on stations across the country, and there are some viewers from the various age, education, income, and sex categories.

These claims notwithstanding, the electronic church remains uniquely a southern phenomenon. Virtually all the major "televangelists" are from the South or have migrated to the South to establish their ministries: Billy Graham (North Carolina), Oral Roberts (Oklahoma), Rex Humbard (Arkansas), Jerry Falwell (Virginia), Pat Robertson (Virginia), Jim Bakker (North Carolina), Jimmy Swaggart (Louisiana), Richard De Hann (Florida), James Robison (Texas), Kenneth Copeland (Texas), T. D. Jakes (Texas), and D. James Kennedy (Florida). Robert Schuller is the only person with a successful television ministry who is neither from the South nor concerned with a southern ministry. Operating out of Orange County in southern California, he is also the only mainline Protestant to develop a successful television ministry.

The audiences of the electronic church are also drawn disproportionately from the South. Whereas the South has slightly less than one-third of the nation's population, the major television ministries draw in the range of 45 to 55 percent of their audience from this region. The Midwest, with roughly a quarter of the nation's population, provides roughly that proportion of the audiences, with the eastern and western regions of the country significantly underrepresented.

These regional figures probably underestimate the extent to which religious broadcasting, especially television, is a southern regional phenomenon. Much of its appeal outside the South is to people who have migrated from the region. Rex Humbard and Ernest Angley (a lesser light in the electronic church) both built large congregations in Akron, Ohio, with farm migrants from the South who came to the industrial Midwest in search of blue-collar jobs.

Present migratory patterns into the Sunbelt will reinforce the southern character of the audience. Virtually all the syndicated religious television programs have audiences of which two-thirds to three-quarters are 50 years of age or over. Audiences are also disproportionately female. The Sunbelt movement is a disproportionately older migratory flow and, as females survive males by an average of about seven years, the proportion of females in the region will increase. Only CBN, with its *700 Club*, seems to be making a systematic effort to attract a broader audience.

JEFFREY K. HADDEN
University of Virginia

CHARLES E. SWANN
Union Theological Seminary
Richmond, Virginia

Robert Ableman and Stewart M. Hoover, eds., *Religious Television: Controversies and Conclusions* (1990); Paul Apostolidis, *Stations of the Cross: Adorno and Christian Right Radio* (2000); Frye Gaillard, *Race, Rock, and Religion: Profiles from a Southern Journalist* (1982); Jeffrey K. Hadden and Charles E. Swann, *Prime Time Preachers: The Rising Power of Televangelism* (1981); Peter G. Horsfield, *Religious Television: The American Experience* (1984).

Calvinism

Calvinism designates that way of being Christian that has its roots in the life and work of John Calvin (1509–64), the Protestant reformer of Geneva. Its theology is both Catholic and Protestant. It is Catholic in that Calvin reaffirmed the ancient catholic faith, in particular the Apostles' Creed, the doctrine of the person of Jesus Christ as found in the Nicene Creed and the Chalcedonian Definition, and the doctrine of the Trinity. It is Protestant in that Calvin thought he was continuing the work of Luther. He built on the affirmations of Luther's writings of 1520: the supreme authority of the Holy Spirit speaking through Scripture, justification by grace through faith, the priesthood of all believers, the sanctity of the common life, and the necessity of personal decision and responsibility. This theology influenced southern religious developments and also found expression in political attitudes, literary works, and the folklore of daily living.

Calvin's greatest work was a comprehensive statement of Christian faith, *The Institutes of the Christian Religion*, which, beginning as a small book in 1536, was continually revised until Calvin found satisfaction with the final Latin edition of 1559. He also prepared a liturgy and a church order for Geneva that was influential in Calvinist churches. He directed the completion of a Psalter in 1562. As a churchman Calvin was in constant contact with Protestant leaders through-out Europe. His letters comprised almost 11 volumes of his collected works.

Calvinism is sometimes used as a synonym for Reformed Protestantism because Calvin was the latter's dominant personality and, in later history, its most influential figure. Yet the Reformed churches in Zurich under the leadership of Zwingli and Bullinger, in Basel with Ecolampadius, and in the Rhineland all had a part in shaping Reformed Protestantism. In general, the Reformed theology of German-speaking Switzerland and the Rhineland was less passionate and more generous and humanistic, less determined to have an independent church, than Geneva; but each type shared a common perspective in theology.

Calvin's work and theology were shaped by emphases that distinguish it from other forms of Protestantism. Calvin perceived God, the creator of the universe, primarily as energy, activity, power, moral purpose, intentionality. The characteristic response to a God so conceived was not contemplation and the vision of God but action in service of the Kingdom of God and a life that embodies the purposes of God.

Calvin's understanding of God as energy and purpose found expression in God's lordship in history, in which the sovereign God works as creator, judge, and redeemer. Hence, Calvin understood the Christian life as the embodiment of the purposes of God in history. From the beginning, Calvinists were activists engaged in transforming economic, political, and cultural life according to their vision of the Kingdom of God. Calvin sought the coming into being of the holy community in Geneva. The Calvinists carried this vision of the holy community, the embodiment of the purposes of God in society, to Scotland, to Puritan England, and to Massachusetts, where they went on an "errand into the wilderness" to demonstrate the possibility of a Christian society. The Baptists and the Presbyterians embodied Calvinism's influence in the South most clearly, although in neither case so dramatically as with the New England Puritans. Calvinism has always been uneasy with a personal piety defined simply in terms of the relation of the soul to God, but that kind of piety has been in the evangelical South the dominant religious form.

Predestination, the doctrine popularly identified with Calvinism, attributed human salvation to the initiative of God. While Calvinists rejoiced in human freedom, they believed that once the human will becomes sinful it cannot by its own efforts transform itself. A self-centered person can become un-self-centered only when divine grace attracts the self away from itself to God.

The Calvinists defined the chief end of life as the glory of God. Calvin, perhaps with Luther in mind, insisted that God's glory, not the salvation of one's own soul, must be the primary human concern. Later Calvinists were skeptical of revivalists who made the salvation of one's soul the center of attention. Calvinism thus represented an important counterforce to the evangelicalism dominant in the South since the early 1800s.

A second characteristic of Calvinism is an emphasis on sanctification. Luther had rediscovered the primacy of God's mercy over every form of work righteousness: salvation by human merit is beyond human power; our best deeds as well as our worst are flawed by self-interest. As a second-generation Protestant, Calvin faced the criticism that this great emphasis on justification by grace undercut the Christian life. Calvin knew that justification, the fact and experience of forgiveness, is the principal hinge on which Christian life hangs, but he also knew that God's grace is power that renews as well as mercy that forgives. He conceived of the Christian life frequently in military terms as a war against the world, the flesh, and the Devil and as the obligation to obey God's command and fulfill his purposes.

Calvinism has also been marked by a distinctive emphasis on the life of the mind in the service of God and by a skepticism about feelings not subjected to rational scrutiny. Calvinists have always insisted that it is important to know what one believes and to be able to give a reason for one's faith. Catechetical instruction has been characteristic of Calvinistic churches until recent times. Southern Presbyterians and denominations that grew out of that group have especially championed this idea in the region.

Closely related to the emphasis on the life of the mind was a similar emphasis on the task of the minister as teacher and preacher. The Calvinist sermon not only proclaimed the gospel but also educated people in logical, coherent thought and discourse. Important southern colleges, such as Davidson and Rhodes, founded by Presbyterians reflect this strong belief in education.

A fifth characteristic has been the importance of the organized church and the disciplined life. Order was a basic concept for Calvin. Salvation could be understood as the proper ordering of a life, an order that found primary expression in the church. Order was also a personal virtue. Calvinist asceticism and discipline were not based on any depreciation of the world, which the Calvinists knew was God's good creation, but on the need for an economical use of life's resources.

An emphasis on simplicity was pervasive in Calvin's writings and in the manner of his life. In literary expression he never used two words when one would do. In liturgy he protested against pomp and "theatrical trifle." In manner of life he insisted on moderation. Calvin and the Calvinists abhorred the pompous, the pretentious, the ostentatious, the contrived, and the artificial. They insisted on authenticity, clarity, directness, simplicity. The simple for Calvin was closely related to sincerity. It was open to reality. The ostentatious, the contrived, and the pompous covered up reality.

Calvinism was modified and transmitted to later generations through the "school" theology of the 17th century. Scholasticism was a necessary development. Calvin as a preacher did not write theology with care for definition. He left many theological issues poorly defined or unresolved. In addition, Calvinism had to face intellectual challenges from Roman Catholics, from other Protestants, and from later Calvinists whose internal debates had to be resolved. The scholastic theologians with great technical skills gave to Calvinism a clearly defined, logical, coherent form.

Protestant scholasticism also developed a common theological vocabulary, which was carefully defined and generally in the language of ordinary human discourse. This common theological vocabulary, which was influential in the South through the first half of the 20th century, made it possible for people with little formal training to become competent theologians.

Calvinism was mediated to the South largely through the 17th-century scholastic theology. *Institutio Theologiae Elencticae* by Francis Turretin (1623–87), a Genevan theologian, was used as a textbook at such Presbyterian seminaries as Princeton, Union Theological Seminary in Richmond, Va., Columbia Theological Seminary in Columbia, S.C., and at the Southern Seminary of the Baptists in Louisville, Ky. *The Westminster Confession of Faith* (1643–47) was the authoritative summary of Calvinism for American Calvinists in Presbyterian, Baptist, and Congregational churches. It was also one of the most influential books of colonial America. *The Shorter Catechism*, a question-and-answer summary of the Westminster theology, was until World War II the basic text for the education of Presbyterian young people.

The original work of Calvin was modified not only by Protestant scholasticism but by many other influences as it came to the South. Among these were English Puritanism, the Scottish Common Sense philosophy, and the Scots-Irish immigrants who constituted the main body of southern Calvinists.

The most influential expressions of Calvinism in the South are to be found in the work of James Henley Thornwell (1812–62), Robert Dabney (1820–98), and Charles Hodge (1797–1878), a Princeton theologian whose influence was widely felt among southern Presbyterians.

Scholastic theology, for all its technical excellence, was challenged from the late 17th century on by the Enlightenment and by the cultural developments of the 19th century. Yet it maintained a pervasive influence, especially in the South through the first half of the 20th century. The task of giving a statement of Calvinist faith in light of the legacy of the Enlightenment and the social, political, and scientific developments of the 19th and 20th centuries is not yet complete. The most influential 20th-century statements have been the works of the Swiss theologians Karl Barth, *Church Dogmatics* (1932–67), and Emil Brunner, *Dogmatics* (1946–60), and the American theologian Reinhold Niebuhr, *The Nature and the Destiny of Man* (1941–43). No theology now has the pervasive influence that Calvinism did in significant segments of southern society. In a pluralistic society dominated by mass media this may no longer be possible.

Calvinism's influence, however, has extended far beyond its importance as a formal theology. It was one of the fundamental forces creating a distinctive character of the people of the region. W. J. Cash saw popularized Calvinism as part of the major dichotomy of southern psychology—the South was the world's supreme paradox of hedonism in the midst of puritanism. He believed that by the mid-19th century "the whole South, including the Methodists," had moved "toward a position of thoroughgoing Calvinism in feeling if not in formal theology." Arminian free will surely also entered into the character of the region through the large Methodist influence, but the two combined in a peculiar cultural synthesis. Noting Calvinism's part in another cultural combination, James McBride Dabbs talked of "the spiritual pride of the God-selected Calvinist" combining with the pride of "the imperial Englishman" to produce the white southerner. Calvinist belief in human depravity, God's sovereignty, and an ordained universe helped to condition southern enslavement of blacks, he wrote.

Cash called southern Calvinism "puritanism," and so have others. Fred Hobson points out that "Southern 'Puritanism' was vastly different from the New England variety, less structured, less intellectual, more emotional—raw Calvinism, rather than the cerebral Puritanism of the Massachusetts Bay." This faith had a dramatic impact on the southern frontier. Calvinism early became an influence in the region through the prominence of the Scots-Irish on the frontier. It became a particularly significant aspect of southern culture during the Civil War and its aftermath. Calvinism was one factor that led southerners to expect victory for the Confederacy. The belief in God's sovereignty and his determination of the elect led southern whites to see themselves as God's chosen engaged in holy war. As Daniel Hundley said after hearing of Confederate battle triumphs in Virginia, "When God is for us, who is against us?"

Unreconstructed southerners after the war, however, were frustrated, trying to come to terms with defeat in a holy war. They could see no explanation except for the mysterious will of God. Their popularized Calvinism led them to believe they had sinned and God was punishing them for their sins, preparing his people for a greater destiny. Not only ministers but teachers and journalists, generals and common soldiers came to believe that God did not fail them; they had rather been unworthy. Stonewall Jackson was the war's supreme incarnation of a Calvinist warrior, but even the aristocratic Robert E. Lee, according to his biographers, had much Calvinism in his soul.

Calvinism was used in a variety of ways by a variety of people, suggesting its pervasive influence in southern culture. Presbyterian Robert Dabney used it to justify a slave society, and others have used the belief in a God-ordained social order to argue against changes in racial customs and against the rights of labor and of women. But George W. Cable, Ralph McGill, Lillian Smith, and other liberals used Calvinism to justify change; as McGill said in *The South and the Southerner*, he became a racial liberal because his "Calvinist conscience was stirred by some of the race prejudice I saw."

Calvinism also influenced the literary development of writers such as William Faulkner. He once noted that he had used religious symbols in his works because they were all around him in north Mississippi, and Calvinism was perhaps the central religious influence he explored. Faulkner disliked what he saw as a puritanical stress on sober living, the discouragement of fleshly pleasures, and a spiritual self-righteousness, all of which he saw stemming from Calvinism. He portrayed characters made authoritarian and repressively violent by a Calvinist outlook. His Calvinists, or Puritans, as he sometimes called them, show little concern for ritual or piety but believe in God's justice and in human practicality and good works. Characters such as Lucas Beauchamp in *Go Down, Moses* and Mink Snopes in *The Town* believe, for example, less in a divine being of mercy and more in a God of justice. Faulkner did seem to admire especially one emphasis in Calvinism—as it was translated into human behavior in the South—that on the human will and the need for action. *Light in August, Absalom, Absalom!*, and "The Bear" in *Go Down, Moses* represent the most thorough southern literary explorations of Calvinism's influence in southern literature.

JOHN H. LEITH
Union Theological Seminary
Richmond, Virginia

Cleanth Brooks, *William Faulkner: The Yoknapatawpha Country* (1963); W. J. Cash, *The Mind of the South* (1941); James McBride Dabbs, *Who Speaks for the South?* (1964); Fred Hobson, *Tell about the South: The Southern Rage to Explain* (1983); John H. Leith, *Introduction to the Reformed Tradition: A Way of Being the Christian Community* (1977); John T. McNeill, *The History and Character of Calvinism* (1954); James L. Peacock and Ruel W. Tyson Jr., eds., *Pilgrims of Paradox: Calvinism and Experience among the Primitive Baptists in the Blue Ridge* (1989).

Churches, Country

Southern evangelicals were mainly country folk, not city slickers. The religious movement that gave rise to the "southern church" began in rural camp meeting revivals early in the 19th century and retained a distinctly rural accent straight through the 20th century. Although the South always boasted a fair share of the nation's "gentlemen theologians"—erudite, well-educated, urban-based ministers—the mainstream of southern evangelicalism tended toward the bivocational, emotional, and rural. It was among lower-class youth who claimed no firm church affiliation that the early camp meetings flourished. And it was their

Rural Baptist church, Mississippi Delta, 1975 (William Ferris Collection, Southern Folklife
Collection, Wilson Library, University of North Carolina at Chapel Hill)

music and religious aspirations that shaped both early southern hymnody and
later gospel music. Although southern gospel music migrated to the city, a cappella shaped note or sacred harp singing remained primarily a country style.

Sectarianism was also present at the beginning of southern religion. A hy-
brid of the exaggerated individualism and Jacksonian democracy that shaped
southern identity, rural religion probably produced more discord than unity
among evangelicals. Churches of Christ, Baptist, Methodist, and Presbyterian
— in all their bickering, splitting, sectarian manifestations — led the way early.
Pentecostal and Holiness sects followed in their wake. Rural evangelicals were
proud, fiery controversialists, not cuddly, generic "southern evangelicals."

Although plagued by simplistic categorization as otherworldly, rural believers lent their considerable support to a variety of political causes. Begin-

Mount Olivet Chapel, Pineville, La., built in 1857 (Louisiana State Board of Tourism)

ning with small farmer Primitive Baptists who identified with Jacksonian democratic values, rural evangelicals later cast their lot with a variety of late 19th-century political insurgencies: Greenback-Laborers, Grangers, Farmers' Alliances, Populists. The electioneering style of the insurgents as well as their rhetoric, mass meetings, and movement psychology borrowed heavily from rural evangelicalism. As this identification demonstrated, rural Christianity in the South could be a powerful force both for change and for continuity, for rustic radicalism and social justice as well as for social hierarchy and conservative tradition.

By the beginning of the 20th century, rural malaise had spread widely across America. Falling commodity prices, the failure of Populism, migration of rural children to cities, increasing rates of farm tenancy, mechanization of agriculture, the disruption of rural institutions because of school consolidation—all these and more generated a sense of crisis. Between 1870 and 1920 the percentage of Americans who farmed fell from one-half to less than one-quarter of the population. And nowhere was this crisis more apparent than in the South.

Although the South's disproportionate ruralism should have made it the seedbed of the Rural Life movement, the genesis of that reform movement occurred in New England and the Northeast. Paradoxically the region of America that was least agricultural inspired rural life renewal. And the midwives of the movement came from northeastern colleges and religious denominations that had been most influenced by the tenets of liberal theology, ecumenism, and the social gospel.

Successfully lobbying President Theodore Roosevelt, they succeeded in 1908 in establishing the Country Life Commission, which contained two southerners, appointed almost as afterthoughts among the seven members. Their 1909 report to the president incorporated the entire Progressive-era vision for rural America: improvements in education, transportation, mail service, and public health services; a massive survey of conditions in rural America. The rural church won special attention because of its role in either stabilizing or destabilizing rural life. Along with the rural school, the rural church ranked as one of the twin institutions most important to rural people.

What followed from these recommendations was two decades of frantic activity. Virtually every major denomination established a special agency devoted to helping the rural church. These agencies conducted seemingly endless surveys of churches in hundreds of rural counties. Special conferences were held, reports submitted, and solutions proposed.

Documenting the crisis in the rural southern church was the simplest part of the reform effort. A comprehensive 1916 report revealed that half the rural churches in the United States were located in the South. Of 24,500 Southern Baptist Convention (SBC) churches, 20,000 were rural. Of these rural churches, 18,000 conducted preaching services only once a month, and the same number were served by absentee pastors. In the same southern states, nearly 20,000 white Methodist churches attempted to spread the gospel, 16,500 of them in rural areas. Among these Methodist congregations, 15,000 held services only once a month, and 11,000 were served by absentee pastors. Of 3,430 Southern Presbyterian churches, 1,355 were rural, and 271 of these were without pastors. Of a total of 44,300 white Methodist and Baptist congregations, 82 percent were rural; and 90 percent of all rural churches offered preaching services only monthly. Also, 80 percent were served by absentee pastors. And because of their small size and irregular services, rural churches could not pay pastors a living wage. Rural Presbyterians pastors' annual salaries averaged only $857, Methodists $681, and Southern Baptist $334. Black rural churches fared much worse.

The surveys depicted problems in dramatic categories: farm owners generally controlled rural churches, making tenant farmers feel uneasy; as a result, counties with the highest rates of farm tenancy usually had the lowest rates of church attendance; most rural churches employed absentee pastors who did not live in the community where the church was located; few rural churches offered their communities any social outlets beyond monthly preaching (they conducted no Sunday schools, youth or women's programs); rural ministers were the least-educated clergy and the most mobile, averaging a tenure of less than three years; rural churches were declining rapidly in attendance, membership, and contributions as the young moved away and the old died.

Proposed solutions were harder. They usually reflected either a highly idealized, romantic view of rural life or the unrealistic theoretical biases of urban, educated Progressive reformers: provide more education and less emotion (one complaint against the rural evangelical church was that its decline opened the way for the rapid growth of undesirable Pentecostal and Holiness churches); begin Sunday school, youth and women's missionary programs; develop a church budget; consolidate small churches so as to pay ministers decently and develop full-time congregations; emphasize service to the community as well as individual salvation; work to improve rural schools and teachers' salaries; enroll rural pastors in rural sociology and economic courses in agricultural colleges; help these colleges to improve farming practices; encourage rural people to organize in order to modify their individualism and isolation. In short, most rural church reformers were overzealous outsiders who paid little attention to rural values. They used the methods and strategies of urban Progressive reformers because they were professionals who believed in progress through rational study, efficiency, and application of the new science of sociology to the problems of the rural South. Most were influenced by liberal theology, ecumenism, and the social gospel. Like urban educational and health reformers, they were often patronizing, haughty, and insensitive in their efforts to help rural people.

Reform proposals failed because rural evangelicals shared neither the diagnosis nor the underlying assumptions of reformers. Farmers saw no need for massive changes in the way their churches functioned. They rejected the religious assumptions of ecumenism, liberal theology, and the social gospel. They valued sectarianism and were fiercely loyal to small, local congregations, which afforded them a strong sense of community. Just as many rural people rejected fencing laws, hookworm eradication campaigns, consolidated schools, and compulsory school attendance laws, they also rejected outsiders who advised them how to change their churches.

Paradoxically those U.S. rural areas that responded most rapidly and completely to the rural church reform movement experienced the sharpest decline in rural churches. And those sectarian parts of the rural South that rejected such reforms fared best in the viability of rural congregations.

Despite assumptions that the rural church movement was of one piece or disappeared in the 1930s, the movement was quite diverse and continued through-out the century. At the end of the 20th century, Baptists predominated in one-third of America's counties. Most of these 1,322 counties were in or adjacent to the old Confederacy and were rural/nonmetropolitan. In 1994 Southern Baptists operated nearly 21,000 churches in open country or villages with a population below 2,500. Those congregations enrolled nearly five million, a third of total SBC membership, and contributed $1.5 billion to denominational causes. Yet the SBC was at best a reluctant participant in rural church reform.

WAYNE FLYNT
Auburn University

Jeffrey L. Gall, "The Country Life Movement and Country Churches, 1900–1920" (1993); Gary A. Goreham, *The Rural Church in America: A Century of Writings* (1990); Karen A. Stone, "Rescue the Perishing: The Southern Baptist Convention and the Rural Church Movement" (1998).

Civil Rights and Religion

The relation of religion and civil rights in the South is as old as southern culture. Black religious experience, forged from oppression, differs from its white counterpart in the South. The oldest black spirituals had political and civil rights overtones embedded in their religious message. "Wade in the Water," "With My Face to the Rising Sun," "Shall We Gather at the River," and many others had to do with meeting, planning, and escaping. Freedom singing has been a key ingredient in the modern civil rights movement, incorporating gospel music in powerful and moving ways. For instance, the nationally known Freedom Singers were formed out of the often jailed ranks of the Student Non-violent Coordinating Committee (SNCC), and their songs in churches greeted protesters returning from jail.

In black churches, preachers constantly compared the plight of black people to that of the children of Israel. The basic issue of civil rights was seen not in the first instance as legal, sociological, economic, or political but as moral and spiritual. The black church was the organizational building block of the civil rights movement; its leadership was predominantly clergy, ministerial students, and women of strong religious backgrounds.

Black religious leadership in civil rights in the South came mainly from the clergy and seminary students. Kelley Miller Smith, C. T. Vivian, Martin Luther King Sr., Fred Shuttlesworth, Metz Rollins, Ralph Abernathy, and Wyatt T. Walker have been key figures. Of course, Martin Luther King Jr. symbolized most dramatically the mobilizing strength of black religious traditions.

Dexter Avenue King Memorial Baptist Church, Montgomery, Ala.;
the first worship service held in its sanctuary was on Thanksgiving Day 1889.
(Dan Brothers, photographer, Alabama Bureau of Tourism and Travel)

James Lawson was a Vanderbilt Divinity School student when he helped to organize the Nashville sit-ins in 1960 with other seminary students from American Baptist Theological Seminary such as John Lewis, Bernard Lafayette, and James Bevel, all of whom played pivotal roles in SNCC. Andrew Young, a United Church of Christ minister, became Martin Luther King Jr.'s chief assistant in the Southern Christian Leadership Conference (SCLC), along with several other ministers such as James Orange and Jesse Jackson. Charles Sherrod, a divinity student in Virginia, became a key leader in SNCC.

Strong black women with religious backgrounds were also numerous in the civil rights struggle, and their struggle was often exacerbated by the traditional male clergy leadership. Rosa Parks sat down in the front of the bus in 1955 and started the Montgomery movement that produced Martin Luther King Jr. Ella Jo Baker wanted to be a medical missionary and instead became the first full-time executive secretary of the SCLC and founding mother of SNCC. Sharecropper Fannie Lou Hamer joined the civil rights movement in a Mississippi church, became a field secretary for SNCC, and ran for the U.S. Congress.

A common observation is that the civil rights movement in the South lost some of its "soul," or meaning, or heart when it became more secular and popular. Some, such as John Lewis, thought that that happened because of the influx of people from the North, black and white, who had little relationship or kinship to religious foundations or to southern experience.

The white church in the South, overwhelmingly Protestant, at its best experienced guilt and practiced restraint; at its worst, it was the ideological linchpin of racism and segregation. The white southern church has mainly been a conservative, reinforcing agent for traditional values of white southern society. There have been significant exceptions, but often those instances had to do with courageous acts or stands taken by individual white Christians allying themselves to the civil rights movement because of Christian conscience and religious values. Their positions, however, were neither practiced nor condemned by the white institutional church.

Marginal, predominantly white, southern Christian organizations have had an important part in civil rights; among them are Church Women United, the YWCA and YMCA, Councils on Human Relations, the Fellowship of Southern Churchmen, and various churchwomen's and youth groups. Such religiously based organizations, although often ostracized by the southern white church and supported by northern patrons, have served as the "call to conscience" of other southern whites, and often had they not been involved, news organizations might not have paid as much attention to civil rights events. But these marginal organizations, while strategic and courageous, also inadvertently served to help mask the deep differences between black and white religious experience.

Within white southern Christianity the courageous individuals rather than organizations, institutions, or "the beloved community" stood out in support of civil rights. Many protesters had seminary training outside the South and in the 1930s and 1940s were active in farm and labor movements. They were often defrocked, fired by their own churches, and forced to seek employment outside the region. In the 1960s they might have been supported by their national church, while ostracized by the local and regional church; many times they were physically beaten and sometimes murdered.

Southern white religious leadership in civil rights was native and grounded in southern tradition, but also it was conspicuously "against the grain," often isolated, and in danger.

The Commission on Interracial Cooperation was founded in 1919 by Methodist minister Will Alexander. Through the 1920s, 1930s, and 1940s a lineage of Christian-based activists followed, including Alva Taylor, the teacher of many southern organizers at Vanderbilt School of Religion; Don West, a Georgia minister and poet; Myles Horton, a Cumberland Presbyterian from Union Seminary and founder of the Highlander School; Presbyterian Claude Williams; Methodist ministers Ward Rogers and James Dombroski; YMCA leader and Presbyterian Howard Kester; YWCA's Lucy Mason Randolph; also Sam Franklin, Charles Jones, Winifred Chappell, and Harry and Grace Kroger. Many of these leaders worked with the farm labor movements and were in the Fellowship of Southern Churchmen.

In the 1950s and 1960s southern white religious leadership continued out of the Fellowship of Southern Churchmen and the "Y" with Will Campbell, Nelle Morton, Helen Lewis, and others. Thelma Stevens, in the Methodist Church, Hayes Mizell and Connie Curry of the American Friends Service Committee, and Jane Schutt of Church Women United are just a few of the white organizational leaders that emerged in southern civil rights struggles.

Ed King, Mississippi-born chaplain at Tougaloo College, was an important activist in the Jackson movement and the Mississippi Freedom Democratic Party in the 1960s. Bob Zellner, son of an Alabama Methodist minister, was the first white field secretary of SNCC. Jane Stembridge, a Virginian, left Union Theological Seminary to become the first office secretary of SNCC. Maurice Ouillet, a Catholic priest in Selma, Ala., was the only white person there who openly helped the civil rights movement.

Because of continuing black pressures, established religious bodies moved over time to support racial brotherhood, and some even to lend support to ministers persecuted for their stands on civil rights. Nonetheless, the vast majority of white churches in the South remained silent and apart, and many formed the institutional base for evading public school desegregation by founding private "Christian academies" and for promoting reactionary policies through the electronic church and the New Religious Right in the 1970s and 1980s.

In spite of the fundamental role that the southern black church and many southern white Christians played in the struggle for civil rights during the past 50 years, to the present day the southern black church and the southern white church stand far apart. Sunday is still the most segregated day of the week. Ministerial alliances, church boards, and agencies remain segregated, with token representation at best.

Nonetheless, black religion has not become antiwhite, acting on the belief that the liberation of the children of Israel and the teachings of Jesus are universal values. The white religion of the South in its essential Christianity knows that it has no religious basis for racism and oppression and that the stratified southern society that it has sanctified and defended is itself making accommodations with other forces. Religion is the driving force in the region's efforts to promote racial reconciliation, as in the biracial Mission Mississippi, which uses evangelical faith to bring blacks and whites together.

JAMES SESSIONS
Commission on Religion in Appalachia
Knoxville, Tennessee

David L. Chappell, *A Stone of Hope: Prophetic Religion and the Death of Jim Crow* (2004); James H. Cone, *Black Theology and Black Power* (1969); James McBride Dabbs, *The Southern Heritage* (1958); Anthony P. Dunbar, *Against the Grain: Southern Radicals and Prophets, 1929–1959* (1981); Frye Gaillard, *Cradle of Freedom: Alabama and the Movement That Changed America* (2004); Samuel S. Hill, ed., *On Jordan's Stormy Banks: Religion in the South: A Southern Exposure Profile* (1983), *Religion and the Solid South* (1972); Dolphus Weary and William Hendricks, *I Ain't Coming Back* (1990).

Diversity, Religious

Conventional wisdom holds that the South is a bastion of conservative, evangelical Protestantism—the "Bible Belt" of popular lore. Dominated by the Southern Baptist Convention, the region's and the nation's largest Protestant body, and by the United Methodist Church, the South has appeared to be, in sociologist John Shelton Reed's terms, "since antebellum times, monolithically Protestant." At the dawn of the 21st century, statistics buttress this claim, with

Tennessee and South Carolina, for example, showing more than a quarter of their total population identified with some Baptist or Methodist body.

At the same time, a vital and vibrant diversity, never far beneath the surface, suggests that the religious life of the South is rich and varied. For example, just over two centuries ago, Charleston, S.C., boasted a Jewish population second only to that of New York, and Charleston's Beth Elohim Synagogue is among the oldest synagogues in the nation. Roman Catholic pockets in St. Augustine, Mobile, New Orleans, and the surrounding areas have for centuries undercut the hegemony of white evangelical Protestantism; in the early 19th century, Roman Catholic authorities based the nation's second diocese in the South, in Bardstown, Ky. By 2000 Roman Catholicism in the central South had a growth rate far exceeding that of the Southern Baptists, whose growth failed to keep pace with the birth rate, and greatly surpassing that of the United Methodists, whose membership declined in most parts of the South.

Geography fostered another aspect of diversity, especially in more rural areas and in Appalachia. Ambitious preachers for generations have started congregations reflecting their own views. Some coalesced into nascent denominations, but many have remained independent. Groups as diverse as the Alpha and Omega Pentecostal Church, Christ's Sanctified Holy Church, the Sought Out Church of God in Christ and Spiritual House of Prayer, the Christian Purities Fellowship, the Original United Holy Church International, the Pentecostal Full Gospel Church, the General Assembly and Church of the Firstborn, the Macedonian Churches of Virginia, the Two Seed in the Spirit Baptists, the Davidian Seventh-day Adventists, and the Christadelphians, for example, have southern roots and enclaves of strength, even though their presence is often overlooked because the number of adherents remains small. In the mountains, literally thousands of independent congregations of a Holiness and of a Pentecostal stripe survive and thrive, some oriented to serpent handling and others as stridently eschewing such practices, but all fiercely independent. The Lovers of Meher Baba established national headquarters along the Grand Strand of South Carolina in the 1950s; that same area today boasts a rapidly growing Baha'i population, a group whose national literature distribution center is in Tennessee.

Ethnicity has added other dimensions to southern religious diversity. Race became a defining factor in southern religion, as in other aspects of regional life, but it also added to the underlying diversity. In the wake of the civil rights movement, analysts abandoned looking at African American Baptist and Methodist bodies as distorted copies of larger white groups in the same denominational families, recognizing that the African religious heritage had fused with

Protestant ideas and Caribbean styles to craft a distinctive Christian expression. From the 18th century on, when Africans began to adopt and adapt Protestant Christianity, this unique blend has manifested itself. African American preaching styles, known as call-and-response, resonated with tribal patterns of spiritual expression, while preachers themselves often combined practices associated with conjure with those characteristic of the Christian pastor to garner extraordinary power and influence. In some areas, voodoo and, more in the 20th century, Santeria (literally the way of the saints) represented a syncretism of Christian, African, and Caribbean ways of living in a world where supernatural power was vital and real.

From the days of the introduction of slavery, Islam has received the religious allegiance of some cohorts of the African American population, although the conditions of slavery made it difficult for Muslim life to flourish. In most cases, this early devotion to Islam gradually dwindled; it does not provide a direct link to the Islam found in most southern cities today. Although the Nation of Islam that came to national prominence during the era of the civil rights movement continues to attract African Americans to its idiosyncratic fusion of the larger Muslim heritage with ideas of ethnic separatism, the greatest growth in Islam in the South, as elsewhere in the United States, has come from immigrants, especially from the Middle East, who have brought with them the religious culture of their homelands. By 2001 most southern cities counted at least two or three mosques among their religious institutions.

The growth of Islam, along with some other new dimensions of religious diversity in the South, owes much to changes in immigration laws coming in 1965. Earlier federal law greatly restricted immigration from the Middle East, Asia, and much of Latin America. By the last decade of the 20th century, a "new" immigration was changing the texture of southern religious life. In the last decade of the 20th century, the greatest proportional growth in immigration from Latin America, the Near East, and Asia came in the Sunbelt. Twenty-five counties in Georgia, more than any other state, reported an increase of at least 50 percent in immigration between 1990 and 1998.

When the laws were changed, there was already a noticeable Hispanic influence in places like Texas, where thousands of Mexican Americans had established themselves, and Florida, which received a surge of Cuban immigrants in the 1950s and 1960s after Castro came to power. Over the past half century, some Protestant and Catholic congregations in most southern cities have begun offering services in Spanish to reach the increasing Hispanic American population. Some immigrant communities have established shrines and layered traditional Hispanic devotional practice onto patterns familiar to southern Catholics. Today the Hispanic presence is obvious not only where larger enclaves of immigrants exist, such as Miami, but also in smaller communities such as Dalton, Ga., where employment in the area's carpet industry has attracted large numbers of Spanish-speaking immigrants.

Those coming to Dixie from Asia have likewise brought with them their indigenous religious traditions, as did those who came from Europe centuries earlier. Throughout the South, Hindu immigrants from India have established temples, sometimes converting existing religious structures to their own use — the Gujarat Samaj of east Tennessee in Chattanooga, for example, is housed in a former Baptist church complex — but also building temples that reflect contemporary architectural patterns for temple devotion in India, as with the one serving the Hindu American community in Nashville. Because Hindu practice is deeply intertwined with a cultural heritage nurtured from birth and has consequently eschewed aggressive proselytizing, it is easy to overlook its growing presence on the southern religious landscape.

Buddhism has also taken root in the South. Once limited primarily to university towns where meditation practice appealed primarily to an intellectual elite, Buddhist centers have cropped up not only in the larger southern cities but in some smaller communities as well. By 2001, for example, North Carolina was home to more than 30 different Buddhist centers, representing the full range of Buddhist practice from Tibetan to Zen, with about half serving primarily an immigrant constituency and half serving a constituency in which converts predominate. Buddhism has penetrated even the Deep South, with small but flourishing Buddhist centers attracting adherents in such places as Birmingham, Ala., the very heart of the Bible Belt.

Other facets of religious diversity reflect how national trends have an impact on southern religious life. One example must suffice. Spurred by the human rights and liberation movements of the 1960s, women in the South, as elsewhere, began to probe a spirituality that reflects the unique biological experiences of those who are female, often harkening back to pre-Christian religious expressions, and sometimes draws on rituals and constructs associated with Wicca. Many women readily blend practice of feminist and/or Wiccan rituals with a Christian identity in forging a spirituality that endows their experience as women with power and supernatural meaning. While Wiccan covens are found in many of the South's larger cities, some exist in smaller towns and more rural areas such as Auburn, Ala., and Anderson, S.C.

Evangelical Protestantism continues to dominate southern religious life, but beneath the surface diversity and pluralism prevail. In addition to the expressions of that diversity discussed here, one might also point to new approaches to worship in southern Protestant congregations beginning roughly in the last quarter of the 20th century, the increasing popularity of Pentecostal forms of Protestantism such as that associated with the Church of God (Cleveland, Tenn.) and independent healing evangelists whose revivals still draw significant crowds, the rapid growth of bodies such as the Church of Jesus Christ of Latter-day Saints, and much more. All highlight a depth in southern religious life extending well beyond what the image of the Bible Belt suggests.

CHARLES H. LIPPY
University of Tennessee at Chattanooga

Walter H. Conser Jr. and Sumner B. Twiss, eds., *Religious Diversity and America Religious History: Studies in Traditions and Cultures* (1997); Samuel S. Hill, ed., *Varieties of Southern Religious Experience* (1980); Corrie Norman and Donald S. Armentrout, eds., *Religion in the South* (2003).

Ethnic Protestantism

Southern Protestantism arose, almost entirely, from ethnic roots. During the 18th century nearly a million immigrants entered the southern backcountry —the majority of them of Germanic or Celtic ancestry—as well as numerous Pennsylvania Quakers who formed a special English subcultural, if not ethnic, community. Highland Scots also entered the region through Wilmington and settled the upper Cape Fear Valley in North Carolina, and Salzbergers and Huguenots did so through the ports of Savannah and Charleston, respectively. Non-English immigration into the backcountry profoundly shaped the culture of the entire region. In the late 18th century, Presbyterians emerged as the elite in much of the South. Religious pacifism weakened state governments during the Revolution, and Quaker antislavery proved to be a potent witness against human bondage.

Then, suddenly, during the first three decades of the 19th century, ethnic distinctiveness rooted in European heritages became absorbed into a new, dominant southern way of life. Dunkers and many Quakers, who were victims of discrimination, migrated to Indiana, and most Lutheran, Moravian, and Reformed churches and communities adopted the English language. The older coastal aristocracy, largely Episcopal in affiliation, and newer backcountry elites, almost entirely dissenter in religious preference, tended to coalesce. The spread of evangelicalism blurred differences between denominations, even between Episcopalians and other Protestants, and the preservation of social order and communal purity took precedence over maintenance of traditional liturgy, theology, and polity—further reducing the memory of European origins and ethnic identification. Nonetheless, a handful of ethnic churches can still be found in the South. Infinitesimal in number, they reflect values absent in the dominant culture as well as the persistence of some elements of the region's historical cultural mosaic.

The earliest ethnic Protestants in the South were Huguenots in colonial South Carolina. Part of a diaspora of French Protestants following the revocation of the Edict of Nantes (in 1685), they constituted an eighth of the white population of South Carolina in 1700. Educated, energetic, commercially skilled, and soon intermarried with the English stock elite, these French Calvinists became Anglicized after 1910. Most of the 10 Huguenot churches in the province became Anglican, and when George Whitefield delivered a controversial sermon in the "French Church" in Charleston in 1740, the Huguenot minister quietly dissociated himself from Whitefield's revivalism. Despite a fire that destroyed the largest French church in Charleston in 1796 and the looting of its successor building by Union troops in 1865, descendants of the early French settlers kept the church alive until 1950. Then, on 17 October 1982, the Huguenot Church of Charleston reopened with a membership that is half former Episcopalian and the remainder Presbyterian, Baptist, and Methodist. The church continues to be Calvinist in theology and uses a Swiss Protestant liturgy. The minister of the reorganized church is Philip Charles Bryant, a Southern Baptist clergyman and an administrator of the Baptist College of Charleston.

The next oldest ethnic Protestant tradition in the South is that of the Moravians. Dating from the followers of John Hus and organized into the Unity of Brethren (Unitas Fratrum) by Count Nicholas von Zinzendorf in the early 18th century, Pennsylvania Moravians purchased a large tract of land in North Carolina from Lord Granville. There, between 1753 and 1766, they established the towns of Bethabara, Bethania, and Salem and practiced communal management of economic, family, and religious life. Although communalism ceased in the early 19th century and Moravians reluctantly became a Protestant denomination, the churches in North Carolina preserve a wide range of rituals and cultural observances dating from Zinzendorf's practices in Moravia — among them the arrangement of the cemetery into four separate "choirs" for men and women, married and unmarried, using identical flat white grave markers; an Easter sunrise service held in the Old Salem burial ground every year since 1772; lively traditions in Christmas cooking and decorating; and an important musical heritage of brass music and hymnology.

The Waldensians, a dissenting sect founded by the followers of Peter Waldo, a merchant of Lyon in the late 12th century, were among the last ethnic Protestants to reach the South. In 1893, 101 families from nine Alpine Italian towns settled in Burke County, N.C. Their patron in this migration was a Pittsburgh industrialist, Marvin F. Scaife, who owned land in Morganton, N.C. Though at first supported by the Congregationalist Church, they chose to affiliate with the Southern Presbyterian Church in the United States (PCUS). By the early 1920s the Valdese Presbyterian Church had abandoned several distinctive Old World Waldensian practices — leaving the offering plate at the rear door of the church, receiving communion in pairs at the altar, seating men and women on opposite sides of the church, and worshipping exclusively in French. In 1941 the use of French services ended altogether.

The Lutheran Church–Missouri Synod represented the ethnic tradition of conservative German confessionalism brought to the United States by immigrants in the mid-19th century. In contrast with Lutherans who had been in America since the colonial period and had absorbed evangelical and other Protestant patterns of worship and theology, the Missouri Synod insisted on upholding the hierarchical and legalistic formalism of 17th- and 18th-century Continental Lutheranism. The relative isolation of this branch of American Lutherans enabled the Missouri Synod, in a modest way, to serve as an instrument for racial justice in the South. During the late 19th century, the synod's home mission board adopted many black Lutheran churches in the South, which had been denied admission to older Lutheran synods, and in the 20th century it established schools for blacks — Emmanuel College in Greensboro, N.C., and Selma Lutheran Academy and College in Alabama. In 1966 Professor Richard Bardolph, a Missouri Synod layman in Greensboro, drafted the denomination's statement titled "Civil Disobedience and the American Constitutional Order," citing biblical and historical support for defiance of law as a tool of the civil rights movement.

The North Carolina Yearly Meeting of the Religious Society of Friends (Conservative), comprising seven Monthly Meetings in North Carolina and one in Virginia, identifies closely with 17th-century English Quakerism. These Quakers broke away from the larger body of evangelical Quakers in the South in 1904. The formal Discipline of the sect (1956) emphasizes parental diligence, harmony and unity with Monthly Meetings, worship under the Holy Spirit without resort to a professional ministry, protection of children from "pernicious books" and "corrupt conversation," pacifism, wholesome diversions and opposition to alcoholic beverages and gambling, living within one's own resources and avoiding business enterprises beyond prudent risk, and care of the poor within each Monthly Meeting.

Mennonites, who settled in Virginia in the 18th century, were pacifists in both the Revolution and the Civil War. At present, they comprise two bodies in the South, the Virginia Mennonite Conference (67 churches, mainly in Virginia and North Carolina) and the Western Conservative Mennonite Fellowship (16 in North Carolina, 6 in South Carolina, 71 in Virginia, and 11 in West Virginia). The Virginia Conference is a part of the Mennonite Church, and the Conser-. vative Fellowship is an offshoot body culturally close to the Amish in practice and discipline.

The most rapidly growing ethnic Protestant group in the South today is represented by the Korean Presbyterian churches—the product of Presbyterian Church (United States) missionary activity in Korea, an upsurge of Christianity as an indirect form of opposition to political expression since the 1950s, the migration of Korean professionals to the United States, and the existence of Korean American families in this country. Twenty Korean Presbyterian congregations can now be found in seven southern states. Finally, there is the Chinese Presbyterian Church in New Orleans. Founded in 1882 as a language school and mission for Chinese men, it was until the 1950s operated by four dedicated Presbyterian women. In 1958 Grace Yao came from Hong Kong to become director of Christian education. The service is bilingual.

Since the 1960s, Korean immigrants to the United States have founded more that 900 Korean Presbyterian churches in the southeastern United States and more than 800 Korean Baptist Churches. In 1985 and 1993, the U.S. government resettled Montagnard, or Dega, refugees from the Vietnam highlands in Greensboro, Raleigh, and Charlotte, N.C., the majority of whom had been converted by Missionary and Alliance missionaries in Vietnam.

ROBERT M. CALHOON
University of North Carolina at Greensboro

Peter Brock, *Pacifism in the United States: From the Colonial Era to the First World War* (1968); Jon Butler, *The Huguenots in America: A Refugee People in New World Society* (1983); *Concordia Historical Institute Quarterly* (November 1969; February 1971; Summer 1975; Summer 1977; Fall 1979); Damon Douglas Hickey, "Bearing the Cross of Plainness: Conservative Quaker Culture in North Carolina" (M.A. thesis, University of North Carolina, Greensboro, 1982); Hunter James, *The Quiet People of the Land: A Story of the North Carolina Moravians in Revolutionary Times* (1976); George B. Watts, *The Waldenses in the New World* (1941).

Folk Religion

Leading scholar of American folk religion William M. Clements defines it as "unofficial religion," the spiritual experience that exists separate from, but alongside, the theological and liturgical religion of the mainline established churches. Clements has identified 10 traits of the folk church: "general orientation toward the past, scriptural literalism, consciousness of Providence, emphasis on evangelism, informality, emotionalism, moral rigorism, sectarianism, egalitarianism, and relative isolation of physical facilities."

Folk religious events include Sunday school classes, vacation Bible school meetings in the summer, Bible study gatherings, covered-dish suppers, singing services, devotional hours, and all-day services with dinner on the grounds. The church worship service is perhaps the central ritual of folk religion in the South. Worshippers may clap or wave their hands as they listen to spiritual songs like "Over in Glory Land." Some churches have a cappella services, but many include electric guitars, tambourines, and other instruments. Shouts of "Thank you, Jesus" and "Praise the Lord" are heard, as are extended public prayers, testimonials, and drawn-out invitations by the preacher to come forward. Faith healing and glossolalia sometimes occur. The preacher conveys a message of the need for conversion, controlling and directing the raw emotions of true believers. In the South's well-defined oral culture, the folk preacher is a prime performer of the Word, and the religious service is a crucial folk event. Films such as Blaire Boyd's *Holy Ghost People*, which records Appalachian snake handlers; William Ferris's *Two Black Churches*, which shows Sunday morning worship services in rural southern and urban northern churches; and *Joy Unspeakable*, a videotape on southern Indiana Pentecostals, have become important modern tools for studying folk religion.

The relation between southern religion and folk culture is seen in the dynamic of conversion. Born sinful, the individual can be saved by conversion. He or she accepts the rule of Jesus and God, sometimes through a dramatic conversion experience after which the individual gives up aspects of folk culture that are regarded as profane. Thus, the hell-raising "good old boy" becomes the "good man," who is a pious member of the church. Drinking and dancing on Saturday night are replaced by temperance and dignified behavior, though in some Pentecostal churches addiction to spirits is transmuted into being possessed by the Spirit and dancing in the flesh to dancing in the Spirit. As one moves from the evangelical/fundamentalist end of the spectrum, which is most identified with folk religion in the South, to the established Southern Baptist, Methodist, and Presbyterian churches, the dramatic conversion syndrome becomes rare, virtually disappearing as one enters the more liturgical churches, such as the Episcopal (which one southern minister described as "religion in its mildest form").

Some established southern churches, however, include survivals of folk religion. Methodists, for example, may not include in today's services the testimo-

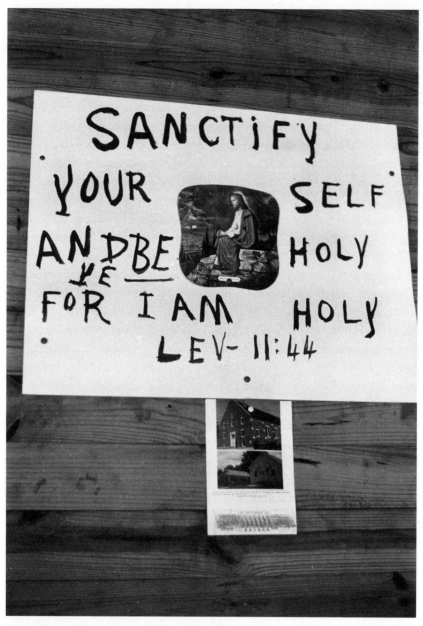

Sign inside Sanctified church, Clarksdale, Miss., 1968
(William Ferris Collection, Southern Folklife Collection,
Wilson Library, University of North Carolina at Chapel Hill)

nials and shouts from the day of John Wesley at Aldersgate, but they continue to sing the old Wesleyan hymns as well as hymns from revivals and camp meetings.

After conversion, fundamentalist Christians may stop singing ballads or country music or blues and shift to hymns, spirituals, and gospel songs; or they may keep on doing the old music, but in secular contexts, such as the bluegrass festival, clearly separating that from the sacred song. Lines are thus drawn between folk and sacred music, even though similarity of form may be detected. Folktales do not normally enter the church, but tale-telling forms, and the love of telling tales, are apparent in southern sermons and testimonies. Religious rhetoric enters secular life through the sermon-speeches of Martin Luther King Jr., Jesse Jackson, and others.

Folk medicine, as exemplified by the root doctor or herbalist, is rarely drawn explicitly into the church, but folk healers integrate religious symbolism into their systems. Within folk religion faith healing stands in a complementary relationship to the individual folk healers in that faith healing is performed by groups in a church, tent, or prayer band.

Hierarchy creeps into the church as it becomes more institutionalized and mainline, but the overriding emphasis of folk religion is on friendliness, togetherness, and hospitality. These qualities have been coded into greeting behaviors, for example, to a greater extent in southern churches than in some of nonsouthern location or sponsorship. Other values that folk churches in the South share with the wider regional culture include a love of the heroic, the theatrical, the charismatic, and the vivid. Such qualities are exhibited by the most popular southern preachers as well as politicians, by southern sermons and worship services as well as in literature. Often overlooked are the compensating senses of irony and tragedy and, for some, a Calvinistic Puritanism. Behind every Elmer Gantry is a Hazel Motes; but behind them are a Cotton Mather and John Bunyan.

Southern familialism finds expression especially in the rural folk churches in family reunions, homecomings, and the decoration of graves. Excepting the family, however, southern folk religion has been remarkably reluctant to identify itself with social units. On the whole, southern folk religion works through preaching and teaching directed at the individual mind, heart, and soul rather than through social or political institutions.

What has been termed here "folk" religion is not confined to the South but instead in myriad expressions is global. For example, the Pentecostal organization Assemblies of God claimed 29 million "members and adherents" around the world in 2000. Statistics aside, one can meet and hear Pentecostals everywhere; at a meeting of a Full Gospel Businessmen's group in Jakarta, Indonesia,

I heard a testimony that, except for the language (Indonesian), was identical with many I have heard in Durham, N.C. On the way to that meeting, I shared a train compartment with a Chinese Pentecostal from Yogyakarta, Indonesia, who was en route to Singapore to join one of the world crusades by North Carolina's Billy Graham. Southern Baptists and others have, of course, long been global via missionary activity, rivaling Catholics and others who are defined as global rather than regional in basis.

JAMES L. PEACOCK
University of North Carolina at Chapel Hill

William M. Clements, "The American Folk Church: A Characterization of American Folk Religion Based on Field Research among White Protestants in a Community in the South Central United States" (Ph.D. dissertation, Indiana University, 1974), in *Handbook of American Folklore*, ed. Richard M. Dorson (1983); Robert Coles, *Psychology Today* (January 1972); William Ferris, *Keystone Folklore Quarterly* (1970); Paula H. Anderson Green, *Tennessee Folklore Society Bulletin* (September 1977); Terry G. Jordan, *Southwestern Historical Quarterly* (Spring 1976); Charles Joyner, *Down by the Riverside: A South Carolina Slave Community* (1984); Newbell Niles Puckett, *Folk Beliefs of the Southern Negro* (1926; 1969); Bruce A. Rosenberg, *The Art of the American Folk Preacher* (1970); Grant Wacker, *Heaven Below: Early Pentecostals and American Culture* (2001).

Frontier Religion

Three primary phases of southern frontier experience occurred — (1) the colonial frontier; (2) the initial trans-Appalachian frontier; and (3) the frontier created by Indian removals. In each period, the religious life of the Southwest was distinct and in certain respects unique in the nation.

After the first century of southern colonial settlement, which amounted to a frontier experience for Europeans, the southern colonial frontier consisted of the western Piedmont and the Great Valley. Settlement of the valley began in earnest in the 1730s, with the massive migration of Scots-Irish and German settlers, who were attracted by the cheap and plentiful land along the Great Philadelphia Wagon Road. Gradually, these migrants began to spread south and east, so that the westernmost sections of the southern Piedmont and the extension of the valley into the Carolinas and Georgia contained perhaps 250,000 settlers by the time of the American Revolution.

These migrants received scant attention from Church of England clergy. The poorly organized established church faced a severe shortage of clergy, the physical barrier of the Blue Ridge, and the non-Anglican background of most of the settlers; it could only watch as the first southern frontier became fertile ground for dissent. Indeed, almost all of the South Carolina backcountry was in one Church of England parish; by 1750 only one Anglican church and two chapels served the upper valley.

The Presbyterian Church dominated the first southern frontier, although Dunkers and Moravians found support among the German migrants. By 1768, 21 Presbyterian churches had been built on the South Carolina frontier; Presbyterians were equally successful in northern and southern frontier regions. Southern colonial governments even provided moderate support for the religious freedom of the migrants. In Georgia, the government ignored the wishes of the Privy Council and provided land for 107 Presbyterian settlers on the Great Ogeechee River. The Virginia government answered a petition of the valley settlers in 1738 by guaranteeing that their religious practices would be tolerated.

These western Presbyterians received the Great Awakening with some suspicion, and most of the frontier response to the religious enthusiasm sweeping the nation took place in the western Piedmont, where the settlers of the valley blended with easterners looking for cheaper land. In the Piedmont, southwesterners in North Carolina listened to the preaching of Shubal Stearns, a Boston-born Baptist, who led a movement that came to be termed the Separate Baptists. The sometimes radically democratic, highly experiential Separate movement spread north and east and by the 1760s had influenced much of the western Piedmont in Virginia as well.

By the end of the colonial period the settlement of the Piedmont and the Great Valley had progressed to the extent that these sections could only very loosely be defined as frontier. Although they were still dominated by Presbyterians, both Regular and Separate Baptists had begun to make inroads, as had Quakers, Moravians, and Dunkers. This first phase of the southwestern frontier experience was unique because of its religious diversity and the high degree of toleration afforded most faiths.

The second phase of the southern frontier experience was the transAppalachian West. Settlers had begun to cross the Appalachian mountain barrier by the 1770s, but the first significant wave of migration into the transAppalachian West came at the end of the Revolutionary War. By 1790, 110,000 people lived in these new southwestern settlements; by 1796 both Kentucky and Tennessee were members of the Union; by the first decade of the 19th century most of the best land in the two states was already densely settled.

In the earliest years of this rapidly developing frontier, the most enthusiastic promoters of religion were Baptist preachers who moved with the migrants, settled farms, and became permanent members of the communities. In one of several such instances, 500 members of the "traveling church" followed the lead of the Reverend Lewis Craig from Spottsylvania County in Virginia to the blue-grass country of Kentucky. Itinerant Methodist preachers, encouraged by the visits of their tireless bishop, Francis Asbury, began to develop small congregations at numerous points along their circuits. Presbyterians remained self-consciously aloof from the other denominations, concentrated as they were in Bourbon County, Ky., the eastern quarter of Tennessee, and the towns and cities springing up on the frontier. Intermingled among these three dominant denominations were scattered Quakers, Episcopalians, and even a few Roman Catholics. Ministers of the leading denominations tried to set themselves up as the moral guardians of the frontier, and some, led by Presbyterian David Rice, even went so far as to propose an end to slavery.

In spite of this religious diversity and activity, ministers in the Southwest of the 1790s complained continually about the lack of piety on the frontier. Most settlers did not attend church, and Deism had begun to be discussed in Nash-ville and Lexington. Increasingly, preachers began to stress watch care within their congregations, rather than expansion and evangelism. In the face of real despair, however, a religious fervor began to emerge, first in 1799 in Logan County, Ky., and then by the next year spreading north and south throughout the region. Presbyterians probably served the most important role in the de-velopment of this Great Revival, but Methodists joined in many of the services. Although Baptists were reluctant to participate in the interdenominational ser-vices, they probably gained the most converts in the awakening.

The Great Revival exerted the greatest influence on southern and national religious development in its stress on complex revivalistic techniques. The Mc-Gee brothers, one a Methodist minister, the other a Presbyterian, served as two of the most innovative leaders of the movement, promoting in particular the concept of the camp meeting. The greatest of these, the 1801 Cane Ridge meet-ing in Bourbon County, Ky., may have brought 25,000 worshippers together to listen to a flock of preachers, who spoke day and night for a week. The meet-ings were not segregated by sex, or in many instances by race, and several black preachers earned their initial reputations speaking at these gatherings.

In the wake of the revival came an inevitable period of reassessment and self-evaluation. In the Presbyterian Church the revival had brought a series of schisms, some members following the Shakers, others forming a new denomi-nation, the Cumberland Presbyterians, and still others, under the leadership of Barton W. Stone, taking a long theological odyssey that eventually contrib-uted to the creation of the Disciples of Christ. As Presbyterians and, to a lesser extent, Baptists and Methodists recovered from the social earthquake of the

Great Revival, the frontier spirit of the region also began to disappear. Instead, the second decade of the 19th century began to witness the development of a regional culture, a regional economy, and a regional self-consciousness.

This resulted in the third phase of frontier religious development in the Deep South. The area of the trans-Appalachian West, south of the Tennessee River, received some initial settlement by the time of the Great Revival, and sufficient migration had occurred by 1817 to allow Mississippi to enter the Union, followed by Alabama two years later. During the 1820s much of the extremely rich soil of the "Black Belt" began to be exploited with the use of large-scale slave labor. Only in the 1830s, however, with the mass expulsion of the Creek, Cherokee, Chickasaw, and Choctaw Indians, did this section begin to lose its frontier quality and develop both lasting settlement patterns and enduring religious, governmental, and economic institutions. Even as late as the end of the 1830s, according to Joseph Baldwin's account in *The Flush Times of Alabama and Mississippi*, much of the area remained wild, reckless, dangerous, uncivilized — in short, a frontier.

Because this section was at once the frontier for South Carolina and Georgia and an extension of settlement for Kentucky and Tennessee, the religious life of the Deep Southwest was an odd mixture of elements. In the first years a series of missionaries from the three major evangelical denominations visited the region, sometimes risking their lives to endure rough conditions of travel, at other times facing hostile reception from early settlers. Some frontier ministers began to adopt the swaggering, unyielding characteristics of many of the settlers, threatening unruly congregations from the pulpit, fighting when they deemed fighting appropriate. A premium was placed on a straight-ahead preaching style, and a thundering voice helped drown out any heckling. In these ways, the pioneer preachers faced the same problems they would have found on other frontiers.

Churches of the southwestern frontier were heir to the factionalism and confusion coming out of the Great Revival period. Perhaps no frontier in American history faced so many religious choices. In addition to mainstream Presbyterians, Baptists, and Methodists, the factions, sects, and new denominations of the frontier included the Cumberland Presbyterians, the Shakers, the Stoneites, the Campbellites, the Republican Methodists, and, perhaps most important, the followers of a Baptist preacher, Daniel Parker, variously termed Hardshell, Two-Seed, or Antimission Baptists. This last group, which radically opposed missions and other benevolent actions as well as the education of clergy, disrupted the already difficult work of more conventional Baptist preachers. As a consequence, the first attempt to organize a state convention in Mississippi failed after five years of constant bickering.

Reflecting the confusion of religious life in the region, slaves remained in the white-run churches, participating in watch-care activities, long after Kentucky and Tennessee churches had begun segregating their buildings and their church services. Yet at the same time that this limited measure of equality existed in some Deep Southwest churches, others had begun to encourage the mission to the slaves with its powerful message of social control. Such confusion of purpose could be seen in other aspects of religious life on this frontier; for example, drinking preachers lived near those in the same denomination who viewed liquor as diabolic. This religious "split personality" from the frontier era continued to characterize the section for decades after. W. J. Cash and other commentators have even attributed paradoxical 20th-century southern characteristics to the survival of frontier ways, and this seems true in regard to religion.

DAVID T. BAILEY
Michigan State University

Joseph G. Baldwin, *The Flush Times of Alabama and Mississippi: A Series of Sketches* (1853); John B. Boles, *The Great Revival, 1787–1805: The Origins of the Southern Evangelical Mind* (1972); Catharine C. Cleveland, *The Great Revival in the West, 1797–1805* (1916); Wesley M. Gewehr, *The Great Awakening in Virginia, 1740–1790* (1930); Robert D. Mitchell, *Commercialism and Frontier: Perspectives on the Early Shenandoah Valley* (1977); Walter B. Posey, *The Baptist Church in the Lower Mississippi Valley, 1776–1845* (1957); Randy J. Sparks, *Religion in Mississippi* (2001).

Fundamentalism

The Fundamentalist movement, as distinct from fundamentalism as a theological orientation, appeared around 1900 among conservative northern Protestants concerned about the development of liberal theology, the social gospel, Darwinian evolution, and secular trends in American culture. With the exception of concerns about the promotion of Darwinian evolution, these trends were largely quiescent in the South until after World War II. The movement made limited progress in the South prior to midcentury because of southern evangelicalism's conservatism. When the social, intellectual, and cultural upheavals that kindled the northern movement began to alter southern culture in the postwar decades, southern evangelicals believed their regional Zion was becoming more like Babylon, and organized Fundamentalism prospered accordingly.

Northern Fundamentalism's earliest forays into the South began with Bible conferences held by members of its core constituency, most notably, premillennialists associated with evangelist Dwight L. Moody's interdenominational revivalist network. Moody's protégés, particularly Amzi C. Dixon, Reuben A. Torrey, James M. Grey, Cyrus I. Scofield, and Lewis Sperry Chafer, played significant roles in shaping Fundamentalism and in exporting it to the South. They were participants in the prophecy and Bible conference movement, which began in 1876 when northern Bible teachers, typically Presbyterians and Calvinist Baptists, met at Swampscott, Mass. In 1878 James H. Brookes, the movement's founding father, produced a 14-article creed depicting embryonic Fundamentalism's central theological concerns. Significantly, this creed included dispensational premillennialism, which taught that the historical eras depicted in the Bible represented distinct ages culminating in Christ's second coming to establish a millennial kingdom. The movement's annual assemblies settled at Niagara, N.Y., between 1883 and 1898 and were thereafter identified as the Niagara Bible Conference. Other high points of the movement's infancy were the publication of *The Fundamentals* between 1910 and 1915, 12 booklets providing a broad and temperate defense of Protestant orthodoxy, and the 1919 founding of the World's Christian Fundamentals Association to conduct an offensive against theological liberalism and Darwinian evolution.

Southerners contributed little to organized Fundamentalism as it coalesced prior to 1917. Only four of the contributors to *The Fundamentals* were from the South: President Edgar Y. Mullins of Southern Baptist Theological Seminary, Professor Charles B. Williams of Southwestern Baptist Theological Seminary, and Presbyterian ministers Alexander W. Pitzer of Salem, Va., and Hiram M. Sydenstricker of West Point, Miss. Nor were there many southerners among the movement's early leaders. The exceptions were Amzi C. Dixon and J. Frank Norris. Dixon, a Baptist pastor and author from North Carolina, was actively involved in the northern prophetic Bible conference movement, served as pastor of Moody Memorial Church in Chicago from 1906 to 1911, and was the first of three editors for *The Fundamentals*. Norris, the controversial Southern Baptist pastor of First Baptist Church in Fort Worth, Tex., launched a Fundamentalist paper entitled *The Fence Rail* in 1917, shared his pulpit with leading northern Fundamentalist speakers, and became an early leader in the World's Christian Fundamentals Association.

While few southerners were leaders within the Fundamentalist movement, some pastors became, like Norris, conduits through which the northern conference movement penetrated the South. Baptist pastor Leonard G. Broughton, who was converted in 1880 at a Dixon revival service in Raleigh, N.C., established one of the earliest and most significant links between northern fundamentalists and southern evangelicals. In 1898, with Moody's encouragement, he launched the Tabernacle Bible Conference in Atlanta, Ga., hosting annual meetings that featured prominent northern Fundamentalist speakers who attracted huge crowds of people representing every southern state. Pastors and lay Christian workers figured prominently among the conferees. Between 1900 and 1917, numerous conference centers similar to Broughton's arose in urban areas throughout the South and played key roles in the dissemination of northern fundamentalist beliefs and concerns in the region.

Perhaps the most significant northern Bible teacher to enter the South prior to the 1920s was C. I. Scofield's protégé, Congregational minister Lewis Sperry Chafer. While serving as song leader alongside Ira Sankey for Moody's Northfield conferences, Chafer used Northfield as a model for organizing the Southfield Bible Conference Association in 1904 at Crescent City, Fla. Annual conferences continued there into the 1940s. In 1911 Chafer moved to New York to lead Scofield's Oral Extension department in the newly established Scofield School of the Bible. He took responsibility for conducting conferences in the South, and in 1926 he transferred his ministerial credentials to the Southern Presbyterian Church (the Presbyterian Church in the United States). Chafer's writings, approved and promoted by Scofield, were second only to the *Scofield Reference Bible* in spreading dispensational premillennialist thought in the South and in creating a perceived need among southern evangelicals for ministers and teachers trained in the dispensational understanding of the Scriptures.

Fundamentalist efforts to curtail liberalism turned militant in the 1920s, brought to a fever pitch by cultural shocks associated with World War I. Fundamentalists believed that German belittling of Scriptural authority and acceptance of evolutionary philosophy had produced cultural decay and German militarism and that American acceptance of German thought threatened equal ruin for American civilization. In response, they launched rigorous campaigns to ban the teaching of Darwinian evolution in public schools and to purge liberalism from their denominations, particularly within the northern Baptist and Presbyterian churches.

Most southern clergy believed their denominations were essentially sound and declined invitations to join national organizations such as the World's Christian Fundamentals Association or the Baptist Bible Union, groups spearheading fundamentalist efforts to expel denominational liberals. Conversely, southerners readily participated in the movement's struggle against Darwinian evolution. Fundamentalism's successes on this front occurred in the South, with Florida, Tennessee, Mississippi, Arkansas, and Oklahoma passing laws prohibiting the teaching of evolution. After the battle in July 1925 between Williams Jennings Bryan and Clarence Darrow in the Scopes Trial at Dayton, Tenn., Fundamentalism was popularly but wrongly identified as a dysfunctional artifact of rural southernness that was destined to wither and disappear.

Norris and Bob Jones Sr. were the most important exceptions to southern clergy noninvolvement in the first half of the 20th century. Norris, a consummate pulpiteer, controversialist, and crusader, was the father of independent Baptist fundamentalism in the South. In the 1920s, he condemned modernism and warned of its incipient influence among Southern Baptists, launched a crusade against evolutionists at Baylor University, hosted annual Bible conferences at First Baptist Church in Fort Worth featuring northern fundamentalist speakers, and joined northern fundamentalists William Bell Riley and T. T. Shields in forming the Baptist Bible Union. In 1923, weary of Norris and displeased with his northern fundamentalist associations and uncooperative spirit, the Baptist General Convention of Texas expelled his church from its ranks. Between 1930 and his death in 1952, Norris ruled over an independent fundamentalist empire built around First Baptist Church that included the Baptist Bible Seminary and the World Baptist Fellowship, an association of independent churches. Dissidents led by G. Beauchamp Vick and Noel Smith left Norris's empire in 1950 to form the Baptist Bible Fellowship and the Baptist Bible College of Springfield, Mo., alma mater of Jerry Falwell, pastor of Thomas Road Baptist Church in Lynchburg, Va., and the foremost Baptist fundamentalist in the second half of the century.

Southern evangelist Bob Jones Sr., licensed at the age of 14 by the Methodist Episcopal Church, South, and greatly influenced by D. L. Moody imitators Billy Sunday and Sam Jones, was an anomaly among Methodist ministers, who rarely became involved in organized Fundamentalism's crusades. During the 1920s, he enjoyed a national reputation as an evangelist and frequently preached a sermon entitled "The Perils of America," decrying the growing influence of theological liberalism in the churches, America's increasing secularity, and the destructive influence of Darwinism in educational institutions. Jones was particularly disturbed by stories told by distressed parents who observed their children's faith transformed into skepticism at state universities and denominational colleges. In 1926 he founded Bob Jones College in St. Andrews, Fla., an interdenominational fundamentalist college that settled permanently in Greenville, S.C., in 1947, where it evolved into Bob Jones University (BJU). In the following decades, Bob Jones Jr. presided over BJU and promoted a stringent separatist fundamentalism that alienated many fundamentalist leaders, including the Independent Baptist evangelist John R. Rice of Murfreesboro, Tenn.,

BJU board member and founder of one of the nation's leading fundamentalist periodicals, *The Sword of the Lord.*

In contrast to the strong separatist variety of fundamentalism spawned by Norris and the Joneses, Lewis Sperry Chafer promoted a moderate fundamentalism in the South that rejected separatism. In 1924 Chafer founded Dallas Theological Seminary (DTS) in Dallas, Tex., which institutionalized the prophetic and Bible conference movement and rapidly emerged as the heart of the dispensational wing of American fundamentalism and the focal point of interdenominational fundamentalism in the South. Graduates of DTS launched interdenominational Bible institutes in the region and used fellow alumni to staff these schools. Several of these institutions continue to exist as Bible colleges and are attended by numerous southern evangelicals. Chafer particularly saw the seminary as a means to reverse liberal trends within the Southern Presbyterian Church (PCUS), but his dream failed to materialize because of the PCUS's formal rejection of dispensational premillennialism in the 1940s, fueling the founding of independent Bible churches across the South led by DTS graduates. By 1998 DTS supplied staff to a significant number of educational institutions and more than 7,000 churches in the South, of which roughly 37 percent were independent Bible churches.

Separatist and nonseparatist varieties of fundamentalism prospered in the South after World War II, but the separatist wing, dominated by independent Baptists, continued to fragment over such issues as the rise of neoevangelicalism, Billy Graham's ecumenical evangelism, and cultural taboos growing out of the sixties cultural revolution. By the 1970s independent Baptists were divided into a host of separatist fellowships. Among the larger groups on the far right were the Baptist Missionary Association and the American Baptist Association, both based in the Southwest and related to 19th-century Landmarkism. The more centrist Baptist Bible Fellowship and World Baptist Fellowship grew apace, each founding hundreds of independent Baptist churches in the 1940s and 1950s. Their ranks were augmented in 1956 when Baptist pastors Lee Roberson of Highland Park Baptist Church in Chattanooga, Tenn., and Harold Sightler of Tabernacle Baptist Church in Greenville, N.C., established the Southern Baptist Fellowship, with Roberson's Tennessee Temple Schools system serving as an institutional base.

Because of perceptions of national moral collapse in the 1960s and 1970s, some Baptist fundamentalists rejected extreme separatist opinions and reentered the political arena, making alliances not only with neoevangelicals but also with Pentecostals, charismatics, Catholics, and Jews. Led by Jerry Falwell's Moral Majority, they became part of the New Religious Right, an assortment of political action organizations that helped place Ronald Reagan in the White House in 1980. Thereafter, these organizations worked through the Republican Party to restore Judeo-Christian influence in the nation, tackling among other things prayer and Bible reading in the public schools, abortion, the drug culture, pornography, film violence, the Equal Rights Amendment, homosexuality, the death penalty, gun control, and national defense. By the 1990s, Pat Robertson's Christian Coalition had supplanted the Moral Majority as the most visible symbol of the movement's social and political agenda. The Religious Right contributed to the mobilization of a politically inactive segment of the population, placed moral issues on the national agenda, and stimulated an ongoing debate about the relationship between religion and politics.

More recently, Albert Mohler, Richard Land, and other conservatives within the Southern Baptist Convention (SBC) have emerged as visible and influential leaders in the struggle against liberal cultural trends. Their sense of cultural crisis and desire to undertake a prophetic countercultural ministry developed in the 1970s and 1980s from engagement with northern evangelical thinkers Carl F. H. Henry and Francis Schaeffer. After gaining control of SBC agencies during the 1980s under the leadership of Paige Patterson, Paul Pressler, and Adrian Rogers, conservatives used these agencies to foster confessional uniformity along neoevangelical lines and to address cultural issues ranging from abortion and gender issues to postmodernism.

Similarly, the Presbyterian Church in America, which was organized in 1973 by conservatives who had failed to reverse liberal trends in the Presbyterian Church in the United States, was equally engaged in America's cultural wars. D. James Kennedy, minister of the Coral Ridge Presbyterian Church in Fort Lauderdale, Fla., quickly emerged as the denomination's most vocal and influential culture warrior. In 1974 Kennedy launched Coral Ridge Ministries, a radio, television, and print ministry, adding the Center for Christian Statesmanship in 1995 and the Center for Reclaiming America in 1996. With the premise that human beings possess a cultural mandate to subdue and rule the earth as God's coregents, Kennedy's multiple ministries emphasize the necessity of reclaiming America for Christ, a task uniting evangelism and political activism in an effort to return America to the Christian heritage left by the founding fathers.

Clearly, thousands of southern fundamentalists abandoned their regional biases when national trends began to transform southern culture and united with mainstream American evangelicals in their attempts to restore Christianity's cultural influence. The groundwork for this religious realignment was accomplished through several avenues: involvement with northern evangelicalism through interdenominational ministries such as Dallas Theological Seminary; conservatives taking degrees at fundamentalist schools in and outside the South; or church members and pastors reading influential northern periodicals such as *Christianity Today* or the works of leading northern evangelical thinkers such as Carl F. H. Henry and Francis Schaeffer. By these and other means, major segments of conservative southern fundamentalism are now assimilated into a national evangelical coalition that evolved from the seeds of northern fundamentalism.

B. DWAIN WALDREP
Southeastern Bible College

Joel A. Carpenter, *Revive Us Again: The Reawakening of American Fundamentalism* (1997); Mark Taylor Dalhouse, *An Island in the Lake of Fire: Bob Jones University, Fundamentalism, and the Separatist Movement* (1996); Jerry Falwell, ed., *The Fundamentalist Phenomenon* (1981); William R. Glass, *Strangers in Zion: Fundamentalism in the South, 1900–1950* (2001); John C. Green, Mark J. Rosell, and Clyde Wilcox, eds., *The Christian Right in American Politics: Marching to the Millennium* (2003); Barry Hankins, *God's Rascal: J. Frank Norris and the Beginnings of Southern Fundamentalism* (1996), *Uneasy in Babylon: Southern Baptist Conservatives and American Culture* (2002); David Edwin Harrell Jr., *Pat Robertson: A Personal, Political, and Religious Portrait* (1987); Samuel S. Hill and Dennis E. Owen, *The New Religious Right in America* (1982); Edward J. Larson, *Summer for the Gods: The Scopes Trial and America's Continuing Debate over Science and Religion* (1997); George M. Marsden, *Fundamentalism and American Culture: The Shaping of 20th-Century Evangelicalism, 1870–1925* (1980); C. Allyn Russell, *Voices of American Fundamentalism* (1976); Ernest R. Sandeen, *The Roots of Fundamentalism: British and American Millenarianism, 1800–1930* (1970); B. Dwain Waldrep, "Lewis Sperry Chafer and the Development of Interdenominational Fundamentalism in the South, 1900–1950" (Ph.D. dissertation, Auburn University, 2001).

Islam

Muslims have spread throughout the South, becoming a part of the religious landscape of many southern cities as well as influencing rural areas. Muslim immigrants and African American Muslims have organized mosques in cities of various sizes, ranging from Biloxi, Miss., to Richmond, Va., establishing sites for communal prayers, religious schools, and community services. In smaller towns where only a few Muslims reside, families often gather in homes to celebrate Islamic festivals.

The history of Islam in the South extends from at least the 18th century, as some of the Africans brought to the South were Muslim. Omar bin Said, for example, was a well-educated Muslim from present-day Senegal who was a slave in North Carolina. His autobiography, written in Arabic, provides insights into the experiences of some of the first Muslims in the region. Christian slave owners, however, prohibited many expressions of Islam, forcing those traditions underground when they survived at all.

In the 1930s, Master Fard and his disciple, Elijah Muhammad, began the Nation of Islam to return African Americans to what Fard described as their original religion. While the Nation of Islam did not conform to the dominant versions of Islam, it incorporated some elements of traditional Islamic practices and ideas. The movement spread to the South with the opening of Mosque Number 15 in Atlanta.

Elijah Muhammad's son Warith Deen Muhammad led the Nation of Islam toward the practices of the largest segment of Muslims in the world, the Sunnis, and renamed the organization the Muslim American Society. Among predominantly African American mosques in the South, most follow the vision that Warith Deen Muhammad presented. In Atlanta, a leading African American mosque operates Warith Deen Muhammad High School, which teaches Arabic and Islamic religious studies along with a college preparatory curriculum. Some followers of Elijah Muhammad rejected Warith Deen Muhammad's leadership and created movements, including Louis Farrakhan's Nation of Islam, that have a smaller presence in the South.

Immigrant Muslims from Southeast Asia, India, the Middle East, and North Africa, most of whom have immigrated since 1965, often form mosques separate from those of African American Muslims. The al-Farooq Masjid in downtown Atlanta formed in 1980 to serve international Muslims. The mosque developed a cemetery that follows Islamic traditions and added two religious schools in the early nineties. In 2003 the community began building a multimillion-dollar mosque that, when completed, will add a minaret and two domes to the landscape of downtown Atlanta. This mosque has also opened other mosques in the suburbs of Atlanta as Muslims have spread beyond downtown.

The character of the mosques varies depending on the makeup of the Muslim community. A mosque in Charlotte, N.C., for example, that largely attracts Muslim immigrants from South Asia incorporates women more equally into the services than the Islamic Center in Greenville, S.C., whose leadership is predominantly from the Middle East. Some mosques in the region incorporate African American and immigrant Muslims, while some minority groups within Islam have created their own institutions, such as the Ismaili Center in Atlanta, which follows a particular branch of Shi'a Islam.

Even where numerous mosques exist, some Muslims maintain some traditions through other organizations. During Ramadan, the month of fasting prescribed in Islam, South Asian Muslims in the Raleigh, N.C., area conduct their own celebrations for the breaking of the daily fast. In Atlanta, the Indian American Cultural Association, which incorporates Hindu, Muslim, and Christian Indian Americans, celebrates 'Id al-fitr, the Islamic festival at the conclusion of Ramadan. Sufi saints, who emphasize mystical experiences of the divine and have related to Islam historically, have also formed organizations across the South that attract followers with various ethnic and religious backgrounds.

Beyond these organizations, Muslims' presence in the South has altered the region. While pork is important in southern culture, Islam prohibits it. Instead of pork, goat meat is important in the cultures of many Muslim immigrants and is often important in their culinary traditions, especially during festivals. Consequently, some farmers in the South have begun raising goats in response to the increasing demand for goat meat. Muslims have also influenced trade in the region as specialty stores supply their particular needs. Throughout the South, Islam has demonstrated its vitality and growing influence.

STEVEN RAMEY
University of North Carolina at Pembroke

Jane Idleman Smith, *Islam in America* (1999).

Jewish Religious Life

Jewish religious identity in the South is complicated and defies easy categorizations. The different Jewish immigrant groups that arrived from the colonial era through the 20th century brought with them diverse customs, traditions, and belief patterns, creating different American southern Judaisms. These religious ideologies and practices were modified by region, surrounding populations, a constant influx of Jewish immigrants and transplants, and, perhaps most important, changing religious ideologies taking place in the larger South.

The first Jews in the South came between 1654 and 1820 and were of Sephardic and Ashkenazic origin. They hailed from Portugal, England, Jamaica, Holland, Curaçao, Brazil, and Poland. Jews arrived in the southern colonies expecting and for the most part receiving the same toleration that England had demonstrated. These earliest Jews formulated a southern Judaism that reflected and incorporated southern gentile Christian and Masonic practices, ideals, architecture, and Revolutionary democratic ideologies. Synagogue structures resembled Christian churches. Synagogue politics reflected political ideas of the

Jewish Religious Service, Waco, Tex., 1890s
(Waco Jewry Collection, Baylor University, Waco, Tex.)

day, including the democratic election of synagogue leadership and the development of congregational constitutions.

Although somewhat more accepted than other minority religions, Jews in the early Republic were subject not only to Christian norms in southern economic, political, and social arenas but also to bouts of anti-Semitism. Anti-Semitism, in concert with philo-Semitism and proselytization, encouraged southern Jews across the 19th century to modify their Judaism to gain increased acceptance in southern society. Inhibiting the cohesiveness of the various southern Jewish communities during the colonial and early Republic eras were the schisms between Ashkenazic and Sephardic Jews, who each privileged their own religious practices and customs. During this first migration, southern Jews praised the American setting for its religious tolerance and religious freedoms, and they were the first Jewish communities based on voluntary affiliation.

The second migration of Jews, in the mid- and late 19th century, consisted of émigrés primarily from Germany, Bohemia, Moravia, Galicia, Alsace, and parts of eastern Europe. Like their predecessors, these Jews came for economic opportunities. American life, which drew distinctions between the public and private in promoting the separation of church and state, along with the Haskalah, or Jewish Enlightenment, markedly influenced the practice of Judaism both in southern synagogues and in southern homes, and beginning in 1824 in Charleston's Beth Elohim Congregation, American Reform Judaism drastically altered Jewish ritual. Influenced by European reform ideologies, contemporary Christian practices, and dominant American ideologies, southern synagogues followed Congregation Beth Elohim's lead and instituted English-language services, revamped prayer books, accepted the rabbinical sermon, allowed mixed seating, and abandoned the traditional prayer shawl and head covering. Scholars have suggested that a desire to Americanize and fit in with their Protestant neighbors also encouraged these changes. In keeping with changing gender roles, southern Jewish women, in an effort to maintain some sense of traditional Judaism, took an active role in synagogue life, including raising funds for clergy, religious items, schools, benevolent societies, cemeteries, and synagogue construction.

Religious differences in this period in the South emerged because of ideological differences. Reform Judaism taught that modifying Judaism to fit the southern context would preserve Judaism as well as encourage southern gentile tolerance of Jews. Orthodox Jews saw this new Judaism as virtually indistinguishable from Protestantism and feared that it, coupled with what they perceived to be dangerously high rates of intermarriage, spelled Judaism's death knell.

Changes in southern Judaism, though, did not occur solely because of internal reasons. Anti-Semitism flared in the 19th-century South because of national and international events, including the Mortara case and charges of profiteering during the Civil War. The majority of 19th-century southern Jews understood that preserving their Judaism while succeeding in the South economically, politically, and socially required modifications. Jews continued to observe Jewish holidays and maintain religious practices but most often did so in accordance with the South's economic and social schedules and prescriptions. Southern Jews preferred to retain the elements of Jewish tradition that did not interfere with their secular lives.

During the first half of the 19th century and reflecting the influence of the

Second Great Awakening, southern Jewish clergy tried to preserve Judaism by assuming greater power in the individual lives of their congregants. The Charleston synagogue, for example, imposed sanctions to encourage its congregants to observe religious laws and rituals and to discourage exogamy. To ensure the perpetuation of Judaism, many religious communities established schools that emphasized key Jewish ideologies. Curricula centered on connections between virtue and religious observance, on traditional Jewish observance and Jewish history. Additionally, because the federal government did not provide welfare services, southern Jewish communities assumed the primary role of caring for orphans, the disabled, the poor, and widows. Benevolent and voluntary societies were established in major southern cities.

The third migration, predominantly from eastern Europe, encouraged massive changes in southern Judaic practice and culture. During the late 19th century, the Conservative Jewish movement developed as response to perceived laxity in Reform Judaism and the rigidity of Orthodox Judaism. The Jewish South underwent crises in Judaic faith. Subsequently, many southern Jews privileged religious pluralist ideologies, thereby encouraging a secularization of Judaism and a decline in Jewish observance. These particular southern Jews sought to practice their Judaism not through religious practice but through good works and liberal political activities. Aside from national social ideologies, southern events also encouraged changes in Jewish culture and practice. Anti-Semitism in the obvious form of the Leo Frank case (1913–15) and in more subtle forms including anti-Zionism and Jewish conspiracies encouraged southern Jews to modify Judaic practices to those that would be accepted by the majority culture.

Southern Jewish practices, customs, and traditions were also influenced by southern locales, and distinctions must be made between southern Jewish religious culture in larger urban southern cities, rural areas, and on the frontier. Southern Jews in cities such as Charleston, Savannah, Richmond, Memphis, and Atlanta tended to adhere to stricter customs, ideologies, and practices regardless of whether they identified themselves as Reform, Conservative, or Orthodox Jews. Jews on the southern frontier and rural areas in the 19th century found it exceptionally difficult to uphold religious dietary requirements and Jewish observances and rituals. Those Jewish communities that emerged in the rural areas or farthest away from transportation and trade routes often greatly modified their practices and customs to suit the context. Observance of kashruth laws and Sabbath observances was made more difficult for these Jews. Rather than sacrifice their Judaism, they created, modified, and implemented innovative practices that would retain the spirit of Judaism. Other customs were dispensed with by some southern Jews because they viewed them as impractical or irrelevant.

Late 20th-century and early 21st-century southern Jewish religious life has undergone tremendous change. Vibrant southern Jewish communities that emerged in smaller southern towns are dissipating in part because of economic reasons and a desire by second- and third-generation Jews to live in the thriving southern Jewish metropolises of Atlanta and Memphis. Small towns continue to hold services, community events, and religious schools. Big southern cities, however, house larger Jewish communities with enormous Jewish networks, community centers, Jewish-oriented businesses, and several synagogues. Like their earliest counterparts, contemporary southern Jews continue to balance and modify their religious identities and practices to suit the larger regional context.

JENNIFER A. STOLLMAN
Salem College

Myran Berman, *Richmond's Jewry, 1769–1976* (1979); Mark Elovitz, *A Century of Jewish Life in Dixie: The Birmingham Experience* (1974); Eli Evans, *The Provincials: A Personal History of Jews in the South* (1973); Steven Hertzberg, *Strangers within the Gate City: The Jews of Atlanta, 1845–1915* (1978); Bertram Korn, *The Early Jews of New Orleans* (1969); Bobbie Malone, *Rabbi Max Helter: Reformer, Zionist, and Southerner* (1860–1929); Louis E. Schmier, *Reflections of Southern Jewry: The Letters of Charles Wessolowsky, 1878–1879* (1982).

Latino Religion

Specific forms of Latino Catholicism have a long historical trajectory in the geographic extremes of the South, but in the past decade, Latino religion has become increasingly pervasive and varied throughout the region. Tejano (Mexican Texan) religion dates from Mexico's ceding of Texas to the United States, which was completed with the Compromise of 1850. In the late 19th century, mestizos in the region, whose indigenous ancestors had been evangelized by Franciscans during Spanish military expeditions, identified as Catholic but had tenuous ties to the institutional church. As the U.S. Catholic Church assumed ecclesiastical control of the region, many factors hindered Tejano participation in the church: only a handful of functioning parishes already existed in the region; Tejanos had a long history of anticlericalism, which resulted from the Catholic Church's alignment with Spain against Mexican independence; and as Anglo-American clergy arrived in Texas, most brought with them a strong bias against Mexican Texans, with a few notable exceptions (such as the Oblates of Mary Immaculate, who worked extensively with Tejanos in the south Texas borderlands). Nevertheless, many Tejanos practiced a vibrant home-centered religion that revolved around devotions to Mary and the saints, as well as a range of syncretic practices such as *curanderismo*, a blend of Catholicism with ancient Mesoamerican healing rites that continues to thrive among Mexicans in the South.

Between 1910 and 1940, Tejanos were joined by hundreds of thousands of Mexican immigrants, who had been pushed from the interior of Mexico by the Mexican Revolution (1910–19) and Cristero Rebellion (1926–29). The new Mexican government's persecution of the Catholic Church and popular revolts in support of the clergy resulted in the exile of Catholic faithful, nuns, and priests. Once in Texas, these exiles worked together to build their own churches, parochial schools, and service centers. Nevertheless, many remained under-served by Catholic diocesan structures, which remained focused on "Anglo" (non-Mexican) Catholics. In some regions of Texas, religious (order) priests were given the responsibility of ministering to Mexicans in separate churches. In 1954 the Oblates of Mary Immaculate constructed a large shrine in the Lower Rio Grande valley to honor the Virgin of San Juan, to whom many Mexican immigrants in the area had a powerful devotion. Currently, almost one mil-lion visitors pass through the doors of the Shrine of Our Lady of San Juan del Valle annually, making it the most visited Catholic pilgrimage destination in the United States.

As Texas was beginning its secession from Mexico, another form of Latino popular religiosity was establishing a presence in the South: that of Cuban im-migrants to Florida. The first Florida Cuban communities formed in Key West in 1831 and Ybor City, Tampa, in 1886. Both of these communities were com-posed of cigar makers and their families, who were supporters of Cuban inde-pendence from Spain and of José Martí's Partido Revolucionario Cubano. As in Mexico, support of the revolution was generally accompanied by a strong does of anticlericalism, since the Cuban Catholic Church aligned with Spanish colonial powers. Nevertheless, Ybor City's first Catholic church was established by a Jesuit priest in 1890, and a second Cuban parish opened in 1922. Although the church was widely regarded as a weak and relatively insignificant institu-tion in Ybor City, some evidence exists that home-based popular religiosity and African-based syncretic religious practices thrived there.

In 1961, as a result of the Cuban Revolution, two-thirds of the Catholic clergy of Cuba were evicted, and they were accompanied by almost 80,000 anti-Communist exiles. These exiles, and hundreds of thousands more in the years to come, took refuge in the primarily Protestant, typically southern city of

Miami. With the help of exiled clergy, they quickly set about re-creating some of their religious institutions, including numerous Catholic schools and student associations, in Miami. Unlike their Mexican counterparts in Texas earlier in the century, they also encountered a Catholic diocese that was very eager to assist them, provided a wide range of material resources, and expected them to rapidly and fully assimilate into already existing "American" parishes. In 1966, perhaps to temper well-documented Cuban Catholic resistance to this plan for assimilation, the bishop of Miami established a shrine for Our Lady of Charity, Cuba's patroness. This sacred site annually attracts hundreds of thousands of pilgrims, making it the sixth largest Catholic pilgrimage site in the United States.

Currently, the South Florida Shrine of Our Lady of Charity and the South Texas Shrine of Our Lady of San Juan del Valle anchor Latino religion in the South. Both extremely popular pilgrimage destinations juxtapose Cuban or Mexican nationalism with tensions between heterodox and orthodox Catholicism, since they are inevitably sites for practices associated with Santeria and *curanderismo*, respectively. Santeria has steadily grown in popularity in Miami as a result of both the Mariel boatlift in the early 1980s, which brought proportionally more practitioners of Afro-Cuban religions than earlier migrations, and U.S. Supreme Court proceedings of 1993, which increased the status and publicity of Santeria in the United States. Such practices are strongly sanctioned and often dismissed as "superstition" or worse by the Catholic hierarchy, which uses the popular shrines to evangelize Latinos, encouraging them to practice a more orthodox and church-centered Catholicism.

In the past decade, the exponential growth of the Latino population in the traditional "Bible Belt" has meant that Latino religion is no longer confined to the South's geographic extremes. According to the 2000 U.S. Census, six of the seven states that have experienced a more than 200 percent increase in "Hispanic" population since 1990 are located in the historically "Baptist South" (North Carolina, South Carolina, Georgia, Alabama, Tennessee, Arkansas). Two of the states in which this increase has been most profound are Georgia and North Carolina, where the foreign-born population has exploded as a result of changing migration patterns of Mexicans and increasing presence of immigrants from throughout Central and South America, particularly Guatemala, Honduras, El Salvador, Colombia, and Peru. What constitutes contemporary "Latino religion" in these states is, in fact, the religion of very recent Latin American immigrants, most of whom are young, mobile, and undocumented residents of the United States. Many can also be characterized as transmigrants because they maintain close ties to their place of origin. Such ties are often religiously mediated through Catholic activities like feast-day celebrations for local, regional, and national saints or through the connections that evangelical and Pentecostal churches have to parent organizations in their members' place of origin.

As they reshape the religious contours of these southern states, new immigrants radically impact the presence and role of the Catholic Church, change the traditional mission fields for established Protestant churches, and introduce a range of new religious practices and organizations. Georgia and North Carolina are home to four of the six Catholic dioceses in the United States with the fastest-growing Hispanic membership (Charlotte, Atlanta, Raleigh, and Savannah). Currently, 46 percent of the churches in the Archdiocese of Atlanta offer Spanish masses, and the Diocese of Raleigh offers such masses in 61 percent of its churches. Beyond offering mass, the Catholic Church is struggling to respond appropriately to these newcomers and defend against what it perceives to be the dangerous lure of Pentecostal and evangelical churches. The most popular strategies used by the church to be more inviting to Latinos and counteract the appeal of Protestant churches are to offer a broad range of social services and to establish charismatic worship groups.

There are two primary sources of Latino Protestant congregations in the South. The first, and less prevalent, type results from a perceptible shift in the home mission field of well-established denominations. An association of Hispanic Baptists in Georgia, for instance, now includes more than 70 congregations, many of which are associated with the Southern Baptist Convention. In Georgia and North Carolina, Lutherans, Episcopalians, Methodists, and Presbyterians have all worked to establish Latino congregations, often recruiting Latino clergy from other parts of the United States, but they have been less successful than their Baptist counterparts. Baptist churches offer less arduous routes to both ordination and the formation of new congregations, and non-Catholic Latino churches in the South appear more likely to thrive when they are independent and pastored by Latino newcomers. The second, and more prevalent, type of Latino Protestant congregation in the region is an extremely heterogeneous collection of small evangelical and Pentecostal groups that are unaffiliated with an established denomination in the region and pastored by Latin American immigrants. Interestingly, some such churches, such as Iglesia de Cristo Ministerios Elim or La Luz del Mundo, have been brought with migrants from Guatemala and Mexico, respectively, to the South.

Home-based popular Catholicism continues to be the most pervasive (and varied) form of Latino religiosity in the South. Most recent Latin American immigrants to the region, like their predecessors, practice a religion that does not necessitate regular participation in particular churches. However, for many immigrants, religious organizations have assumed another kind of responsibility. In many parts of the South, Latino immigrants have arrived in destinations that are sometimes violently unwelcoming. Even when not resistant to their presence, southern cities and towns offer few, if any, services, advocacy groups, or even public gathering places for Latinos. In some such places, churches fill all these roles, becoming sites for the defense and protection of undocumented immigrants, in particular. As they strive to provide much more than spiritual assistance to a minority group experiencing persecution and discrimination, these Latino religious organizations follow a route paved by African Americans in the South, along which churches become, for marginalized groups, centers of economic, social, educational, and political life.

MARIE FRIEDMANN MARQUARDT
Emory University

Gilberto M. Hinojosa, in *Mexican Americans and the Catholic Church, 1900–1965*, ed. Jay P. Dolan and Gilberto M. Hinojosa (1994); James Talmadge Moore, *Through Fire and Flood: The Catholic Church in Frontier Texas, 1836–1900* (1992); Lisandro Pérez, in *Puerto Rican and Cuban Catholics in the U.S., 1900–1965*, ed. Jay P. Dolan and Jaime R. Vidal (1994); Thomas A. Tweed, *Our Lady of the Exile: Diasporic Religion at a Cuban Catholic Shrine in Miami* (1997), *Southern Cultures* (Summer 2002); Martha Woodson Rees and T. Danyael Miller, *Quienes Somos? Que Necesitamos? Needs Assessment of Hispanics in the Archdiocese of Atlanta* (25 March 2002); Manuel A. Vasquez and Marie Friedmann Marquardt, *Globalizing the Sacred: Religion across the Americas* (2003).

Literature and Religion

Religion has influenced the imagination of southern writers in fundamental ways. Both aesthetically and thematically, religious practice in the region has helped writers render a particular place and time as a target for their satire and as a prism through which they interpret human experience. Often southern writers' debts to the religious beliefs and practices of their region are unacknowledged, perhaps even unconscious. William Faulkner asserts such influences exist, nonetheless: "The writer must write about his background. He must write out of what he knows and the Christian legend is part of any Christian's background, especially the background of a country boy, a Southern country boy. I grew up with that, took that in without even knowing it. It's just there. It has nothing to do with how much of it I might believe or disbelieve—it's just there." Southern writers, whether or not they expressly address religious issues, engage questions that preoccupy southern culture, questions that often arise in the practice of religion.

The South historically has been more homogeneous and orthodox in its beliefs than other regions. Survey data by sociologist John Shelton Reed showed that 90 percent of southerners surveyed identified themselves as Protestant, as opposed to 60 percent of nonsoutherners. The same study found more agreement in religious beliefs among these southern Protestants than among nonsouthern Protestants or Catholics. Within this homogeneity, there is, however, individuality—institutionalized in the many Protestant denominations—producing colorful variants in religious behavior. This individuality within an overwhelmingly Protestant culture resulted from the particular emphasis of the southern church as it parted from the pluralistic patterns of the North. The Baptist and Methodist movements that swept across the largely rural South after 1755 often featured preachers who delivered dramatic, emotional pictures of the struggle to escape sin and achieve salvation. With common roots in the New England Calvinism of the Great Awakening, this expressive religion stressed personal piety and the preeminent importance of achieving one's salvation. Appealing to the often isolated poor, it cared little for abstract theology or issues of ethical responsibility within the society. No church-state was envisioned. In the hospitable, fertile southern landscape, preachers taught that one must struggle inwardly with an inherent sinfulness. This sense of human frailty and limitation combined with the hedonism of a rich, frontier culture led to what Samuel S. Hill has called a pattern of "confession, purgation, and going out to sin again."

As private morality became more exclusively the domain of the church, engagement with issues of public morality became less frequent. The explanation lies with the South's commitment to slavery. Because the southern church avoided confronting the immorality of the institution of slavery, it could not validly address issues of ethical responsibility in the larger society. Instead, spokesmen of the church defended the institution as consistent with God's plan, vilifying its critics as ungodly in motivation and action and reaffirming the position that the church should concern itself only with issues of personal piety and salvation. Also, the southern church undertook elaborate missionary efforts to teach the slave community to share its outlook.

When writers of the Southern Literary Renaissance looked to the social history of the South for reasons behind its 20th-century ills, they blamed the church's preoccupation with matters of personal behavior and its carefully defended historical blindness to slavery. Writers like Faulkner, Allen Tate, Flannery O'Connor, and Erskine Caldwell created communities of self-righteous churchgoers and hypocritical preachers practicing a narrow, spiritless religion insensitive to the moral issues with which these writers were concerned. Mark Twain had earlier laid the ground for satirizing the formal practice of religion in the South as a fountain of intolerance; Faulkner tilled the same soil in his depiction of the good Baptist ladies of Jefferson who close the door to those who violate the standards of personal behavior endorsed formally by the church. Once questioned about his own religious beliefs, Faulkner said what other southern writers seemed to be implying in their portrayal of institutional religion: "I think that the trouble with Christianity is that we've never tried it yet." These writers created worlds where issues of public morality had to be engaged; adherence to strict codes of personal piety was insufficient. As Robert Penn Warren wrote at the end of *All the King's Men*, the challenge was to immerse oneself in "the awful responsibility of time."

Yet even as they attack the self-satisfied attitudes of the southern religious establishment, many of these writers accept views basic to regional religious belief. For example, Flannery O'Connor, a writer who makes this gap between belief and practice the focus of her work, finds in the southerner's belief in the Devil, in the reality of evil, an important article of faith. From the perspective of her own orthodox Roman Catholic beliefs, O'Connor keenly perceives the fundamentalist Protestant experiences of the majority of southerners. She introduces her collection of short stories *A Good Man Is Hard to Find* with a quotation from Saint Cyril of Jerusalem: "The dragon is by the side of the road, watching those who pass. Beware lest he devour you. We go to the Father of Souls, but it is necessary to pass by the dragon." O'Connor believes she addresses a modern world in which evil is dismissed as sociological or psychological aberration. In the South, particularly the rural Protestant South, this Roman Catholic writer ironically recognizes another point of view.

Episcopal bishop Robert R. Brown writes that southerners "believe more in the reality of Satan than in the reality of God," and John Shelton Reed's research shows that by a significant margin (86 percent to 52 percent) southerners are more likely than nonsoutherners to say they believe in the Devil. Southern writers, too, insist on the reality of evil. They present it as active, powerful, inescapable, irreducible, threatening the individual from within as well as from without. They also criticize ideas of social reform dependent on a view of humankind as essentially good. Writers such as Faulkner, Warren, Katherine Anne Porter, Carson McCullers, and Truman Capote join O'Connor in representing evil as violence, grotesque psychological distortion, selfish pride, or despair. These storytellers find in the individual's confrontation with evil the conflict from which dramatic fiction arises.

Another common theme that reflects the debt of southern writers to their religious environment is closely allied to this acceptance of the existence of evil: human beings are flawed, limited, imperfect. "Man is conceived in sin and born in corruption," says Warren's Willie Stark, "and he passeth from the stink of the didie to the stench of the shroud." The viewpoint is essentially conservative, even pessimistic if contrasted with visions of a more idealized human nature. Without explicitly referring to original sin, southern writers create characters more sinning than sinned against. Mr. Thompson of Katherine Anne Porter's "Noon Wine" or Horace Benbow of Faulkner's *Sanctuary* awaken to their own capacity for violence and evil. Individuals resist or succumb to their own selfish pride, their greed, their bestial natures. It is a mistake, however, to label such a vision of human beings as pessimistic or deterministic. Within the context of the accepted religious beliefs of their culture, southern writers turn their attention to how one conducts life given these imperfections. The measure of the spiritually healthy individual is in his or her ability to recognize limitations and then to involve oneself with the world and its complexities.

In the emotional style of southern evangelical Protestantism lie the clearest connections to the South's creative literature. The southern writer could have and often did turn to the preacher for models of imaginative, moving uses of language. Faulkner once speculated about the appeal of the Southern Baptist movement: "It came from times of hardship in the South where there was little or no food for the human spirit — where there were no books, no theater, no music, and life was pretty hard and a lot of it happened out in the sun, for very little reward and that was the only escape they had." The southern preacher dramatized the struggles of good and evil in vivid, concrete stories, enlivened by expressive flourishes, which allowed the congregation to forget for the moment their day-to-day fight to survive. In the competitive world of the itinerant preacher, he who could touch the imagination as well as the conscience of his congregation thrived. Every writer who grew up in the South, then, breathed in this dramatic, emotional atmosphere.

The preacher offered southern writers literary tools and visions that guided them in confronting central questions about life. Writers worked scenes of camp meetings and revivals into their stories. Johnson Jones Hooper, for example, introduces the character Captain Simon Suggs to a camp meeting, where he becomes the object-lesson sinner for the preacher. Mark Twain presents a camp meeting through Huck Finn's eyes as the duke and the king, Huck's con-artist companions, prey on the gullible there assembled. Flannery O'Connor in "The River" shows the preacher Bevel, who baptizes a small boy so that he will "count now." Recently, Lisa Alther has portrayed the modern youth revival and evangelist Brother Buck, who couches his message in extended football metaphors of Christ Jesus Thy Quarterback, the Celestial Coach, and the water boys of life. And Faulkner shows the power of the preacher to raise his audience to new levels of self-recognition in *The Sound and the Fury* with the sermon of the Reverend Shegog.

Faulkner chose to depict a black preacher when he wanted to express a redemptive quality in the religion practiced in the South. Samuel Hill has pointed out that the black church developed along lines different from those of white Protestantism, in that "the theology of black people's Christianity was shifting, not away from glorious heaven, to be sure, but away from the threats of hell. It remained a religion of salvation, but less and less from eternal punishment and more from alienation from Jesus. . . . [Black people] created an authentic folk variant of a traditional religion. It featured expressiveness, joy, fellowship, moral responsibility, pious feelings and the hope of heaven." Yet black southern writers, like their white counterparts, respond with ambivalence when portraying religious practice in the region.

Richard Wright in his autobiographical *Black Boy* depicts the women of his family as threatening him with God's punishment for his transgressions. In *Native Son* religion weakens black rebellion with promises that suffering in this life will be rewarded in the next. But in the short story "Fire and Cloud," Wright presents the Reverend Taylor as a man who lives his religious commitment as social action. In his picture of the Reverend Homer Barbee in *Invisible Man*, Ralph Ellison illustrates the rhetorical power of the black preacher even as he suggests that it is used to misdirect the attention of the congregation from their exploitation. Alice Walker, however, seems to capture the spirit of what Hill called the joyful folk variant of traditional southern religion in *The Color Purple*. Shug Avery celebrates a personal religion, independent from any formal church, which asks only that one express love for God's creation. It is one of the most positive, albeit unconventional, expressions of religious feeling in southern literature.

H. L. Mencken once characterized the South as the "bunghole of the United States, a cesspool of Baptists, a miasma of Methodism, snake-charmers, phony real-estate operators, and syphilitic evangelists." Southern writers have populated their work with hypocritical preachers, self-righteous congregations, rigid Calvinists, and spiritually twisted fanatics. They have, nevertheless, drawn their vision of human limitation and a world in which good and evil contend from the most basic beliefs of southern religion. Perhaps as the distinctions between the South and other regions fade, southern writers will become more indistinguishable in their response to their community. In the work of Walker Percy, a southerner and a Catholic, there is attention to philosophical and theological issues that cannot be said to be strictly southern. Contemporary writers continue, though, to explore themes rooted in the religious life of the South. Clyde Edgerton writes humorously of southern preachers and parishioners, Mary Ward Brown explores the psychology of charismatic believers, and Lee Smith tells darkly comic tales of religion in Appalachia. Dennis Covington wrote of serpent handlers in *Salvation on Sand Mountain*, conveying how he became caught up in the religion's drama.

Other recent southern writers who write of religion include James Wilcox, Randall Kenan, and Larry Brown. Steven Stern has carved out a special sacred literary geography, with short stories and novels about the Pinch district of Memphis, peopled by a Jewish community that sees itself isolated in the South and truly a lost tribe.

ROBERT R. MOORE
State University of New York at Oswego

Robert H. Brinkmeyer, *The Art and Vision of Flannery O'Connor* (1989), *Three Catholic Writers of the Modern South* (1985); Doreen Fowler and Ann J. Abadie, eds., *Faulkner and Religion* (1991); Samuel S. Hill, *The South and the North in American Religion* (1980); Fred Hobson, *The Southern Writer in the Postmodern World* (1991); C. Hugh Holman, *The Immoderate Past: The Southern Writer and History* (1977); Susan Ketchin, *The Christ-Haunted Landscape: Faith and Doubt in Southern Fiction* (1994); Rosemary Magee and Robert Detweiler, in *Encyclopedia of Religion in the South*, ed. Samuel S. Hill (1984); Perry Miller, *Errand into the Wilderness* (1956); John Shelton Reed, *The Enduring South: Subcultural Persistence in Mass Society* (1972); Louis D. Rubin Jr., in *The Added Dimension: The Art and Mind of Flannery O'Connor*, ed. Melvin J. Friedman and Lewis A. Lawson (1977); Lewis Simpson, in *The Cry of Home: Cultural Nationalism and the Modern Writer*, ed. H. Ernest Lewald (1972).

Missionary Activities

Religious revivalism swept the South in the early days of the Republic and brought with it an intense belief in the millennium — the thousand-year reign of Christ on earth that would commence when all peoples of the world had been given a chance to accept Christ. By natural extension foreign missions joined domestic missions to Native Americans in the effort to carry out the Great Commission: "Go ye therefore, and teach all nations, baptizing them . . . ; [and] teaching them to observe all things whatsoever I have commanded you" (Matt. 28:19–20). Richard Furman, pastor of the First Baptist Church of Charleston, S.C., adjoined nationalism to religion in 1802 when he asserted that the United

States would "participate, largely, in the fulfillment of those sacred prophecies which have foretold the glory of Messiah's kingdom. . . . Hence God has prepared this land for a great mission, to lead the world into the millennium." Nationalism thus reinforced religious belief and determined the religiocultural nature of American foreign missions.

The formal organization of at least one major denomination in the United States resulted from the missionary impulse. Baptists believed so strongly in the autonomy of the individual congregation that they had resisted all efforts to form even statewide organizations. Yet they established a national body when confronted with the need to support foreign missionaries. Adoniram Judson and his wife and Luther Rice, Congregationalists, had been sent to India by the American Board of Commissioners for Foreign Missions (ABCFM) in 1812. During their voyage they became convinced that baptism of believers was scripturally correct, so they requested and received baptism by immersion from a British Baptist on their arrival. Luther Rice returned to the United States to inform the ABCFM of their actions, whereupon the board severed its connection with them. Rice toured Baptist churches, North and South, requesting support for the Judsons. The need to sustain these missionaries already in the field led to the organization, in 1814, of the General Missionary Convention of the Baptist Denomination in the United States of America for Foreign Missions. Richard Furman, long an advocate of this effort, was elected its first president, and other Baptists from southern states who supported both foreign missions and a national organization for Baptists also served in positions of responsibility.

Frontier Baptists were not as enthusiastic about foreign missions as their eastern brethren. Indeed, in the early 19th century there were more differences between rural and urban Baptists than there were between northern and southern Baptists who lived in cities, and this was most likely true of other denominations as well. Until American sectional issues caused divisions in three Protestant bodies—Methodists in 1844, Baptists in 1845, and Presbyterians in 1861—southerners were among the early missionary volunteers and worked alongside their colleagues from the North. The three new southern denominations quickly established foreign missions as a major part of their program, with China as one of the first fields to be manned. Missionaries from each denomination had worked there before the separation, and China loomed large in the millennial view. It had more people than any other country; they had to be reached before the millennium could begin.

Several circumstances retarded the southern missionary effort in China. Before the Peking Treaties of 1860 missionaries had been confined to a few treaty ports. Access to the interior, even when obtained, could not be exploited until the financial strains of the Civil War and Reconstruction ended. By that time missionary efforts in India and the Near East, without imperial restrictions on the free movement and activities of foreigners, had become well established and drew heavily on mission budgets. Throughout the 19th century American support for foreign missions — in expenditure, personnel, and capital construction — went for the most part to the Near East and to the Indian subcontinent.

Qualitatively, if not quantitatively, southern missionaries of the past century made significant contributions to China in particular and to the missionary enterprise in general. A southern Methodist from Georgia, Young J. Allen, arrived in Shanghai in 1860. During his long tenure in China he became one of the most influential American missionaries through his magazine, *The Globe*. Written in Chinese, it became a vehicle to inform readers, non-Christian as well as Christian, of the Western scientific knowledge so many of them sought beginning with the Self-Strengthening movement of the 1860s and particularly after China's humiliating defeat by Japan in 1895. A young woman from Virginia, Charlotte "Lottie" Moon, served as a missionary to China and became the inspiration for extensive fund-raising activity by the Women's Missionary Union of the Southern Baptist Convention. The Lottie Moon Christmas Offering annually collects millions of dollars, which the Foreign Mission Board uses to maintain the largest number of American Protestant missionaries now in the field.

Perhaps the most influential missionary activity of the late 1800s occurred in the southern United States. In 1880 an American ship's captain, Charles Jones, discovered a young Chinese stowaway on his vessel, and when he docked in Wilmington, N.C., he entrusted the boy to the care of the pastor of the Fifth Avenue Methodist Church there. The lad, named Soong, was converted and took as his Christian name that of the captain. He remained in the United States to receive an undergraduate and ministerial education. In 1886 Charlie Jones Soong returned to China an ordained Methodist minister and became involved in the revolutionary movement of Sun Yat-sen. One of his sons, T. V. Soong, and three of his daughters, Ai-ling, Ching-ling, and Mei-ling Soong, were educated in the United States and became internationally known figures in Chinese political life.

Southern missionaries in the first half of the 20th century generally were indistinguishable from those of other regions of the United States. They volunteered for the same mission fields — Latin America, Africa, the Middle East, South and East Asia — and engaged in the same kinds of activities: evangelization, education, medical missions, and social work. Independence granted to former colonies and the establishment of Socialist governments in the Third

World from about 1950 created a divergence between the missionary emphases of southern and northern denominations. The latter mainly joined the National and World Councils of Churches, which stressed the social gospel, with cultural and technological aid projects predominating. Southern denominations have retained a more evangelical focus in their missions overseas. These lines, however, should not be too sharply drawn. As of the early 1980s the evangelical bodies supported more than three times as many foreign missionaries as the "liberal" churches and American Catholics combined. As governments sensitive to foreign presence have discouraged, if not forbidden, foreign missionary activity, many of today's missionaries seek out the 16,000 tribal groups in remote areas around the world who have not heretofore been reached with the gospel. This may be the greatest change in Protestant missionary strategy of the past two decades. Some missionaries who would have been denominational missionaries now work in nondenominational agencies in countries that do not welcome foreign religious workers.

In addition, the Southern Baptist Convention has undergone enormous changes as a result of conservative theological and political dominance since 1979, and its missionaries must now subscribe to biblically inerrantist doctrines, leading to their presenting Christianity in different ways than before. The traditional Baptist view of the priesthood of believers would, for example, be downplayed. Longtime Southern Baptist missionaries have chosen to give up their assignments rather than subscribe to these new understandings.

GEORGE B. PRUDEN JR.
Armstrong State College

Ecumenical Missionary Conference: New York, 1900, 2 vols. (1900); John K. Fairbank, ed., *The Missionary Enterprise in China and America* (1974); Kenneth Scott Latourette, *A History of the Expansion of Christianity,* vol. 6, *The Great Century in Northern Africa and Asia A.D. 1800–A.D. 1914* (1945); *Time* (27 December 1982).

Modernism and Religion

In American religious studies the term "modernism" describes a style of Christian theology that attempted to adjust traditional religious doctrines to the intellectual demands of the modern world, especially to biological evolution and historical-critical study of Scripture. Although the term is often used to describe the beliefs of all who make such adjustments, it is usually reserved for the liberal theology of the early 20th century (1920–40).

Modernism has not been a significant position among southern theologians. The predominant southern orientation has been theological orthodoxy. Even before the Civil War, southern theologians, especially in the culturally influential Presbyterian Church, tended to adopt more traditional theological positions than their northern counterparts. This was partly because of the conviction that the Bible, if interpreted literally, supported the institution of slavery. The Civil War reinforced this preexistent conservatism in two ways. First, the revivals that periodically swept the Confederate armies solidified the evangelical churches as the expression of southern piety. These revivals, often led by lay preachers, stressed biblicism as a key element in religion. Second, the defeat of the South and the subsequent forcible reunion of the country forced the former Confederates to find new ways to express their loyalty to the Lost Cause. An amalgamation of sentimentality, conservatism, and southern identity took place — a southern civil religion — that inhibited intellectual change and adventure.

James Woodrow (1828–1907), professor of Natural Science in Connection with Revelation at Columbia Presbyterian Seminary in South Carolina from 1861 to 1886, was one of the first southerners to approach the question of the relationship between the new biology and Christian theology. As a result of the publication of his position, controversy arose over the issue from 1884 to 1886, which, although not leading to his conviction for heresy, resulted in his dismissal from the school. Crawford Howell Toy (1836–1919), professor of Old Testament at Southern Baptist Seminary in Louisville, Ky., had been trained as a biblical critic at the University of Berlin. While teaching the Bible at Southern, he referred to the views current in Europe on such matters as the authorship of the Pentateuch and Isaiah. Fearful of controversy, his colleagues asked for his resignation before the trustees could force the issue by dismissing him. William Whitsitt (1841–1911), president of Southern from 1895 to 1899, was likewise persuaded to resign after he applied modern historical techniques to Baptist history.

Among Methodists, a migration of students from Randolph-Macon, Wofford, and other colleges to Germany after the Civil War and to the Johns Hopkins University after its founding in 1876 created a noticeably larger contingent of progressive thinkers in that denomination than among Presbyterians or Baptists. In 1875 Alexander Winchell was brought to the new Vanderbilt University and within four years came to advocate publicly Darwin's theories. He was dismissed in 1879 after a prolonged controversy. Nonetheless, Vanderbilt became a center for advanced biblical study as well as for the Christian interpretation of evolution. The struggle that separated Vanderbilt from the Methodist Church was technically over the issue of who had the right to govern the school, but theological factors were also involved. The elevation of Emory to university status and the establishment of its Candler School of Theology as a response to the Methodist loss of Vanderbilt were also partially antimodernist developments.

During the 1920s the nation as a whole witnessed a battle between modernists and fundamentalists. On the one hand, it was a struggle within various denominations for control of each church's teaching and government. Although these struggles took place primarily in the North, they influenced those southern churches that had miniature fundamentalist-modernist controversies.

In southern Methodism, Bishops Candler, Denny, and DuBose were continually critical of liberal theology, which they saw as a threat to historical Methodist belief, and they were in contact with Harold Paul Slvan, a New Jersey pastor who led the conservative wing in the northern church. In the Southern Baptist Convention, the issue of whether evolution should be taught in the denomination's schools was hotly debated in the twenties, and in 1925 a new confession of faith — the Baptist Faith and Message — was adopted to guard against liberal ideas in the church.

The controversy was even more marked in the Presbyterian Church in the United States. This southern denomination had a series of trials in the early 20th century that prepared the way for the major controversy in the 1920s. The Reverend William Caldwell, who moved to Fort Worth from Baltimore, was at the center of a debate on biblical inerrancy that lasted from 1900 to 1909, and F. E. Maddox was suspended from the ministry in 1909 for heresy. Darwinism was continually denounced in the church press, and evolution was an issue before the 1920s made antievolutionism a popular crusade. The internal Presbyterian controversy in the 1920s revolved around the Bible Union of China, which charged that modernism had infected the mission field. Much of the controversy concerned Nanking Theological Seminary, a joint enterprise of the northern and southern churches. In addition, the question of whether a candidate needed to affirm his acceptance of biblical inerrancy was also hotly discussed. Feelings on this issue were so high that Walter Moore, president of Union (Richmond), withdrew his nomination of Harris Kirk, a Baltimore pastor, for a faculty position at the denomination's seminaries. By 1930, however, the debate was quieted, although it reemerged from 1938 to 1940 in a controversy over the theology of Ernest Trice Thompson of Union Seminary. When the general assembly declined to investigate the doctrinal views of the faculty of the church's seminaries in 1940, the battle ended.

The other side of the debate in the 1920s was over the teaching of evolution in the public schools. In North Carolina, this debate was particularly hard fought. The presidents of Wake Forest College (Baptist) and Duke University, William

Louis Poteat and William Preston Few, took the position that freedom of inquiry was essential to education and resisted the passage of the law. For many Baptists and Methodists, their advocacy of academic freedom branded them as modernists and brought them much criticism in the church press. Their alliance, however, helped to block the passage of the act. The issue was fought more dramatically in the neighboring state of Tennessee, whose law prohibiting the teaching of evolution in the public schools resulted in the Scopes Trial in 1925.

The comparatively small number of modernists in the southern churches did not prevent "modernism" from becoming symbolically important in southern religion. The denunciation of modernists became a stock element in much southern preaching, and Bible colleges and similar institutions used the fear of modernism as a way of promoting their own cause. For many southerners, resistance to modernism was a central element of their faith. As part of the system of symbols by which southerners have ordered their religious lives, modernism — real or imagined — has been one of the dominant forces in the 20th century.

GLENN T. MILLER
Southeastern Baptist Theological Seminary

Kenneth K. Bailey, *Southern White Protestantism in the 20th Century* (1964); Norman F. Furniss, *The Fundamentalist Controversy, 1918–1931* (1954); Willard B. Gatewood Jr., ed., *Controversy in the Twenties: Fundamentalism, Modernism, and Evolution* (1969); Robert T. Handy, *Religion in Life* (Summer 1955); William R. Hutchison, *The Modernist Impulse in American Protestantism* (1976); George M. Marsden, *Fundamentalism and American Culture: The Shaping of 20th-Century Evangelicalism, 1870–1925* (1980).

Native American Religion

For millennia, religious practices enabled Native Americans in the Southeast to maintain or restore vital balances disrupted by human action or the actions of other living beings. Across the Southeast, Native Americans perceived spiritual values and meanings in a wide range of activities, events, and phenomena. They found holiness in a comet's sweep across the sky, the earth's rumbling in a quake, turbulence in a river, and the flight of a bird. Their dreams foretold the future, warning of impending sickness and death or, more auspiciously, a successful hunt. Their systems of belief and morality shaped how they understood weather, birth, courtship, healing, death, horticulture, warfare, and diplomacy. Their pottery, baskets, clothing, jewelry, stories, place-names, art, and architecture invoked creation stories, mythic beings, and cosmic symbols. Their sacred sites, holy times, and festivals embodied their distinctive spiritual orientations toward the world.

Embedded so deeply in daily life and diffused so widely across so many activities, Native American religions were very influential, but ironically, they were to some extent invisible as religion. Many native peoples did not think of religion as a separate thing or coin a word to name it. On the other hand, if there was not a well-bounded or tightly circumscribed phenomenon called "religion" in ancestral Native America, there were among many peoples special ceremonies, sacred buildings, and ritual specialists that stood out, possessed special names, and evoked extraordinary treatment. This was especially the case in nonegalitarian social formations, such as the Mississippian society that flourished a thousand years ago along that river and to the east.

Mississippian society (900–1550 C.E.) consisted of chiefdoms, alliances of villages, and outlying farmsteads dominated by particular chiefly lineages that exacted tribute from or waged war with other chiefdoms. Although remarkably unstable, these polities produced some monumental architecture, most notably, large flat-topped earthen mounds that served as political and spiritual foci. Some of the most spectacular of these were located at Moundville, Ala. These ceremonial mounds, although constructed over many years by communal labor, were not open to the general public. On these square-topped platforms, priests and chiefs performed vital ceremonies to pay homage to the chiefly lineage, to gather power for warfare against other chiefdoms, and to orchestrate the community's agricultural activities. Centuries later, these mounds, in spite of a lack of care and in the face of serious threats posed by modern development, still comprise the largest religious structures ever built in the Southeast. Their silent monumentality belies the dynamism of the societies that constructed them.

Long before contact with Europeans and well before the Mississippian period, Native men and women changed their traditions in many ways, some local and almost invisible, others far more dramatic, systemic, and public. Because Native traditions were holistically connected to the rest of life, any significant change in one aspect of life could produce profound religious repercussions. When corn moved from Mexico to the American Southwest and then later to the Southeast, it arrived not simply as a plant but as an embedded part of a distinctive and highly spiritualized cultural tradition. Symbols and rituals, gods and ceremonies accompanied the plant, as a cultus came with the corn. Corn gave rise to the Mississippian religiopolitical system and other maize-centered religious practices, stories, and sacrifices. Corn changed in fundamental ways how people lived, related, and believed. All of this occurred long before Columbus.

After contact with non–Native Americans, mound building declined significantly. Disease epidemics brought by Europeans and the violence of conquistador armies caused the greatest loss of life ever experienced in the Southeast and severely disrupted Mississippian society and its religious system. Nevertheless, if mound building declined, many Mississippian beliefs, values, and practices survived and helped shape the traditions of post-Mississippian groups such as the Muskogee (Creek), Choctaw, and Cherokee Indians. Hunters did not forget to offer pieces of meat to fire, and women took care to sequester themselves during their menses. And everyone kept tending corn and, in annual communal ceremonies, celebrated its significance as a gift from self-sacrificing sacred beings.

With the spread of Spanish missions in La Florida during the 16th and 17th centuries, many southeastern Indians learned the rites and tenets of Catholicism. Missionized Native Americans continued to play a version of the ballgame and to hold on to other precontact traditions. They also occasionally revolted against priestly authority. Over time, a complex, hybridized world — part Spanish, part Native American — emerged in these missions. It did not last. At the beginning of the 18th century English-led armies from South Carolina destroyed all the missions and enslaved or deported the Christianized Native Americans. For the next century, few missionaries of any sort sought to convert southeastern Indians, but Christianity, especially Protestant Christianity, continued to percolate into Indian country, brought by traders, settlers, agents, and runaway slaves. They shared stories from the Bible.

Different Native American groups in the Southeast responded differently to Protestant Christianity. The Creek Muskogees, for example, expressed a very low tolerance for Christian preaching and harassed Protestant missionaries when they arrived in the early 19th century. Indeed, among the Creeks, anti-colonial American Indian prophets found a receptive audience. These prophets rejected the economic dependency associated with the deerskin trade and decried class divisions emerging among southeastern Indians. In 1811 a significant faction of Creeks, known as the Redsticks, launched a dramatic movement to restore the symbolic boundaries between Indians and whites. Political revolt became a sacred cause involving 9,000 Muskogee men, women, and children, but American armies and their Choctaw, Cherokee, and Creek allies crushed this revolt decisively, destroying dozens of villages in the process and changing the future of the region and all its peoples.

In the wake of the Creeks' defeat, all southeastern Indians faced intensified threats to their political and cultural sovereignty. Having witnessed the
Creeks' defeat and recalling other, earlier defeats experienced by Cherokees and
others, southeastern Indians knew that overt revolt against the invasion of their
lands was hopeless. Some left, moving west. Others, especially among the Choctaws and Cherokees, began welcoming Protestant missionaries in their midst,
attending their schools, translating hymns, and converting to Christianity in
small numbers. Missionaries condemned, initially to no avail, popular practices, including the ballplay, traditional medicine practices, conjure, and all-
night dances. Methodist and Baptist itinerants soon outnumbered the missionaries from the American Board of Commissioners for Foreign Missions and
from the Moravian Church, and in the long run, most southeastern Indians
joined these evangelical branches of Christianity, modifying them in the process in ways that have yet to be fully studied or appreciated. Enduring Indian
removal in the late 1830s and the Civil War, southeastern Indians somehow
survived in the region and also in Oklahoma. By the end of the 19th century,
most of them had become Protestants. Baptists predominated among the native
peoples of Virginia as they did elsewhere. Methodists also abounded among
many southeastern Indian groups, but Mormons won the hearts of Catawbas.
Regardless of the denomination, in the era of Jim Crow individual churches
served as important symbolic centers for rural Indian communities and helped
them negotiate the challenges of living in a rigidly biracial society that had little
room for peoples who were not black or white.

Protestantism continues to prevail among southeastern Indians today. Most
are conservative Christians, not unlike their non–Native American neighbors,
with whom they often intermarry. Some Native men and women consider their
Christian confession to be at odds with ancestral traditions or, at the very least,
think religions exist on parallel paths and should not be mixed. Among Creeks
in Oklahoma, one is expected to affiliate either with a church or with a ceremonial square ground, but not both at the same time. In contrast, eastern Cherokees connect being truly Cherokee with being truly Christian. To win the highest respect among the eastern Cherokees, one needs to be able to read the
Cherokee New Testament or sing Cherokee hymns. In the past, the syllabary
was also used by individual conjurors to scribble down formulas related to
matters of witchcraft and sorcery. While this esoteric knowledge might also be
considered part of Cherokee religion, it is occult, secretive, and not shared in
public. The knowledge recorded in those writings is feared, not revered like the
Cherokee translation of John or the Cherokee version of "Amazing Grace."

After centuries of struggle just to survive as distinct peoples, some southeastern tribes today are thriving economically, thanks to their own entrepreneurial talents. Now possessing the economic and political means to exercise much fuller self-determination, several tribes have created formalized educational programs and institutions to revitalize ancestral language, arts, and culture. Poarch Creeks hired an Oklahoma medicine man to teach their young in Alabama the Muskogee language. Eastern Cherokees have sought to buy back lost lands, protect sacred sites, and establish positive ties with the Cherokee Nation in Oklahoma, symbolically healing the longstanding breach between east and west.

Old challenges still exist, and new ones will no doubt emerge that will directly or indirectly affect Native American religions. Mass communications, electronic media, improved transportation systems, and increased exposure to tourists make it more difficult to revitalize distinctive cultures and indigenous languages. The good news, however, is that in spite of terrible travails—epidemic diseases, invasion and loss of most of their lands, forced removal from their sacred ancestral landscapes and geographic separation from their kin, racial subjugation, transgenerational poverty, and social marginalization—some southeastern Indian peoples have finally regained some security in the Southeast. It is as if the world of southeastern Indians, long imbalanced, has finally begun to be righted.

JOEL MARTIN
University of California, Riverside

Margaret Bender, *Signs of Cherokee Culture: Sequoyah's Syllabary in Eastern Cherokee Life* (2002); Vernon Knight Jr., "The Institutional Organization of Mississippian Religion" (1986); Bonnie G. McEwan, ed., *The Spanish Missions of La Florida* (1993); William G. McLoughlin, *Cherokees and Missionaries, 1789–1839* (1984); Joel Martin, "Creek (Muskogee) Religion: Rebalancing the World in the Contradictions of History," in Lawrence E. Sullivan, ed., *Native Religions and Cultures of North America* (2000); Joel W. Martin, *Sacred Revolt: The Muskogees' Struggle for a New World* (1991); J. Anthony Paredes, ed., *Indians of the Southeastern United States in the Late 20th Century* (1992).

New Age Religion

The term "New Age" suggests a broad and open spirituality connected to notions of unity between spirit and body. No institution, church organization, or governing board claims authority over New Age religion and its many meanings, so definitions of the term vary widely. The term comes from 1960s Britain, where groups dissatisfied with institutional religion and seeking more meaningful forms of spirituality and a wider range of forms of worship developed new or reinterpreted forms of religious practice and belief. The term "New Age" proved especially attractive in and since the 1960s to American Baby Boomers, who felt a great sense of freedom to choose from among religious practices, adding those they liked and discarding others, outside the authority of religious institutions. Organized broadly around bookstores, publishers, seminars, and conventions and locally around groups that follow some of the range of New Age practices, New Age religion is particularly eclectic, drawing beliefs and practices from numerous Eastern, Western, African, and American Indian religions and adding other practices.

New Age religion has not had an especially friendly welcome in the South. The leading groups of evangelical Protestants do not look with favor on a movement that discounts the importance of sin, thinks optimistically about human potential, and feels free to draw from all religious traditions and current movements. Opposition, however, has usually been mild, except when evangelical groups believe New Age practices include witchcraft or Satanism, especially with the growing popularity of Wiccans. Some New Age believers' concentration on personal transformation parallels—even if it rarely intersects with—evangelicals' emphasis on the need for a new birth. New Agers often insist that true transformation comes from within the consciousness of the individual, while evangelicals stress that humans are essentially flawed and that change comes only from God. Also, healing is something most religious groups sponsor, some through huge medical complexes and others through special healing services, so the New Age interest in religious healing is not without precedent or parallel in other groups.

Florida, it is clear, is the most active area in the South for New Age religion, thought, and practice. A national organization called the New Age Directory has an online list of New Age learning centers and classes, bookstores and health food stores, healers, chiropractors, massage and acupuncture therapists, yoga and zen centers, and psychics, mediums, and astrologers. According to this list, Florida had 280 New Age sites in 2003, while the closest other southern state, Texas, had 165. The other states with substantial numbers of New Age sites were North Carolina (95), Virginia, (79), and Georgia, (60). The other southern states ranged from South Carolina, with 33 sites, down to Mississippi, with just 6.

The South has a few leaders and centers of New Age activity. Popular New Age author Marianne Williamson grew up in Houston, but the church she helps lead is in Michigan. In her 1997 volume *The Healing of America*, Williamson writes broadly as an optimistic American hoping that love, peace, diversity, spirituality, and conscience can overcome a range of American problems. But she introduces her life with a specifically southern story of the day Martin Luther King Jr. was killed and her Texan father "spat out the words, 'Those bastards.'" Williamson described that as the day she lost her innocence and started her journey toward healing, both herself and the country. In Birmingham, the American Institute of Holistic Theology offers online classes in healing, divinity, parapsychic science, and holistic child care. The far-from-typical Florida town of Cassadaga, the site of a spiritualist community that dates from the 1890s, has since the 1990s increasingly become a center for a range of New Age interests. As scholar Phillip Charles Lucas wrote of a trip to the Cassadaga Spiritualist Camp Bookstore, "leaflets advertise lessons in rainbow shamanism, advanced mediumship, astral projection, psychic development, trance channeling, psychometry, healing angels, Reiki healing, and skotography (the photographing of spiritual entities). In the bookstore proper are book displays on subjects such as numerology, tarot, tunes, dreams, meditation, UFOs, Eastern mysticism, Edgar Cayce, 'A Course in Miracles,' angels, alternative medicine, and the philosophy of spiritualism."

New Age religion does not seem to have made a great impact on southern literature, although some well-known works mention New Age practices, sometimes with tongue in cheek. Florida novelist Carl Hiaasen set part of *Lucky You* (1998) in the fictional town of Grange, where numerous sincere and insincere people seek miracles, sometimes for tourists. In two southern sports movies, *Bull Durham* and *Semi Tough*, the latter based on a novel by Dan Jenkins, female characters try to raise their consciousness through meditation, sometimes to the amusement of male characters. In a more serious vein, Alice Walker's interests in meditation, healing, and practices from various world religions, including Buddhism and Native American religions, show her attraction to New Age religion.

TED OWNBY
University of Mississippi

Catherine L. Albanese, *Nature Religion in America from the Algonkian Indians to the New Age* (1990); Philip Charles Lucas, *Cassadaga: The South's Oldest Spiritualist Community*, ed. John J. Guthrie Jr., Phillip Charles Lucas, and Gary Monroe (2000); Wade Clark Roof, *Spiritual Marketplace: Baby Boomers and the Remaking of American Religion* (1999); Bruce J. Schulman, *The Seventies: The Great Shift in American Culture, Society, and Politics* (2001); Marianne Williamson, *The Healing of America* (1997).

Pentecostalism

American Pentecostalism comprises many diverse organizations, some of which are predominantly southern in both membership and influence. Much of the drama of early Pentecostal history occurred in the South, among the socially disinherited whose yearnings for spiritual perfection and otherworldly ecstasy had made them participants in the Holiness movements that had swept the region intermittently for decades.

Pentecostalism became a definable movement after 1901 when a consensus on the evidence of the baptism with the Holy Spirit emerged among the followers of Charles Parham, a Kansas Holiness preacher. The simple assertion that glossolalia (or speaking in tongues) was always the initial evidence of a crisis experience indicating a baptism with the Holy Spirit separated Pentecostals from others who shared the same concern for vital spiritual experience.

For five years this doctrine was preached primarily in Kansas, Oklahoma, and Texas, until in 1906 William Seymour took the message to California. From a warehouse on Azusa Street in Los Angeles the distinctive Pentecostal assertion spread and shaped a movement that would have long-term significance for American religion across the nation, especially in the South.

Out of the fluid religious culture of the late 19th century came several currents that would converge in 20th-century Pentecostalism. The conviction of some individuals about the imminence of the second advent made them yearn for both "enduement with power for service" and holiness. The focus on restoration that had been a creative force throughout the American religious experience motivated others to desire the contemporary realization of the charismatic experiences of the New Testament church. Others were led through the healing revivalism of people like John Alexander Dowie and Mary Woodworth-Etter to stress the present manifestation of the spiritual gifts cited in I Corinthians 12–14. Another group, influenced by the loosely organized Wesleyan Holiness movement, stressed a "second blessing" of encounter with the Spirit resulting in holiness of heart and life. All these emphases became significant for Pentecostalism. Each stressed intangible blessings and otherworldly benefits and consciously discounted material possessions. Each had a consequent appeal to those who were "dispossessed" in this life.

These approaches to spirituality stressed the Holy Spirit and had some conception of a crisis encounter with the Spirit. There was no consensus among believers, however, as to incontrovertible evidence of the Spirit's special gifts, and those who responded to Parham's assertion of such evidence and thus became Pentecostal were thereby alienated from others in the religious culture whose concerns and heritage most closely resembled their own.

Cross atop Sanctified church, Clarksdale, Miss., 1968 (William Ferris Collection, Southern
Folklife Collection, Wilson Library, University of North Carolina at Chapel Hill)

In the South restorationist and Holiness thinking created a setting favorable
to the Pentecostal message. Holiness teaching stressed the necessity of a work of
grace, subsequent to the conversion experience, in which the individual would
be sanctified. It focused on the Holy Spirit and on a definite religious experience
subsequent to conversion. By 1906 outspoken southern Holiness advocates had
largely left their original base in the Methodist Episcopal Church, South, to
form independent groups, many of which had precise understanding not only
of valid spiritual experience but also of appropriate Christian general behavior.
Prohibitions against pork, coffee, colas, chewing gum, tobacco, alcohol, dancing, "spectator sports," and mixed bathing were common, as were directives
regarding jewelry, short hair for women, and many types of clothing. "Holiness" came to be associated with specific external evidences. Across the South,

small Holiness groups, local in character and different in emphasis, struggled to survive. Among these who already claimed a "second blessing" of sanctification were some to whom a "third blessing" of enduement with spiritual power seemed plausible.

Among the hundreds who visited Los Angeles in 1906 to observe the Pentecostal movement were two whose importance to southern Pentecostalism would be central—G. B. Cashwell of the Pentecostal Holiness Church, a Holiness group based in Falcon, N.C., and Charles Harrison Mason of Memphis, Tenn., who shared leadership with Charles Price Jones in the predominantly black Church of God in Christ. Both claimed an experience of Spirit baptism and returned to the South as advocates of the Pentecostal message. Southern Holiness preachers had already been advised of the Los Angeles Pentecostal revival through articles and letters in such widely circulated Holiness periodicals as *The Way of Faith*, and many responded with interest to the teaching. Cashwell traveled widely, primarily among rural southeastern Holiness groups, with some ministry in urban centers like Memphis and Birmingham. One result of his ministry was the coalescence of several small southern Holiness groups to form the Pentecostal Holiness Church in 1911. Another would be the uniting with the Pentecostalism of Ambrose J. Tomlinson and the restorationist Church of God that he led. Ultimately, at least three important Pentecostal groups would result from this connection—the Church of God; the Church of God of Prophecy (both with headquarters in Cleveland, Tenn.); and the Church of God, World Headquarters, with offices in Huntsville, Ala.

Mason's acceptance of the Pentecostal message divided the Church of God in Christ. Mason assumed leadership of the Pentecostal majority; Jones renamed his Holiness followers the Church of Christ (Holiness) U.S.A. and moved his headquarters to Jackson, Miss.

The earliest division among Pentecostals centered around their understanding of sanctification. Initially, Pentecostal leaders had insisted that sanctification was a discrete experience, a "second work," which always preceded the baptism with the Holy Spirit. After 1910 increasing numbers accepted teaching associated with William Durham, a Chicago pastor who understood sanctification as progressive, and perfection as impossible, and who developed his ideas under the heading "the finished work of grace." For several years controversy raged between "two-work" and "one-work" Pentecostals. Southern Pentecostal groups accepted the older "two-work" understanding of sanctification, and the "finished work of grace" became associated with the newer Assemblies of God.

Organized in 1914, the Assemblies of God drew together into a loose association some of the many independent Pentecostal missions across the country. Two important centers of its early strength were Alabama and Texas, but its constituency was always broader than any single geographic region. About 35 percent of its current membership is in the South. The Pentecostal Holiness Church and the several Pentecostal Churches of God, on the other hand, are overwhelmingly southern in membership, essential Holiness in doctrine, and centralized in polity. These southern Pentecostal groups were scarcely touched by the second dividing crisis in Pentecostal history—the oneness controversy.

Oneness Pentecostalism stresses the name of Jesus, claiming that Jesus is the name of Father, Son, and Spirit. This insistence, with its variant conception of the Trinity, as well as several other doctrinal traits, split the Assemblies of God and gave rise to an array of new Pentecostal groups, none of which has a strong southern base.

One distinct segment of Pentecostalism, then, is an integral part of the southern experience. Wesleyan in theology and centralized in structure, it remains largely confined to the South. The Church of God (Cleveland) and its several offshoots also incorporate a strong restorationist motif that Pentecostalism in other parts of the country does not include. The Church of God in Christ remains predominantly black and maintains its headquarters in Memphis. Its initial southern base has been extended to include outreach in major metropolitan black communities across the nation.

Although Pentecostalism is not exclusively a southern religion, some of its institutions have been shaped by their southern roots and continue to have their principal outreach in the South. Southern Pentecostalism incorporates theology and polity that set it apart, at least to some extent, from the movement at large. It has validity in the culture while perceiving itself as part of a force that transcends culture to provide spiritual vitality to the church.

EDITH L. BLUMHOFER
Evangel College

Robert Mapes Anderson, *Vision of the Disinherited: The Making of American Pentecostalism* (1979); Charles Conn, *Like a Mighty Army Moves the Church of God* (1977); William Menzies, *Anointed to Serve: The Story of the Assemblies of God* (1971); John T. Nichol, *Pentecostalism* (1966); Cheryl Sanders, *Saints in Exile: The Holiness-Pentecostal Experience in African American Religion of Culture* (1996); Vinson Synan, *The Holiness-Pentecostal Movement in the United States* (1971); Grant Wacker, *Heaven Below: Early Pentecostals and American Culture* (2001); Daniel G. Woods, "Living in the Presence of God: Enthusiasm, Authority, and Negotiation in the Practice of Pentecostal Holiness" (Ph.D. dissertation, University of Mississippi, 1997).

Politics and Religion

To the extent that there has ever been any truth to the term "Solid South," it has come from the distinctive relationship between religion and politics that has been a defining feature of the region. Pervasively Protestant, dominated from early times by evangelical groups, southern religion has tended strongly toward tradition and orthodoxy, being more biblical in belief, more emotional in practice, and more moralistic in its attitudes about the world than religion in other parts of the country. Over the past century, this conservative religion has contributed to the conservative politics of the region, as an alliance between evangelical and mainline white Protestants has provided a strong core of support for conservative political parties beginning with the southern Democrats of the early 20th century and continuing with the Republicans of our own time. Even so, the relationship between religion and politics in the South has been far from monolithic, as demonstrated especially by the divergent religious and political views of black and white Protestants. Moreover, with recent inmigration southern religion has become less overwhelmingly Protestant, and this growing religious diversity has been reflected in the increasing political influence of Catholics, in particular, but also of other faiths as well as the secular unchurched.

From the time of earliest European settlement, Protestantism has exercised dominant political power in the South. Although Roman Catholics arrived first, establishing a foothold in Spanish Florida from the early 16th century, English-speaking settlers brought the Church of England with them, and it gained state support in every southern colony beginning with Virginia in 1624. Although institutionally weak in many areas, especially along the southern frontier, the Anglican church was strong enough in the most populated places to effectively assert its authority to collect parish taxes and compel attendance at some services, sparking determined protests from religious dissenters led by Baptists and Methodists. Following the American Revolution, these separatist sects flourished, encouraged by sympathetic political leaders such as James Madison, who led the campaign to disestablish Anglicanism (now the Protestant Episcopal Church) in Virginia and who penned the provision in the Bill of Rights preventing the establishment of a state church in the new nation. While some evangelicals continued to engage in political protest, including resistance to slavery, many more accommodated to mainstream norms, and by the early 19th century most had adopted attitudes that sanctioned and even sanctified the patriarchal slave-owning family. In the antebellum period, evangelicals became still more supportive of the existing social order, as Baptists, Methodists, and Presbyterians articulated a biblical defense of slavery and broke from their national church organizations to form distinctly southern denominations. By 1861 any separation between church and state had all but disappeared, as southern clergymen in large numbers supported the Confederacy, describing the impending war as a crusade for righteousness and a "baptism in blood."

After the Civil War, Protestant political hegemony continued but came to be manifested in a variety of ways, with differences dependent on race and to some extent class and gender. Among white Protestants, church leaders contributed to the creation of a southern civil religion, the "religion of the Lost Cause," which combined Christian and Confederate imagery to reiterate the righteousness of the war and provide spiritual support for the racial segregation of the postwar period. Mixing moralism with a sense of white superiority, middle-class church members participated in prohibition and Sunday closing campaigns while also advocating the creation of Jim Crow laws. In some churches, particularly those in the poorest parts of the rural South, Populists applied religious rhetoric in attempts to achieve economic reform. By the 1920s, however, with fundamentalism becoming a force in the South, increasingly conservative churchgoers directed their energies to outlawing the teaching of evolution in the public schools and defeating Al Smith, a Catholic, in the presidential election of 1928. Black Protestants, in contrast, responded to their loss of political power in the post-Reconstruction period by relying on newly created African American church denominations to act as agencies of social change: teaching literacy, providing social services, and creating a black leadership class, including many women, to exercise influence within the increasingly segregated black community. Some southern church women, black and white alike, brought about political reform through their participation in the antilynching crusade and the suffrage movement. Finally, a few Protestants—sometimes combining with Catholics and Jews—created interdenominational and interracial organizations such as the Southern Christian Tenant Farmers' Union and the Fellowship of Southern Churchmen to work for economic reform and racial progress.

In the mid-20th century, the South emerged from regional seclusion to play a more prominent role on the national stage, in large part because of its ability to combine religion and politics in new ways. From the time of the Montgomery bus boycott, the black church was inextricably tied to the civil rights movement, providing not only its biblically based philosophy of nonviolent protest but also an extensive infrastructure of buildings, community support, and politically skilled preachers led by Martin Luther King Jr. With few exceptions, white church leaders provided little support for the movement, and local pastors like the Reverend Jerry Falwell insisted that the church separate itself from politics and concentrate instead on the winning of souls. By 1980, however, with the growth of evangelical and fundamentalist church membership, and with increasing concern among religious conservatives about social issues such as abortion, homosexuality, and changing roles for women, Falwell was exhorting his followers to become active in politics by participating in the movement of preachers and politicians that would come to be called the New Religious Right. Led by television evangelists Falwell and Marion "Pat" Robertson, institutionalized in national organizations such as the Moral Majority and Christian Coalition, and making use of local churches to distribute election guides and mobilize conservative voters, this religious-political movement rapidly became a force in national and regional politics, providing strong support for Ronald Reagan in the 1980 and 1984 elections while mustering millions of votes for conservative candidates in elections at the state and local level. With Pat Robertson's failure in the 1988 Republican presidential primaries, the movement lost strength, falling victim to tensions between Falwell's fundamentalists and Robertson's Pentecostals and to the endemic tendency of evangelicals to avoid politics altogether. Yet in spite of divisions and defections, the New Religious Right continued to exercise political power, primarily within the Republican Party, so that studies from the 1990s showed that activists associated with the movement controlled or held substantial influence in nine southern state party organizations and that voters sympathetic to it constituted up to 35 percent of the Republican electorate in some southern states.

In the South today, religion and politics continue to combine in distinctive but constantly changing ways. Maintaining the strong support of evangelicals and fundamentalists while also reaching out to mainline Protestants as well as to growing numbers of southern Catholics and Jews, the Republican Party has sought to solidify its control over the politics of the region. Simultaneously, black churches have continued to carry on the legacy of the civil rights movement, acting as part of a coalition of minorities — including Hispanic Catholics, Jews, and seculars — that provides the core constituency of the Democratic Party in the South. The result has been religious and racial polarization, as seen in the presidential election of 2000, when Republican George W. Bush won the support of 84 percent of observant white evangelicals in the South while Democrat Albert Gore received the vote of 96 percent of southern black Protestants. Beyond electoral politics, however, patterns are more complex and diverse. On some social issues white and black evangelicals hold similar views and at the state and local level have made alliances in campaigns against casino and racetrack gambling, the sale of liquor by the drink, and state-sponsored lotteries. Catholics have contributed to the complexity as well, combining with conservative evangelical Protestants to protest abortion while also acting in liberal interfaith alliances to oppose the death penalty. Other religious groups, even those small in size, have exercised disproportionate political power in other ways, as when Santerians in Florida won a precedent-setting case in the U.S. Supreme Court allowing them to engage in animal sacrifice as part of their religious practice. The growing presence of religious groups new to the region, including large numbers of Latino Catholics and small but steadily increasing numbers of Buddhists, Hindus, and Muslims, portends even less predictable political ramifications. For the foreseeable future, with the continued growth of evangelical and fundamentalist churches, and with the rapid in-migration of new faiths, the South promises to become both more distinctive and more diverse in its religious politics, and alliances of believers can be expected to play a defining part in southern politics in the 21st century.

MICHAEL LIENESCH
University of North Carolina at Chapel Hill

Kenneth K. Bailey, *Southern White Protestantism in the Twentieth Century* (1964); John C. Green, in *The 2000 Presidential Election in the South*, ed. Robert P. Steed and Laurence W. Moreland (2002); John C. Green, Lyman A. Kellstedt, Corwin E. Smidt, and James L. Guth, in *The New Politics of the Old South*, ed. Charles S. Bullock III and Mark J. Rozell (1998); Christine Heyrman, *Southern Cross: The Beginnings of the Bible Belt* (1996); Evelyn Brooks Higginbotham, *Righteous Discontent: The Women's Movement in the Black Baptist Church, 1880–1920* (1993); Samuel S. Hill, ed., *Religion and the Solid South* (1972); Samuel S. Hill, *Southern Churches in Crisis* (1966); C. Eric Lincoln and Lawrence H. Mamiya, *The Black Church in the African-American Experience* (1990); John Shelton Reed, *The Enduring South* (1972); Charles Reagan Wilson, *Baptized in Blood: The Religion of the Lost Cause, 1865–1920* (1980).

Preacher, Black Folk

During the Great Awakening of 1800 and for years after, many itinerant preachers found that their listeners for religious services often numbered in the thousands. To accommodate such large congregations, the camp meeting was institutionalized. These large-scale worship services were especially successful in the border states of Kentucky and Tennessee, where many clergymen from the North traveled. This new form of divine worship, sometimes attracting as many as 20,000 or more at events such as the one held at Cane Ridge, Ky., included black as well as white worshippers. Although this form of worship never caught on in the Northeast, it was highly successful in the South and Southwest. Many black ministers were inspired to preach at such gatherings, though at first only

Elder Tatum at the Rocky Mount Primitive Baptist Church in Panola County, Miss. (David Wharton, photographer, Center for the Study of Southern Culture, University of Mississippi)

to other blacks, and a characteristic oral style of delivery emerged from this experience.

These sermons were characterized by the preacher's chanting the Word of God rather than delivering it conventionally. The sermon began traditionally enough with a statement of the day's text and its application to contemporary morals. Then, as the preacher got further into the day's message, he began to chant his lines, the metrics and time intervals of the lines becoming more and more regular and consistent, and as he became further imbued with the Holy Spirit, the preacher's delivery slid into song. The sermons were—and still are —characterized by an increase in emotional and spiritual intensity, expressed by the gradual transition from conventional pulpit oratorical style, through chanting, to highly emotional singing. Many black folk preachers are excellent singers and have had several years' experience with church choirs, if not on the professional stage. Quite a number have been choirmasters, and nearly all these men have from an early age attended church services in which music played a major role. A musical sense has thus been acquired, and its rhythms, intonations, timbres, and verbal phrasing are inextricable parts of the tradition. Foreign visitors to black church services in the early 19th century remarked not only on the minister's chanting but on the congregation's equally emotional responses. Such witnesses were appalled by the unbridled emotionalism of such services.

The African heritage of black preachers influenced the style of their performances and of the congregations' responses. The African folksong tradition of call-and-response was carried over; not only was the preacher directly in this tradition, but in holy services the congregants felt free to call out to the preacher, or to the other congregants, as the Spirit moved them. The service became, and is still, however, something more than the regulated, orchestrated, and patterned response of one individual or group to another; in black services each member of the congregation actually creates his or her own sacred communion simultaneously with the holy service that is proceeding. Members of the congregation call out spontaneously, and such exclamations may not have been anticipated by the minister.

During a service in which the preacher has been successful in arousing the Spirit of the Lord or in bringing the congregation to a high emotional level, individual cries are frequent, some of the congregation will enter an altered state during which they may lose consciousness or dance seemingly involuntarily, and the preacher will be visibly ecstatic as well. Many people laugh aloud; a few cry unashamedly. When the service is over, they will say that they have had a happy time.

Research on this phenomenon suggests that while much of the sermon cannot possibly be heard distinctly, something is being communicated, and the congregation will feel that it has received God's Word. This may happen because many of the congregants know the Bible almost as thoroughly as does the preacher, and they creatively anticipate the preacher's message; also, in these services the congregation participates actively and creatively in the service, and congregants may for long periods be "hearing" their own celebrations.

Both preacher and flock share many common traditions, not only inherited Christianity but also an African American interpretation of that faith flavored by the experience of living in the South. Few preachers have had extensive seminary training, and many of their beliefs, like those of their congregations, are derived from popular traditions. For instance, many preachers prefer to use popular, folk versions of stories and parables in Scripture. Hence, although their Christianity is in the main "official," it is heavily influenced by folkloric elements. In some urban areas these preachers are often known as "old-time country preachers," though many of them have migrated away from the rural South to the urban North. The Reverend C. L. Franklin, for instance, became most famous after he left the South and moved to Detroit.

The ministers do not use manuscripts but believe that when they are in front of congregations the Holy Ghost is using them to communicate his message to the people. This spontaneous preaching style is accurately and movingly reproduced by William Faulkner in the last portion of *The Sound and the Fury*. In those pages the Reverend Shegog from St. Louis delivers a moving sermon in a style indistinguishable from the authentic oral performance. Significantly, this sermon is placed near the novel's conclusion; Faulkner recognized the great emotive and spiritual power that is the potential of this medium and chose to end his book on an affirming note.

Some white preachers also still preach in this mode; the style is not the exclusive property of one ethnic group. But the practitioners are mostly black and usually Methodist or Baptist. The practice is characteristically southern, though many preachers have now moved to the cities of the North and to the Pacific Southwest. These preachers continue to evoke the South in their services. Many professional black singers have vocal qualities that carry heavy echoes of this preaching style. Examples are Aretha Franklin (daughter of the Reverend C. L. Franklin), Sarah Vaughn, and Lou Rawls. Much of the "Motown sound" owes a debt to southern country preaching.

The influence of black folk preachers on the nation extends well beyond the contributions of musical entertainment and the popular arts. The Reverend Martin Luther King Jr. was a "spiritual" preacher whose "I Have a Dream" speech was in large measure a sermon on racial equality; he is well known for this oral performance, which profoundly moved his listeners, regardless of their race or ethnic backgrounds. Today, this art is most prominently practiced by Chicago's Jesse Jackson, a southerner by birth and raising. His address to the Democratic National Convention (1984) was a spontaneous sermon, a moving oration delivered by electronic media to the nation and the world.

BRUCE A. ROSENBERG
Brown University

Richard Allen, in *Black American Literature: 1760 to present*, ed. Ruth Miller (1971); Paul C. Brownlow, *Quarterly Journal of Speech* (December 1972); Gerald L. Davis, *"I Got the Word in Me and I Can Sing It, You Know": A Study of the Performed Afro-*

American Sermon (1986); Charles V. Hamilton, *The Black Preacher in America* (1972); Albert J. Raboteau, *Slave Religion: The "Invisible Institution" in the Antebellum South* (1978); Joseph R. Washington Jr., *Black Religion: The Negro and Christianity in the United States* (1964).

Preacher, White

White southern religion, once considered a monolithic, unidimensional structure, is now recognized as diverse and filled with ambiguities. Previously accepted stereotypes have been challenged by recent scholarship, which points out the diversity of southern culture in general and of southern religion in particular. Accordingly, the tendency to categorize all southern preachers as overzealous evangelists espousing a fiery brand of fundamentalism must be called into question as well. Ministers of southern white Protestant churches have been represented among the ranks of the theological elite, multimedia practitioners of the gospel, and country parsons alike. There are as many images as there are preachers, and the effort to discuss the image of the southern white preacher seems, at least initially, a futile one. Yet one quality distinguishes southern white preachers from their neighbors and also from their northern colleagues — and that is precisely their image. Whatever their social situation or professed beliefs, wherever they may live and work, awe and reverence accompany them. Theirs is a powerful image; it is one of authority.

Certainly this distinctiveness is a matter of degree rather than of kind. Protestants in America, Robert S. Michaelsen has pointed out, "have looked to their ministers as the defenders of morality and the representatives of spirituality. They have expected them to stand out as examples of what people ought to be morally and spiritually." If this depiction is accurate in the country as a whole, then it is even more apt as a description of conditions in the South. The centrality of Protestantism in southern culture gives preachers their legitimacy as articulators of truths, and they in turn provide religion with its shape and power. For people who are devout believers in God, as large numbers of southerners profess to be, his earthly representative is an awesome figure. Although the image of preachers has consistently been one of authority, their role in southern culture has not been static. Indeed, it is possible to trace certain trends in southern history by examining the unfolding of the image of authority.

During the early days of the South, this sparsely populated region with its scattered outposts demanded a preacher who was an itinerant man of God. As he traveled from place to place, he served as a cultural bonding force. Although southern religion had not yet developed a distinct and separate identity, the

Fundamentalist preacher, Red Banks, Miss., 1968 (William Ferris Collection, Southern Folklife Collection, Wilson Library, University of North Carolina at Chapel Hill)

region's faith and its self-understanding were gradually becoming inextricably interwoven. Simplicity ruled in those hard times: the minister was one called by God. Educational or professional preparation was incidental to his activities. Peter Cartwright, an early Methodist minister, once explained that when a man went into the ministry he did not seek a seminary; rather, he "hunted up a hardy pony of a horse . . . and with his library always at hand, namely Bible, Hymn-Book and Discipline, he started, and with a text that never wore out or grew stale, he cried 'Behold the Lamb of God.'" The sacred works identified him wherever he roamed.

The preacher's image was enhanced as the revivals swept through the South in the early 19th century. Now he had to be a skilled exhorter who could bring sinners into the fold in large numbers and with rapid precision. Although all southerners did not by any means participate in these massive spectacles, the revivals exerted a significant force on southern society. The growth in church membership was impressive, and, though a variety of denominations emerged, within and among the churches there was a strong sense of shared values and beliefs. The feeling of community that evolved contributed to the prestige of the minister in the South; he was the official exponent of religious and regional beliefs. His sphere of power extended beyond the domain of the church steeple.

In the words of John Holt Rice, an early 19th-century Presbyterian minister, the preacher's work "embraces every duty, in every situation."

Increasing population density resulted in churches that were established permanently in a particular place, with a wide influence over the inhabitants there. The popular Methodist and Baptist denominations became part of the status quo: the clergy became more educated, church members more affluent, and the churches' attitude toward the world more accepting. As a consequence, the minister of a church with prestigious community members exercised considerable influence over local and regional affairs. His presence at group meetings and political gatherings was not merely perfunctory; he represented the forces of the divine.

With the emergence of the issue of slavery and the subsequent Civil War, the white minister in the South articulated a solid defense of his region's way of life. In so doing he gained even greater prestige and visibility. Although controversies over proper education and appropriate qualifications erupted from time to time, the white preacher — no matter what his background — was an important regional spokesman. At times, however, as villages grew into cities and towns in the antebellum period, his image became fragmented. On the one hand, he was to converse with other professional members of his community and maintain a rational and sophisticated demeanor; on the other hand, he was to represent the simple way of life and belief of the rural past. The result was often a dwindling sense of inner assuredness for individual preachers. All the same, in the days of Reconstruction, the preacher's power expanded significantly as large numbers of southerners turned to churches for a rationale to explain defeat. In 1885 a noted Methodist editor claimed that "there is no part of the world in which ministers of the Gospel are more respected than in the Southern states."

In the first half of the 20th century the white Protestant preacher continued to exercise considerable influence in the South. Erskine Caldwell, the popular southern novelist whose father was a minister, asserted that "in the 'twenties and 'thirties . . . a Protestant minister was frequently called upon to act as a social welfare worker, a marriage counselor, a financial adviser, an arbitrator between feuding families, a psychiatric consultant, and as a judge to decide what was and what was not moral conduct."

Public opinion surveys suggest that ministers remain among the most respected figures in the contemporary South. Increased professional obligation has decreased the intimacy in the relationship between pastors and parishioners, and the resurgence of fundamentalism has strengthened moralistic dimensions of religious leadership. Such southern writers as Flannery O'Connor and Erskine Caldwell created images of charismatic preachers, and television ministries have popularized real-life examples, such as Jimmy Swaggart and Jim and Tammy Faye Bakker. Although the South lags behind other areas in the ordination of women, women ministers are increasingly present in pulpits of Episcopal, Methodist, and Presbyterian churches, building on a longer tradition of women preachers and healers in Pentecostal churches.

ROSEMARY M. MAGEE
Emory University

Erskine Caldwell, *Deep South: Memory and Observation* (1972); Peter Cartwright, *The Autobiography of Peter Cartwright: The Backwoods Preacher* (1856); *Christian Advocate* (17 October 1885); Samuel S. Hill, ed., *Southern Churches in Crisis* (1967); E. Brooks Holifield, *The Gentlemen Theologians: American Theology in Southern Culture, 1795–1860* (1978); Susan Ketchin, *The Christ-Haunted Landscape: Faith and Doubt in Southern Fiction* (1994); Robert S. Michaelsen, in *The Ministry in Historical Perspectives*, ed. H. Richard Niebuhr and Daniel D. Williams (1956).

Protestantism

Southern Protestantism and southern culture are as inseparable as bourbon and fruitcake. The South stands out both as a discernible cultural entity and as an equally unique religious region. Indeed, it is the most religious and Protestant area of an extraordinarily religious nation. Southerners tend to be more active in religious organizations and more orthodox in measurable belief than any of their fellow citizens. Evangelical Protestants often make up 80 to 90 percent of the "churched" population, and most call themselves Baptists and Methodists. Yet there is also great diversity — independent churches, all the major organized denominations, a rapidly growing number of Pentecostal/charismatic churches, and numerous small, proudly independent associations and congregations, which are properly denominations unto themselves.

The South has given rise to distinctively American and even regional styles of religion. This pattern results from a combination of geography (America's early and hence formative frontier), economic conditions (extremes of plantation wealth, slavery, and rural poverty), great mobility (geographic and economic), and a fierce individualism. Protestantism in the South is also nostalgic, smoldering, and languorous. It seeps an ethos haunted by guilt, defiance, a deep attachment to sacred places and heroes, a strong positive sense of mission, and a painful memory of the bitter combination of chosenness and inexplicable defeat.

The southern Protestant (the Cane Ridge Revival) ethos decisively began with the extended period of revivalism that swept in waves over the South from

1799 until 1820. Baptists and Methodists, far more adaptive to frontier conditions than their Presbyterian and Episcopalian competitors, quickly became the dominant organizations and remain so today. The influence of revivalism is everywhere in southern religion. Emotive, rhetorically persuasive preaching designed to produce personal crisis and conversion is central. There are, consequently, traditions of great preaching and great preachers—charismatic leaders whose personalities often serve as the bonding agent of their personal churches. Worship focuses on the production of palpable religious experiences for congregation-audiences. Christianity tends to be reduced to the simplicity of sin, guilt, conversion, and forgiveness, always centered around individual salvation. An individual's religious life is intensely focused on the conversion experience. It is an event continually recalled and even relived through revivalistic rededication, the evangelical equivalent to the Catholic sacrament of penance. Additionally there are presumptions of perfectibility or at least thorough transformation. One "gets saved" or is "born again" or "gets right with God."

The shadows of slavery and segregation have fallen heavily across the social gospel, limiting but not eliminating social responsibility. For more than 150 years voluntary societies as well as churches have fought for temperance, printed and distributed literature and Bibles, and built settlement houses and educational institutions; yet they were always reluctant to confront the fundamental structure of a society based on a system of racial oppression. Revivalism insists that one attend to the immediate demands of piety; it "verticalizes" one's religion from God above to humans below, enclosing it in what James McBride Dabbs calls "a limited, private world" free from the complexities of social and political life. Additionally, because the revivalistic style takes people out of their normal context and places them as individuals before the righteous God, it has had the power to suspend their usual social rules, including those of hierarchy. This creation of "liminality" (a state "in between" classifications) allowed slaves to instruct their masters in religious matters, urge their conversion, and assume, for the duration of the liminal period, a position of superiority. The "limited world" made possible the experience of socially safe bonds of genuine affection between slaves and owners, black and white, offering an illusion of solidarity that eased the white conscience and soothed black anger. The South's limitation of the ethical dimensions of Christianity to the private realm required a moralistic ethical style—the connection of specific biblical "principles" to specific individual moral choices, often in an ad hoc and surprisingly legalistic way.

Assurance is a final and defining characteristic deeply embedded in the evangelical tradition. The assurance of the believer involves a certainty of salvation arising from the varied sources of conversion, Scripture, and experiences of God's presence. It appears almost as an evangelical personality style or perhaps a state of being—warm, confident, immediately and openly religious, intensely yet comfortably intimate with a somewhat domesticated deity but also quite unquestioning and rather unteachable.

For many white Protestants the line between Christian religion and Christian civilization has often been too fine to discern. Ironically, during the periods of slavery and legal segregation, southerners were in the forefront of those celebrating America's Christian identity and even claiming to have attained a high degree of social perfection. From this perspective the Civil War was a noble and tragic effort undertaken in defense of a last bastion of Christendom. After the war southern Protestantism became a "suffering servant" and a "saving remnant," a moral and religious preservative with a mission of national salvation. World War I, fought against the German originators of academic biblical criticism and liberal religion, was seen as a triumph of American, Protestant, southern, and Baptist values. Defeat, however, was snatched from the jaws of victory in the aftermath of World War II, culminating in a liberal betrayal of American mission and manhood in Vietnam. This evangelical civil religion continues to inform and motivate numerous southerners and their churches.

For African Americans, too, the entwinement of religion and culture has run deep. Slave religion and later the black churches have always served social and political purposes, often providing black people with their primary source for social cohesion and political mobilization. Black churches have given leadership, continuity, and organization to the black community ever since emancipation. They launched the civil rights movement of the 1950s and 1960s and a presidential candidacy in 1984, permanently changing southern society at its most basic levels. The enthusiasm of the South's black population for the white vision of a Christian America has been understandably limited. Slaves took the evangelical Protestantism handed them by their captors and adapted it to their own special needs and circumstances. Unlike southern whites, blacks attended to the prophetic dimensions of Christianity, finding the self-esteem and strength necessary to withstand the dehumanization of slavery and segregation in the knowledge that Jesus, too, had felt the oppressor's lash. Christianity confirmed for slaves what they had always known, that slavery was wrong, and what they had always hoped, that it was not permanent. Slaves quickly determined that they were considerably closer to the example established by Jesus than were their owners, and they soon found their own version of Christianity superior to that of the whites. Out of their suffering the slaves created a form of evangelicalism considerably more celebratory than its white counterpart.

Much remained the same—the intensity, the experiential focus, simplicity, and informality—but there were crucial differences. Whereas white Protestantism consistently appealed to authority, particularly that of the Scriptures, the religion of African Americans tended to allow authority to remain tacit while celebrating God's love and their deliverance. In the words of Eugene D. Genovese, whites sought forgiveness from Jesus and blacks sought recognition.

As America entered the final decades of the 20th century, southern Protestantism again stood at the center of action, emerging as the most modern and energetic American religion. In worship, the triumph of popular culture has been nearly total. Up-tempo rhythms played with guitars, drums, and assorted keyboards and horns all electronically amplified overwhelm the senses. In many churches worship has come to consist of music and sermons, with songs sliding into prayer and prayer into song as smoothly as Scarlet O'Hara slipped into velvet. The advent of the church growth movement with the resulting development of megachurches whose members are numbered in the thousands has allowed for the professionalization of liturgical production unattainable in smaller venues. The goal of intense religious experience is still the same as at Cane Ridge. The production values are a world apart.

In the face of the rather contradictory currents of disintegrating regionalism, growing cultural uniformity spurred by electronic media, and an ever increasing social diversity, proponents of Christian civilization reemerged in the 1980s, creating new voluntary societies aiming to save America for Christendom and the world. After the unsuccessful presidential bid of television evangelist Pat Robertson in 1988, the New Religious Right, represented primarily by Robertson's Christian Coalition, had settled into a supportive relationship with the Republican Party much like that of the labor unions with the Democrats. The political participation of evangelicals increased significantly, especially at the local levels, where candidates sought to bring "traditional family values" into society by running for seats on school boards and county commissions. The banner issues of abortion and prayer in the public schools generated much interest but little success after almost a quarter century of lobbying.

The political effort of southern evangelicals represents, in itself, a significant secularization of conservative southern Protestantism. Political action requires joining forces with the unsaved, focusing one's attention on questions other than salvation, and mixes hefty amounts of civil religion with biblical Christianity. As the nation set forth into the next millennium, evangelical political activists still clung to a nostalgic mythology of an original Christian America, which is their God-given responsibility and honor to restore. In some ways this represents a new social gospel, requiring responsible action in the larger world outside the church. It is, however, a gospel more concerned with dominion than service, control than empowerment. For evangelicals, religious purity and political effectiveness have proven difficult to keep in the same choir.

In related developments, southern evangelicals have discovered that their religious style with its heavy emphasis on ministerial action and congregational consumption translates easily into television. By the 21st century the nation had beheld the rise and self-immolation of numerous evangelical media empires, with no lack of replacements waiting in the wings. A growing worldliness and even a materialistic spirit are evident in contemporary evangelicalism, particularly in in its video incarnations. Tangible rewards — physical or even financial healing — are routinely promised to those who support the ministries with the donations. Prophetic voices on the evangelical left warn that idolatry is inherent in the very idea of Christian civilization. Their voices go largely unheard by both secular and religious nationalists. Moderates have sought to build an island of common ground where religious people and values can impact the public realm without striving to dominate it. Protestantism in the South has become less regional. The faithful are being called to arms over issues emanating from California. Cultural and geographic isolation have become impossible to maintain. Rapid population growth, diversification, and continued social and economic mobility promise a future of continued conflict and realignment. What will emerge is always in doubt, but in the South one can rest assured that there is a good chance it will include dinner on the grounds.

DENNIS E. OWEN
University of Florida

Kenneth K. Bailey, *Southern White Protestantism in the Twentieth Century* (1964); John B. Boles, *The Great Revival, 1787–1805: The Origins of the Southern Evangelical Mind* (1972); Joel A. Carpenter, *Revive Us Again: The Reawakening of American Fundamentalism* (1997); Dennis Covington, *Salvation on Sand Mountain* (1995); John Lee Eighmy, *Churches in Cultural Captivity: A History of the Social Attitudes of Southern Baptists* (1972); Christine Leigh Heyrman, *Southern Cross* (1997); Samuel S. Hill, ed., *Encyclopedia of Religion in the South* (1984), *Religion and the Solid South* (1972), *Southern Churches in Crisis* (1967); C. Eric Lincoln, ed., *The Black Experience in Religion: A Book of Readings* (1974); Donald Mathews, *Religion in the Old South* (1977); John Shelton Reed, *The Enduring South: Subcultural Persistence in Mass Society* (1972); Justin Watson, *The Christian Coalition* (1999); Charles Reagan Wilson, *Baptized in Blood: The Religion of the Lost Cause, 1865–1920* (1980).

Restorationist Christianity

This style of Christianity that self-consciously seeks to ignore historical Christian forms and traditions and to reproduce primitive Christianity has flourished in the American South, but it is not unique to the South. Restorationism has deep roots in British Protestantism and appeared with particular vitality in the left wing of that heritage, especially among the Puritans, Baptists, Quakers, and, later, the early Methodists. Thus, restorationist traditions that persist in America today—in addition to the modern heirs of the Swiss and German Anabaptists—include Mormons, various types of Baptists, various Holiness and Pentecostal groups, Christian Churches, and Churches of Christ.

At least two factors influenced the openness of southern Christianity to the restorationist impulse in the 19th century. First, the Baptist and Methodist dominations of southern religion created a climate of deference both to the Scriptures and to Christian antiquity. Second, the stubborn persistence of the southern frontier until well into the 20th century in some regions (for example, Appalachia and the Ozarks) created a cultural situation particularly resistant to modernity and especially amenable to various types of primitivism. When Baptists and Methodists with a primitivist theological orientation settled in large numbers on the southern frontier, it was perhaps inevitable that this potent religious/cultural mix would spawn numerous restorationist movements, some of which would coalesce into lasting denominations.

Four major movements, all with a self-conscious restorationist orientation, emerged in the South after 1800: the Churches of Christ; the Primitive or Antimission Baptists; the Landmark Baptists; and southern Pentecostalists, especially the Church of God (Cleveland, Tenn.) and to a lesser extent the Assemblies of God.

Churches of Christ emerged in Tennessee, Kentucky, and southern Ohio under the leadership of Barton W. Stone in the first decade of the 19th century and by 1825 had made headway into northern Alabama. Reflecting in many ways the quest for liberty that characterized the American Revolution, participants in this movement threw off the yoke of history and bondage to historical traditions, rejected the authority of creeds and clerics, used the primitive church as portrayed in Scripture as a model for their individual and ecclesiastical behavior, and styled themselves simply "Christians" and their congregations "Churches of Christ." Stressing personal piety, they argued that a universal emulation of the primitive church would bring Christian unity through God's power.

Although Stone and some of his "Christian" colleagues had Presbyterian roots, the vast majority of both members and leaders in the new movement

Place of Prayer and A. J. Tomlinson grave site, Route 294 between
Ducktown, Tenn., and Hiawassee Dam, 1960s (Charles Reagan Wilson Collection,
Center for the Study of Southern Culture, University of Mississippi)

came from the ranks of Separate and Regular Baptists, whose allegiance both
to Scripture and to the primitive church made them restorationists in their own
right. This was particularly true of the Separate Baptists, who determined to
follow the Bible as their only confession of faith in the mid-18th century. They
followed Shubal Stearns to North Carolina and Virginia in 1755 and later in the
century migrated to Kentucky and Tennessee, where they increased the ranks
of the Christian movement. The Stone movement had approximately 13,000
members in the late 1820s.

By 1823 Alexander Campbell began to influence both Baptists and the
"Christians" of Kentucky and Tennessee, largely through his new periodical,
The Christian Baptist. Campbell critiqued Baptist practices that he believed
were not authorized by the New Testament. He proposed a "lost" primitive
church order to replace corrupt human practices that, if adopted, would usher
in Christian unity. Campbell's contribution in this region was essentially twofold. To begin, he was by then a significant link in the growing, nationwide resistance to the new missionary societies of the North and East, viewed by many
as flagrant attempts to extend the power of the New England Standing Order
throughout the nation in the wake of disestablishment. Campbell's opposition
to ecclesiastical societies, clerics, and creeds greatly strengthened both the restorationist and the antimissionist sentiments already present among both Bap-

tists and Christians. Uniting with many Stone churches in the 1830s, Campbell's followers superimposed on the primitivist piety of the Stone movement a hardheaded, rational, commonsense approach to the restoration ideal that has characterized Churches of Christ ever since. By 1860 the Churches of Christ flourished in middle Tennessee under the leadership of Tolbert Fanning and David Lipscomb. During the Civil War and through World War I, the group was strongly pacifist. By the end of the 20th century pacifism eroded as Churches of Christ accommodated to southern culture.

Because of post–Civil War migration patterns, Churches of Christ are today concentrated not only in southern Kentucky, middle Tennessee, and northern Alabama but also in other portions of southern Missouri, Tennessee, Arkansas, Oklahoma, and Texas.

The Primitive or Antimission Baptists arose out of the same ideological matrix that provided such a fertile field for the growth of Churches of Christ: a passion for liberty, an expectation of the millennium, a rejection of the power of the older ecclesiastical establishments and of their missionary societies, and a consequent affirmation of the freedom and simplicity of the primitive church as a model for Baptists of the 19th century. The antimission agitation, based on a fear of eastern ecclesiastical power and of state-church resurgence, was a nationwide, interdenominational phenomenon in the 1810s and especially the 1820s, led by Deists like Elihu Palmer, Christians like Elias Smith and Alexander Campbell, Baptists like John Leland, Methodists like Peter Cartwright and Lorenzo Dow, and interdenominational figures such as Theophilus Ransom Gates, whose *Reformer* (1820–35) was a veritable clearinghouse for antimission sentiment from a wide variety of sources. Antimission arguments from these and other leaders typically contrasted the elaborate extraecclesiastical and interdenominational agencies and societies of that age with the simple, congregational autonomy of the early Christians.

Although opposition to eastern ecclesiastical power was nationwide, it was especially strong in the Jacksonian South, where rural religionists resented the efforts of eastern missionaries and "dandies" to save the frontier from barbarism. Further, among some Regular Baptists in the South, opposition to missions was buttressed by a rigid predestinarianism: after all, why organize mission societies if the eternal fate of humankind is already determined? These Baptists appealed both to the structure (no societies) and to the theology (predestination) of the primitive church to legitimate their positions, and throughout the 1820s these questions were debated in Regular Baptist churches and associations throughout America and especially in the South.

The key early leaders of Baptist antimissionism were John Leland, Daniel

Parker, and John Taylor. By 1820 most Baptist churches in Tennessee and northern Alabama apparently had adopted the primitivist, antimission posture, and the Kehukee Association of North Carolina followed suit in 1827. By 1832 the primitive antimissionists began the process of separating into a distinct denomination. Their greatest early success was in Tennessee and northern Alabama, but they also experienced significant growth in Georgia, Virginia, North Carolina, Kentucky, and Texas.

It is ironic that the Primitive Baptists drank so deeply from the well of optimistic postmillennialism that sustained the early antimission agitation nationwide, for when these Baptists blended their opposition to mission societies with their rigid predestinarianism, they emerged as stridently pessimistic and premillennial—a perspective reflected in their first widely circulated periodical, the *Signs of the Times* (1832–35). Like the Churches of Christ, they believe that instrumental music is not authorized by the New Testament, and so their worship is characterized by a cappella singing and a distinctive style of music.

Although Primitive Baptists began as a white denomination, they eventually had even greater strength among blacks than among whites. By 1900 the black church had become more progressive than the white church, employing both Sunday schools and conventions, and by 1936 the black church had considerable strength in Alabama, Florida, Tennessee, Georgia, Texas, and North Carolina. In 1993 the black National Primitive Baptist Convention of the U.S.A. claimed 250,000 members. The white church, on the other hand, enjoyed its greatest early success in Tennessee and northern Alabama but also experienced significant growth in Georgia, Virginia, North Carolina, Kentucky, and Texas before experiencing decline to around 49,000 members in 1990.

A third restorationist tradition emerged in 1851 in Tennessee—the Landmark Baptists. Like the Churches of Christ, this tradition drew its greatest strength from the revivalistic Separate Baptists and focused almost exclusively on questions of ecclesiology and particularly on the identity of the "true church." The Landmark leader, James Robinson Graves of Nashville, argued that the true church had existed in an unbroken chain throughout Christian history and had always borne the marks of congregational autonomy, ecclesiastical democracy, and baptism by immersion. Any religious body organized since apostolic days was no church whatsoever, and the true church could be traced by the "trail of blood"—those martyrs who have refused throughout Christian history to be seduced by modernity.

The term "Landmark" was taken from a tract by James Madison Pendleton, "An Old Landmark Reset," which raised and answered negatively the question of whether Baptists should invite pedobaptists to preach in their pulpits. A third significant leader was Amos Cooper Dayton, who articulated fundamental Landmark themes in a two-volume novel, *Theodosia Ernest* (1857). Though Landmarkism had gathered significant strength in Tennessee and parts of the Old Southwest by 1880, it was not organized into a formal denomination until 1905, when Ben M. Bogard and others led in establishing the General Association of Landmark Baptists in Texarkana, Ark., renamed in 1924 the American Baptist Association. By 2000 the American Baptist Association claimed its greatest strength in Arkansas and Texas, with lesser strengths in Oklahoma, Louisiana, and Florida.

Not until the late 19th century would the restoration sentiment again incarnate itself in lasting and major institutional forms and structures in the South. This later development was the Holiness/Pentecostal phenomenon that grew largely, though not exclusively, from Methodist soil and was, like the earlier antimission agitation, a national phenomenon. John Wesley, and later his Holiness followers, believed they were restoring the power of the Holy Spirit modeled in the book of Acts. The evangelical experience of perfection had been lost in history but was being restored by the Holiness movement. The restorationist underpinnings of the Holiness revival, which preceded the Pentecostal phase of the movement, were implicit in the Holiness rejection of modern trends in established denominations. But some Holiness denominations, such as the Church of God, Anderson, Ind. (1880), made the restorationist appeal to the primitive church both explicit and fundamental.

During the last two decades of the 19th century, a more radical phase of the Holiness movement was developing — a phase that appealed especially to the poor and disinherited and that emphasized the baptism of the Holy Ghost as a third work of grace (following justification and sanctification), physical healing, and premillennialism. By 1906 and thereafter, most of these more radical churches also accepted glossolalia (speaking in tongues) and emerged as Pentecostalism, separate from the more moderate Holiness movement.

Although Pentecostalism, like the Holiness movement, was a nationwide phenomenon, it is significant that many of the Holiness churches in the South became Pentecostal. A clue to why this occurred lies in the otherworldly rejection of history that was implicit in early Pentecostalism and that appealed powerfully to the disinherited of a still alienated and impoverished South. This otherworldly dimension was evident in two central themes of early Pentecostal theology. First, whereas the Holiness phenomenon had been rooted early in an optimistic postmillennial perspective, Pentecostalism embraced a more pessimistic premillennial theology anticipating an imminent second coming of Christ. Second, implicit in Pentecostalism's emphasis on the baptism of the

Holy Ghost and glossolalia was a restorationist perspective that looked beyond the present age to the primitive church and made the power of Pentecost available to disinherited southerners some 19 centuries later. This was true of the four major southern Pentecostal traditions in the early 20th century: the Church of God (Cleveland, Tenn.), the Pentecostal Holiness Church, the Fire-Baptized Holiness Church, and the predominantly black Church of God in Christ.

Restorationism was explicitly acknowledged in some of the movement's early literature such as B. F. Lawrence's *The Apostolic Faith Restored* (1916). And it came to full flower especially in the Church of God (Cleveland, Tenn.), a major Pentecostal denomination that emerged at the turn of the century in the mountains of southwestern North Carolina. By 1903 the acknowledged leader of the embryonic Church of God was an Indiana Bible salesman, A. J. Tomlinson, who stamped the young church with the conviction that the true church had disappeared in the Dark Ages but was now being recovered in the mountains of Tennessee and North Carolina. The Church of God, Tomlinson taught, had no man-made creed, was not a denomination, and took the Bible as "our only rule of faith and practice." Further, in due time Christ would organize his millennial kingdom at Burger Mountain (North Carolina), and Christians from all denominations would flow into the true Church of God. Like the Churches of Christ, the Church of God had strong pacifist sentiment during World War I, but this gradually disappeared as the group accommodated to mainstream southern culture. The various factions of the Church of God had particular strength in Georgia, Florida, North and South Carolina, Tennessee, and Alabama, with lesser strength in Texas, Mississippi, Kentucky, Virginia, and West Virginia.

The Assemblies of God, a nationwide denomination, was established in Hot Springs, Ark., in 1914; it maintains its headquarters in Springfield, Mo., and continues to have a strong presence in the South. The ruling General Council of the Assemblies of God was modeled after the Jerusalem council of Acts 15. The denomination's early restorationism emphasized that its members were citizens of another kingdom and so were uninterested in politics and had strong pacifist sentiments during World War I. As with some other restorationist groups, pacifism quickly disappeared as the denomination became more affluent. While the Assemblies of God muted the more radical forms of restorationism, considerable restorationist sentiment still can be found in healing and tongue speaking.

The forms of restorationism that have flourished in the South range from the rational and cognitive Churches of Christ to the charismatic and experiential Pentecostals, but all share in common the goal of transcending history and restoring primitive Christianity. The American South with its distinctive religious ethos will continue to nurture restorationist sentiment.

MICHAEL W. CASEY
Pepperdine University

Edith L. Blumhofer, *Restoring the Faith: The Assemblies of God, Pentecostalism, and American Culture* (1993); Michael W. Casey and Douglas A. Foster, eds., *The Stone-Campbell Movement: An International Religious Tradition* (2002); Mickey Crews, *The Church of God: A Social History* (1990); Richard T. Hughes, *Reviving the Ancient Faith: The Story of Churches of Christ in America* (1996); Richard T. Hughes and C. Leonard Allen, *Illusions of Innocence: Protestant Primitivism in America, 1630–1875* (1988); Byron Cecil Lambert, *The Rise of the Anti-Mission Baptists: Sources and Leaders, 1800–1840* (1980); Beverly Bush Patterson, *The Sound of the Dove: Singing in Appalachian Primitive Baptist Churches* (2001); Vinson Synan, *The Holiness-Pentecostal Tradition: Charismatic Movements in the 20th Century* (1997); Robert G. Torbet, *A History of Southern Baptist Landmarkism in the Light of Historical Baptist Ecclesiology* (1980).

Revivalism

This phenomenon is characterized by an emphasis in religion on a renewal of interest in belief and practice, marked by the conversion of new members and the rededication of existing members to the church. In the South revivalism has set the dominant tone for Protestant Christianity since the early 19th century, informing the main religious concerns of mainstream denominations and smaller organizations alike.

Southern revivalism has occurred at two levels. One is composed of the spectacular general awakenings of society, which at several periods of the region's history have brought significant numbers of people into connection with various southern denominations. These awakenings have provided the foundation for revivalism at a much less spectacular but more profound level, consisting of an ongoing effort by southern religious organizations to maintain their goal of bringing new members into the church continuously and taking shape most clearly in gatherings called "revival meetings," which are held regularly throughout the South.

Four major periods of general revival have occurred in the South. The first, throughout what were then the English colonies of North America in the mid-18th century, was known as the Great Awakening. It was followed by the Second Awakening, or Great Revival, which centered on the southern frontier between about 1795 and 1805. A third, beginning in the latter part of the 19th century, was also national in scope and involved such noted evangelists as Dwight Moody and Billy Sunday. A fourth began in the mid-20th century and has been strongly identified with the southern evangelist Billy Graham.

The revivalism that is an ongoing phenomenon of southern religion involves a tendency on the part of southern religious organizations to view evangelism as their primary activity, with other aspects of the religious life interpreted in terms of the evangelistic impulse. To a great extent, revivalism at this level has become the religion of the South, for it crosses denominational lines to unite in sympathies and purposes members of most religious organizations, particularly those of the region's dominant communions, the Methodist and Baptist churches.

This revivalistic thrust of southern religion has had major implications for the specific content of religious ideas and practices in the region. Because southerners have understood such a thrust to involve, above all, the conversion and salvation of individual souls, their religion has had an extremely individualistic orientation. Questions of faith, belief, and sinfulness have all been interpreted in terms of the individual's religious state, and the church itself has been considered more a gathering of converted individuals than a community that, as such, has important relationships with God.

The roots of this religious individualism are theological and may be traced not only to the traditional Protestant concern for salvation but, more specifically, to the triumph in the Second Awakening of an Arminian theology of free and universal grace. According to this theology, God has called everyone to salvation, but each individual must heed and follow God's call. The mission of the church, given this, is to make each individual aware of this call and its significance. Thus, theology not only demands an evangelical focus in religion but also ensures that evangelism will be directed toward the individual and individual salvation rather than toward any religious collectivity. Supplanting the older Calvinist notions of predestination and irresistible grace, Arminianism would, by the early 19th century, underlie the practical religion of even such nominally Calvinist bodies as the Presbyterian and Baptist churches and, because of its popularity, would contribute greatly to the growth of the Methodist Church, which had embraced it wholeheartedly. Arminianism has, since that time, been the theology of southern Protestantism, the underpinning of its evangelical efforts.

Accompanying a theology that defines the church's duty as reaching individual souls has been an emphasis on personal experience as the most significant element in the religious life. This, too, has its roots in the Second Awakening, when revivalistic denominations made the direct experience of conversion a test for church membership and even sought evidences for such experience in the spectacular physical "exercises" that often accompanied conversion. Although such exercises have become rare in mainstream churches since the middle of the 19th century, the stress on personal experience remains important, and the talented revivalist still tries to bring even the most affluent mainstream congregation to tears. Strong feeling is a significant element in southern revivalistic religion.

This stress on personal experience can be seen in one of revivalism's most important contributions to southern religious practice, the gospel hymns. Originally composed, for the most part, during the late 19th-century revival, these songs have entered into all the mainstream denominational hymnals, having virtually replaced more traditional hymns for use even in Sunday morning services. Simple in message and stressing God's love for every individual, these gospel hymns evoke a highly personal and emotional sense of the nature of faith. More spectacularly, the stress on personal experience has contributed to a mid-20th-century charismatic revival. A development in the larger Pentecostal movement, which had its American beginnings around 1905, this revival has adopted traditional techniques and emphases from the southern revival heritage but has elaborated on them through an emphasis on such charismata as divine healing and speaking in tongues. Although most mainstream Protestants tend to desire more decorous forms of experience, the charismatic movement's main concerns are well within the southern revival traditions of evangelism and an individualistic, personal faith.

Southern revivalism has led the region's churches, in general, to adopt a stance toward society that differs markedly from that of religious organizations outside the South. Whereas American religion has been dominated, since the antebellum period, by a liberal Protestantism that has sought to respond to social issues and problems—from temperance and antislavery in the antebellum period to modern problems of race and war—southern churches and religious leaders have tended to avoid questions having deep social roots and to deal mainly with problems that can be addressed from the standpoint of the sinfulness of individuals and their need for conversion and salvation. Thus, southern churches have generally not participated in efforts for social change, even when they have been politically active, as with the conservative efforts of the Virginia-based Moral Majority, but have continued to focus on evangelism as their primary mission in the world.

DICKSON D. BRUCE JR.
University of California at Irvine

John B. Boles, *The Great Revival, 1787–1805: The Origins of the Southern Evangeli-
cal Mind* (1972); Dickson D. Bruce Jr., *And They All Sang Hallelujah: Plain-Folk
Camp-Meeting Religion, 1800–1845* (1974); David Harrell, *All Things Are Possible: The
Healing and Charismatic Revivals in Modern America* (1975); Samuel S. Hill, *South-
ern Churches in Crisis* (1967); Anne C. Loveland, *Southern Evangelicals and the Social
Order, 1800–1860* (1980); William G. McLoughlin Jr., *Modern Revivalism: Charles
Grandison Finney to Billy Graham* (1959); Donald Mathews, *Religion in the Old South*
(1977).

Roman Catholicism

From the first Catholic settlers in colonial Maryland to the recent influx of
Spanish-speaking and Asian Catholics, "southern" Catholics have traditionally occupied an ambivalent place in the region as they struggled to balance a
universal faith with their own peculiar ethnoreligious differences in a social environment that often has been hostile toward them. After the American Revolution the American Catholic Church, composed of roughly 35,000 native Catholics located largely in Maryland, Kentucky, and Pennsylvania and under the
leadership of John Carroll, the first American bishop (1790), had sought social
and cultural assimilation into American life. By the mid-19th century, however, the American Catholic Church had veered away from the genteel Anglo-
American Catholicism of John Carroll's generation. The annexation of "Latin"
Louisiana and the Gulf areas and, more important, massive European immigration, chiefly Irish and German, beginning in the 1830s, fixed the multiethnic
character of American Catholicism thereafter. Ethnic disputes over liturgical
rites, ecclesiastical jurisdictions, and customs came with immigration. They
racked Norfolk, Charleston, Richmond, and New Orleans congregations in the
early 19th century and prefigured more serious divisions within the American
church throughout the century.

With force of numbers and an English-speaking advantage, the Irish gained
control of the American church hierarchy. Coming during the devotional revolution under way in Ireland at midcentury, which stressed piety through regular devotions and worship, and respect for clerical authority, the Irish had the
energy and discipline to impose their ways on the church. Indeed, they largely
subdued German elements in Baltimore and New Orleans during the 19th century. In lower Louisiana, however, the European immigrants confronted an entrenched French Catholic population heavily tinged with Continental French
liberalism and with Spanish and African cultural strains. The French Creoles
lost the contest for control over the church, but enough Creole customs sur-

vived in the increasingly austere American church to give Louisiana Catholicism a Mediterranean flavor that exists even today.

Without endorsing ethnic pluralism, the American church muted cultural tensions by establishing nationality parishes, in effect conceding a measure of cultural diversity in parish life while it insisted on greater uniformity in formal church practices and pushed Americanization through education. The cultural development of the church in the South, however, diverged from the national pattern when immigration to the South virtually ceased after the Civil War. A period of relative internal stability in the southern church followed the end of the war and lasted through World War II. Overall, the southern church escaped the cultural and social tremors of the "new immigration" wrenching Catholicism in northern communities, except in Louisiana, where the arrival of southern Italians to work in the sugar fields in the 1890s created fresh cultural tensions in the local church for a generation. By moderating its internal ethnic and ecclesiastical stresses, the southern church slipped into a respectable obscurity in the region until the 1960s.

Catholics remained a religious minority everywhere in the South outside of Louisiana, while Catholicism became the majority religion in much of the urban North. Conscious of its minority status in the overwhelmingly evangelical Protestant South, the church assumed a low political and social profile. The Catholic emphasis on personal salvation through the sacramental system tended to deflect Catholic concern from social action, and from John Carroll until Vatican II (1962–65) church leaders preached social and political accommodation with the host society — as much to focus their resources on building a church establishment as to fend off nativism and anti-Catholic prejudices. Southern church leaders provided Scriptural justifications for slavery and a conservative social order in the antebellum period, supported secession and the Confederacy, inveighed against Republican rule during Reconstruction, and instituted their own form of Jim Crowism in the 1890s — all in conformity with the dominant regional values and practices. Such actions did not wholly dispel Protestant suspicions concerning Catholic loyalties, however, for nativism and anti-Catholicism flared in the Populist movement in the 1890s and again after World War I and lingered through the 1930s as a political factor in southern life. Effective lay Catholic political resistance — the creation of the Georgia Laymen's League to combat the Ku Klux Klan, for example — and the church's accommodationist policies on race and social issues countered such external threats, but the persistent, if often only latent, anti-Catholic temperament of evangelical Protestantism in the region inclined the Catholic Church toward a policy of social enclosure. Concerned about the corrupting influence of the

Protestant Bible, hymns, and teaching in public schools, for example, Catholic bishops in the late 19th century began to build a parochial school system in their dioceses. Church-sponsored devotional societies, religious and recreational organizations, and the recruitment and training of native-born southerners for religious vocations solidified the southern Catholic culture, although the church's effort to match secular society in social services and schooling led to a proliferation of institutions that sapped the meager financial endowments of an always poor southern church.

In the 20th century the ideology of southern agrarianism reduced differences between Protestants and Catholics in the South and thereby increased the acceptance of Catholics in southern society. The conservative social views of Catholics increasingly assumed an important place in the region's general critique of modernism. Southern Catholic writers — especially Kate Chopin, Flannery O'Connor, William Alexander Percy, Katherine Anne Porter, and Allen Tate — shared a framework of values that was both Catholic and southern. They distrusted abstraction and modern liberalism, particularly its celebration of the rootless individual in search of the American dream; evidenced a strong sense of place; and praised organic, communal society. Like so many non-Catholic southern writers, they idealized a simpler southern past and decried the insidious secularism of industrial, urban America.

Catholicism, which taught the sanctity of marriage and family, also easily allied with the host society in attacking divorce and abortion — moral positions that contributed to the thawing of relations between Catholics and evangelical Protestant groups. During the 1970s, for example, several regional Southern Baptist/Roman Catholic conferences were held in a mutual effort to undo generations of stereotypes and mistrust that had separated the two churches and to build a consensus for social action. The improved position of Catholics in the region's public life in recent years further testified to Protestant tolerance of Catholics and to Catholic integration into southern life. If Catholics did not quite belong in the Protestant South, they were no longer universally condemned as wholly antithetical to it.

Yet, even as Catholicism gained acceptance in the South, liberal forces swept into the church and the region to loosen the anchors of social conservatism and political accommodationism. More than anything else, the church's social posture shifted in response to Vatican II, which, among other influences, modified church hierarchical authority by calling for greater lay initiative in devotions and discipline. It also altered the ritual foundation of Catholic conservatism and cultural consensus by modernizing liturgical practices. Tradition gave way to change, and often confusion, in worship and social vision. Catholics reared in a tradition of docility groped to separate new truths from old errors in belief.

In the South, papal denunciation of racism in 1958 and insistence on social justice after Vatican II posed immediate challenges to local Catholic and southern habits. Catholic segregationist policy had begun to crumble in the late 1940s and early 1950s because of the actions of individual prelates in Washington, St. Louis, Raleigh, and Nashville in desegregating parochial schools, but the rush came in the 1960s when Catholic school desegregation sometimes moved at a pace faster than that in the public sector. Desegregation of other Catholic institutions soon followed. Desegregation, imposed as it was from above, met stiff resistance from white Catholic laity, particularly in the Deep South, where many people defied church orders. The continued practice of segregated worship virtually everywhere in the South revealed the fragmented nature of the new Catholic Church and the tug between church authority and social norms among southern Catholics. The involvement of Catholic religious leaders in the civil rights movement further alienated southern communicants from the official church, even though many southern bishops opposed civil rights activity.

Similarly, the church's grip on lay thinking weakened as parochial schools became battlegrounds of social change. With fewer nuns, brothers, and priests in teaching positions the influence of lay instructors, who did not always share common social values, increased. The creeping secularism in Catholic education led some pastors to question openly the necessity of parochial schools at all. The floodtide of Spanish-speaking migrants and immigrants in the past few decades, especially in the Gulf South and the Carolinas, combined with the migration of northern-born and often better-educated Catholics into the southern Sunbelt, introduced new cultural stresses into the church while pulling it toward new, nonsouthern definitions of social concern. As sections of the South have become "northernized" by industrialization and ethnic pluralism, so too has the southern Catholic Church.

On the face of it, the Catholic imprint on the South has been negligible. A small, scattered Catholic population has not developed a regional influence. Within areas of Catholic concentration, however (particularly Louisiana, the lower Gulf region, Florida, Texas, and parts of Maryland and Kentucky), Catholicism continues to inform local cultural and social life and, in places where Hispanics congregate, to dictate it. In lower Louisiana, especially, where roughly one-third of the population is Catholic, Catholic religious symbols abound in the practice of regular nightly prayers and in more public, if secularized, expressions such as the annual rice and sugarcane festivals, the Yambilee, the blessing of the shrimp fleets, and even Mardi Gras, which is not without religious overtones.

The contribution of diverse, immigrant Catholic cultures to southern character remains incalculable because it is so elusive and fluid. Catholics have always existed as both outsiders and insiders in southern culture, and the tension between their public and private roles has produced subregional permutations wherever Catholics have lived in significant numbers. On the negative side, cultural differences between Catholic and Protestant reinforced or forged stereotypes and rivalries that have threatened the region's social harmony. The accommodation of the Catholic Church and its people to southern social and political norms, in addition to the higher religiosity of southern Catholics compared with their northern counterparts, paradoxically reaffirms the evangelical Protestant core of southern culture with its stress on personal religious accountability and conservative social values.

RANDALL M. MILLER
Saint Joseph's University

Jon W. Anderson and William Friend, eds., *The Culture of Bible Belt Catholics* (1995); Cyprian Davis, *The History of Black Catholics in the United States* (1991); Jay P. Dolan, ed., *The American Catholic Parish: A History from 1850 to the Present* (1987); John Tracy Ellis, *American Catholicism* (1969); James Hennesey, *American Catholics: A History of the Roman Catholic Community* (1982); Gary W. McDonogh, *Black and Catholic in Savannah, Georgia* (1993); Randall M. Miller and Jon L. Wakelyn, eds., *Catholics in the Old South: Essays on Church and Culture* (rev. ed., 1999).

Social Activism

"Social activism" is hardly the first thing that comes to mind when thinking of religion in the South. Historically, most southern Christians have emphasized obedience to the powers that be, political quietism and conservatism, personal (as opposed to social) morality, and a suspicion of social activism as a distraction from the real business of saving souls for eternal life. Presbyterian theologians historically defended the venerable doctrine of the "spirituality of the church," and most southern churches—especially white churches but often black churches as well—advised political quietism, insisting that rewards would come in heaven above for those who lived good quiet Christian lives below. Social activists, moreover, often came tainted with that most ugly of epithets—"outside agitator." But the South harbored many inside agitators as well, and most of them came from church traditions. Social activism in the

South quite often came from people with the same evangelical upbringings as those who adamantly defended the social order.

Like religious expression elsewhere, religion in the post–Civil War American South has been both priestly and prophetic. It has often undergirded, and, less frequently, challenged, the social order. If white southern formalized theology generally sanctified southern hierarchies, evangelical belief and practice also at times subtly undermined the dominant tradition. Churches as institutions were conservative, but progressive Christians drew different lessons from southern spirituality than regional religious leaders often intended. The actions of individual churchmen and women outstripped the cautious defensiveness that often marked the public stance of the religious institutions.

Here, a listing of a few examples will have to suffice: Henry McNeal Turner, black religious leader and political activist during and after Reconstruction; Alexander McKelway, Presbyterian crusader against child labor in the early 20th-century South; Edgar Gardner Murphy, progressive Episcopalian theologian and minister in Montgomery, Ala., who spearheaded efforts to improve education for whites in the Progressive-era South; Nannie Burroughs, longtime leader of the black Woman's Convention of the National Baptist Convention, Inc., and founder of the National Training School for Women and Girls in early 20th-century Washington, D.C.; Will Alexander, founder of the Commission on Interracial Cooperation; Ella Baker, daughter of a black Baptist minister and later godmother and honorary founder of the Student Nonviolent Coordinating Committee (SNCC); James Farmer, son of a black Methodist educator, founding member of the Congress of Racial Equality, and participant in the Freedom Rides of the early 1960s; Howard "Buck" Kester, Presbyterian minister, lynching investigator, and founder of the Fellowship of Southern Churchmen; Nelle Morton, a woman from the mountains of Tennessee who served as executive director of the Fellowship of Southern Churchmen and later became a well-known feminist theologian who taught at Drew University; Clarence Jordan, founder of the experimental interracial Koinonia farm in southwest Georgia and author of the well-known *Cotton-Patch Gospels*; Dorothy Tilly, a white Methodist from Georgia who served as the only southern woman on President Truman's national civil rights committee in the 1940s and later formed the Fellowship of the Concerned as a support group for whites supportive of civil rights in the 1950s and 1960s; Fred Shuttlesworth, black minister in Birmingham who survived numerous bombings, beatings, and attempts on his life to fight for civil rights in his often violent community; Foy Valentine, head of the Southern Baptist Christian Life Commission and a denominational leader largely responsible for dragging his huge and conservative organization into a recognition of the need for racial reform in the South; Fannie Lou Hamer, a black sharecropper and stalwart Baptist from Ruleville, Miss., who emerged as a leader of the Mississippi Freedom Democratic Party at the 1964 Democratic National Convention; Martin Luther King Jr., scion of a black Baptist family and leader of the civil rights movement; Casey Hayden (née Sandra Cason), white daughter of Texas Methodists who sprang from the "Faith and Life Community" of the University of Texas in the late 1950s and later was influential in the SNCC, Students for a Democratic Society, and the early feminist movement; Jerry Falwell, founder of the Moral Majority and godfather to the contemporary religious-political right wing; and Jesse Jackson, born to a single mother in South Carolina and later leader of the liberal-left "Rainbow Coalition" of the Democratic Party and spokesperson for numerous progressive causes.

While religious institutions were resistant to change, many religious folk devoted themselves to social change precisely because they perceived God as the author of it. Writing about the rise of southern liberalism, John Egerton explains that churches and universities were wellsprings "for the intellectual and philosophical stimulation out of which some reform movements came — but when the institutions themselves shrank from joining the fray, it was often their sons and daughters, acting in new alliances or as individuals, who moved the dialogue and the action to a higher plane." Evangelical resolve to cleanse the region combined with the social gospel idealism that spread into southern church organizations energized social justice politics.

Coming from both the left (such as the civil rights workers) and the right (including what is sometimes referred to as the "Religious-Political Right"), an outspoken minority of southern Christians historically have moved into social activism in response to what they perceive as a call from God. In doing so, they often have suffered doubts within and retribution without, for historically social activism in the South has exacted a high price from its leaders. Petty daily harassment, economic coercion, beatings, death threats, and even assassination have hounded religious prophets for social change in a region historically hostile to radical seers — especially those committed to racial justice. But the very pervasiveness of evangelicalism in the region also provided the religious language from which these social prophets drew their inspiration. They knew that, as a severe and righteous judge, God would condemn the historical patterns of brutality and injustice endemic to an impoverished and racially segregated region.

Scholars have often — and rightly — seen evangelicalism as a legitimator of the southern status quo, of giving divine sanction to the peculiar social mores of the region. But religious belief could also just as readily be used as a judge of that status quo, as a prophetic voice warning against God's judgment on a people willing to tolerate unrighteousness. Certainly the black prophets listed above, ranging from Henry McNeal Turner to Fannie Lou Hamer, used evangelical language powerfully to invoke God's wrath on a region devoted to the unholy idol of white supremacy. Some of the most religiously self-conscious social activists served in the SNCC in the 1960s. Organizers of the committee felt a higher power suffusing themselves in the movement, earning the respect of the deeply evangelical "local people" with whom they worked. Early black SNCC workers—John Lewis, Diane Nash, and others—combined their black evangelical heritage with lessons in radical nonviolent politics from James Lawson at Vanderbilt University during the 1950s. For Lewis, it was like a "holy crusade," with the blood of civil rights martyrs redeeming the South from its former self-professed Redeemers. The young students who integrated lunch counters in Greensboro and inspired the original SNCC organizing conference also came from the church world. Many whites in SNCC came from churches as well. The committee's "distinctively idealistic belief that fortitude, determined action, and fearlessness would result in momentous social change," Mary King has explained, "stemmed to a great degree from the Protestant upbringings of most of its workers." She connected her vision specifically to Wesleyan theology, that "through grace and redemption each person can be saved," a view that "reinforced our belief that the good in every human being could be appealed to, fundamental change could correct the immorality of racial segregation, and new political structures could be created."

Since the 1960s, social activism in southern religion largely has passed from the civil rights coalition, whose primary focus was racial justice in the South, to the antiabortion right, seen in the rise of figures such as Jerry Falwell, Pat Robertson, and Ralph Reed. Learning from the techniques of the civil rights movement, the contemporary religious-political right has deployed the practices of nonviolent civil disobedience and used the language of social righteousness to command attention for its causes. In this case, though, social activism has been used not so much to pull a backward region forward as to reclaim a "lost" heritage of a once supposedly "Christian America."

PAUL HARVEY
University of Colorado at Colorado Springs

Evelyn Brooks-Higginbotham, *Righteous Discontent: The Women's Movement in the Black Baptist Church, 1880–1920* (1994); David Chappell, *Inside Agitators: White Southerners in the Civil Rights Movement* (1994); Constance Currie et al., eds., *Deep in Our Hearts: Nine White Women in the Freedom Movement* (2000); John Egerton,

Speak Now against the Day: The Generation before the Civil Rights Movement in the South (1994); Paul Harvey, Freedom's Coming: Religion, Race, and Culture in the South, 1865–2000 (2003); Mary King, Freedom Song: A Personal Story of the 1960s Civil Rights Movement (1987); William Link, The Paradox of Southern Progressivism, 1880–1930 (1992); Andrew Manis, A Fire You Can't Put Out: The Civil Rights Life of Birmingham's Reverend Fred Shuttlesworth (1999); William Martin, With God on Our Side: The Rise of the Religious Right in America (1996); Charles Payne, I've Got the Light of Freedom: The Organizing Tradition and the Mississippi Freedom Struggle (1995).

Spirituality

Observers of the contemporary South can see as many "spiritualities" and definitions of the term "spirituality" as there are individual seekers. For many, the term "spirituality," in its broadest sense, denotes "the simple life, well lived." Recently one grandmother, teaching a faith formation class in Kernersville, N.C., drawing on the rich background of her Irish Catholic tradition, summarized the spiritual journey for her teenage students in these words: "There are only two things worth doing in life: to know the truth and to be in love." The rest of their study time together was a commentary on her understanding of this phrase, which was for her a basic truth.

In the past 30 years in the South, spirituality has meant wellness, wholeness; it has stressed that the human person is more than the physical, more than what the eye can see, and so has stressed the importance of understanding and developing mind, heart, and soul as well as body. For many, spirituality has become synonymous with "finding the true self" and "unleashing the potential for truth and love," as well as terms such as "serenity" and "peace of heart."

While not excluding these definitions, people of religious faith, Jews, Christians, Muslims, and others, have wanted to emphasize that their understanding of spirituality is in the first place grounded in a belief in a Supreme Being who is personally and lovingly involved in their daily lives. The nature of that involvement and the response on the part of the believer constitute for them the core of spiritual awareness.

Spirituality in both its popular forms as well as more specifically religious forms has manifested itself in many ways, often overlapping. A few examples will suffice to illustrate how diversity and pluralism are at work, as well as the ecumenical flavor of what is happening today.

The Church of the Covenant (Baptist in origin) in downtown Houston, Tex., constructed a new facility that included a permanent labyrinth on church

Folk sign on Highway 82, two miles west of Indianola, Miss. (Charles Reagan Wilson Collection, Center for the Study of Southern Culture, University of Mississippi)

grounds. In order to nurture their own spiritual growth as well as to be able to serve their congregations better, Lutheran pastors at Lenoir-Rhyne College, Hickory, N.C., formed the Society of the Holy Trinity. Members of the society enter into a covenant to observe common spiritual disciplines and to meet regularly for mutual support and accountability. Jewish congregants, joining themselves to the Tikkun Conference of Jewish intellectuals, writers, and artists, explore what they are calling an "emancipatory spirituality" to "maximize love and caring, ethical and ecological sensitivity, and enhance our capacity to respond to the universe with awe and wonder at the grandeur of creation."

Those recovering from addictions of many kinds gather daily in Twelve Step programs seeking understanding, support, and challenge as they turn their lives over to their understanding of a "Higher Power" at work in their lives. The retired, the elderly, those challenged by mental or physical illness, engaged couples, young marrieds, singles, and those looking to begin a second career are turning to spiritual teachings and disciplines to guide their life journeys. As a result, opportunities such as Cursillo, Marriage Encounter, Stephen Ministries, and Emmaus Walk—to mention only a few—continue to receive the support of many mainline churches and to enjoy a wide following. These experiences more often than not involve their participants in encounters that underscore the ecumenical nature of spirituality in the South today. Boundaries are being redefined, and people are encountering one another in ways that surprise, inform, and delight them.

Once identified solely with the formation of Catholic seminarians, divinity schools are now affiliated with Protestant denominations and are sponsoring extensive academic and formational programs in spirituality. Wake Forest University Divinity School (Baptist in heritage) in Winston-Salem, N.C., for example, recently (1997) appointed a Roman Catholic priest and Benedictine monk an associate professor of spiritual formation. Truett Seminary at Baylor University, Waco, Tex., has developed a systematic program of spiritual formation in which both faculty and students participate.

Many people are regularly using the Internet to interact with others, share prayer requests, and learn more about spiritual disciplines. College students, church groups, ministerial associations, and others are arranging for speakers of many traditions, not the least of these Zen Buddhist and other Eastern paths, to address their study groups on topics pertaining to spiritual growth. Ancient Jewish, Christian, and Muslim traditions of spiritual wisdom, once restricted to religious practitioners with knowledge of ancient languages, are being widely read as publishing houses such as Paulist Press make available translations of spiritual classics.

People of all ages, backgrounds, and occupations are going as individuals or groups to monasteries like Benedictine Subiaco Abbey in Arkansas and Trappist Gethsemani Abbey near Louisville, Ky., or to the Methodist conference center at Lake Junaluska, N.C., for days of study and retreat. "Return to nature" and "encounter God in solitude" are important themes for these seekers of spiritual enlightenment. Personal and group spiritual direction sessions often accompany retreat experiences and are becoming more and more common in their own right.

The town of Asheville, N.C., near the Blue Ridge Parkway, has become a gathering place for a wide variety of spiritual practitioners. In the summer of 1998 one visitor to the Belle Chere weekend 20th annual street festival recently reported seeing Methodists selling bottled water and soft drinks, Hare Krishna devotees with shaven heads and saffron robes distributing copies of the Bhagavad Gita, and diverse religious groups such as the Islamic Society and the Eckankar meditation movement housed in storefront centers and open for business. The lobby of a health-food restaurant posted brochures for "Psychic Tarot Readings," whose "psychic-sensitive" medium was "an apprentice of renowned Native American medicine man and author, Sun Bear."

In order to support the demand for spiritual ministries, a number of organizations have arisen in recent decades to train teachers, spiritual directors, and any who would be "soul friends" in the world of our day. Typical among these are the Shalem Spiritual Development Group, Washington, D.C.; Stillpoint Ministries, Black Mountain, N.C.; and the Trinity Center, Winston-Salem, N.C. Almost every major church body sponsors either programs or offices that address issues of spiritual formation at every level of church life. Music ministry as an important means to spiritual fulfillment cannot be underestimated. The American Guild of Organists and the Hymn Society of America work constantly to lift heart and mind to God through the ministry of sacred music. The Appalachian Ministries Educational Resource Center (AMERC) in Berea, Ky., offers seminarians the opportunity to study and experience aspects of Appalachian life, including the spiritualities unique to that region and culture.

Is spirituality in the South to be identified with the past 30 or 40 years only? By no means. From the arrival of Franciscan Friars in St. Augustine, Fla., in the 16th century, through the itinerant missionary journey of John Wesley in Georgia and the coming of the Moravians to North Carolina in the 18th century, to the Great Awakening among Protestants in the early 19th century, various spiritual traditions and disciplines have been known and cultivated by a myriad of groups as well as individuals.

The contributions of African Americans to spirituality in the South, as enduring as they have been rich, have been characterized by strong religious traditions, both oral and written. Among the characteristic elements of this spirituality are the resonant sounds of their spirituals and other religious music; a joyful, spontaneous, heartfelt worship "in the Spirit," including sacred dance; animated preaching patterns; faithful perseverance through times of darkness and distress; and family/community-centered religious devotion. African American spiritual expression involves the whole person and affirms the legitimacy of human emotion in all its dimensions: joy, sorrow, yearning, love —whatever the life of the individual, or the story of the community, brings to the prayer experience. Physical contact, a cultural reality, denotes warmth and hospitality. Both elements are indispensable to this spirituality.

Although throughout its history many teachers of spiritual wisdom have been counted among its daughters and sons, the African American community recognizes in a particular way its indebtedness to the life, ministry, and writings of Dr. Martin Luther King Jr. People of good will everywhere have acknowledged the teaching he gave, both in word and in deed, even to the laying down of his life for the truth he served.

No presentation of spirituality in the South would be complete without mention of the Native American peoples who have been celebrating the land and the spirit on these shores for countless generations before the arrival of more recent peoples. Native American tribal traditions of storytelling, prayer, and harmony with nature in all its beauty are enriching many outside their own communities who come to them in search of wisdom and contact with the transcendent.

SAMUEL F. WEBER
Wake Forest University

Elizabeth Canham, *Praying the Bible* (1987); Forrest Carter, *The Education of Little Tree* (1976); Michael Downey, ed., *The New Dictionary of Catholic Spirituality* (1993); Tilden Edwards, *Living Simply through the Day* (1977); *Expressions of the Heart: A Moravian Journal of Spirituality* (1999); Richard J. Foster, *Celebration of Discipline: The Path to Spiritual Growth* (1978), *Celebrating the Disciplines: A Journal Workbook to Accompany Celebration of Discipline* (1992), *Richard J. Foster's Study Guide for Celebration of Discipline* (1983); Bradley Hanson, *A Graceful Life: Lutheran Spirituality for Today* (2000); Joy Harjo, *The Woman Who Fell from the Sky* (1994); Mary Ann Hinsdale, Helen M. Lewis, and S. Maxine Waller, *It Comes from the People: Community Development and Local Theology* (1995); E. Glenn Hinson, *A Serious Call to a Contemplative Life-Style* (1974); John F. Kavanaugh, *Following Christ in a Consumer Society: The Spirituality of Cultural Resistance* (1991); Martin Luther King Jr., *Strength to Love* (1963); Bill Leonard, ed., *Christianity in Appalachia: Profiles in Regional Pluralism* (1999), and in *Religion and American Culture: A Journal of Interpretation* (1999); Eric C. Lincoln and Lawrence Mamiya, *The Black Church in the African American Experience* (1990); Thomas Merton, *Seeds of Contemplation* (1949), *The Seven Storey Mountain* (1948); Weavings, *The Upper Room* (1986).

Sports and Religion

Although the devotion of southerners to sports is frequently identified with football in Texas and Alabama, basketball in Kentucky, NASCAR in the Carolinas, and baseball's spring training in Florida, the popularity of these sports developed in the 20th century. Before the Civil War, however, the most popular sports in the South were cockfighting, card playing, hunting and fishing, horse racing, and prize fighting. Because of their association with gambling, most of these sports faced strong moral condemnation from southern ministers and churchwomen. In Georgia before midcentury, Jesse Mercer, editor of the *Christian Index*, urged Baptists and Methodists in particular to shun temptations to play cards or attend horse races. A few decades later in the *Alabama Baptist*, ministers denounced a variety of entertainments including cockfighting, card playing, prize fighting, baseball playing, and novel reading. At the same time in North Carolina, a Methodist affirmed that when a man joined

Cleveland Speedway, Cleveland, Tenn., 1997 (Susan Lee, photographer)

the church, he was expected to give up his worldly amusements and habits, including card playing, and a Presbyterian woman indicated that cards intended for gambling games were forbidden, even when innocently used for other purposes. Although dissipating in its intensity, this attitude continued into the mid-20th century when a Mississippi minister's wife forbade the use of playing cards for solitaire, while allowing that Rook cards, sometimes referred to as "a Protestant Deck," could be used for such a game.

Although horse racing also was suspect because of its association with gambling, it sometimes avoided the stringent condemnation directed toward card playing because horse racing could be justified on the pretense that racing horses improved the stock. Nonetheless, in 1889 a Baptist church in Summit, Miss., boycotted the county fair because it permitted gambling on horse races.

Like horse racing, cockfighting also encouraged gambling by observers as well as participants. Although the sport featured animal brutality and appealed to gamblers, cockfighting was, in significant respects, the quintessential antebellum southern sport, with reports of its appeal in Virginia having been noted as early as 1724. The most popular cockfighting magazine of the 19th century, *Grit and Steel*, was published in South Carolina, and it regularly reinforced the ethic of southern sportsmen—that they disdained cocks that shied away from fighting while praising those that persevered in combat even when mortally wounded. In this sense, the cocks represented southern honor. Southern cock-fights also often bridged both class distinctions and racial barriers by featuring sporting alliances between white landlords and African American tenants.

Although cockfighting might have exemplified antebellum male culture, it was excoriated by women and ministers because of the gambling and rowdy behavior that it provoked. One North Carolina woman who, in the title of her memoirs, identified herself as a deserted wife complained about a number of her husband's sins and shortcomings, chief among them being his cockfight-ing on the Sabbath. And ministers throughout Georgia and Alabama repeat-edly denounced cockfighting. Reflecting the religious mores of the evangelical culture that increasingly disapproved of blood sports, several southern states passed laws by 1900 forbidding prize fighting, and by then all southern states except Florida had passed laws against activities in which excessive pain or harm was inflicted on animals.

In contrast to the religious condemnation of gambling sports by women and ministers, hunting and fishing enjoyed a good reputation among these poten-tial critics, since ministers and church members regularly hunted and fished for food and sport. The killing of game in hunting was not condemned in ways similar to the outcry against sports pitting animals against each other, and by the late 19th century conservationists, rather than religious leaders, promoted laws that imposed bag limits, established off-limits with fences, and determined seasons. Until then, it was not uncommon for hunters to measure the success of their sport in terms of the mass of their kill or for fishermen to use various netting methods and dynamite to increase the size of their catch.

During the last years of the 19th century, the "body, mind, spirit" motto of the YMCA began to influence the preparation of ministers in their personal physical and spiritual exercise, yet southern church leaders continued to decry the moral digressions posed by sports. In opposition to the increasing popu-larity of baseball and football, religious leaders throughout the South initially condemned their play. In 1891 the editor of the *Arkansas Baptist* disparaged baseball because its players were often more devious, profane, and idiotic than other men. And a few years later Baptist and Methodist papers in Virginia, Texas, and Mississippi denounced football because of its brutality, claiming that it was more deadly than warfare. Reflecting such evangelical criticism of sports, turn-of-the-century southern lawmakers passed laws regulating Sunday sports, forbidding team play of football and baseball while similarly restricting indi-vidual play of tennis, golf, bowling, and target shooting.

Suggesting a shift in attitude from the condemnation that southern religious leaders had heaped on sports and recreation throughout the 19th century, the Southern Baptist Theological Seminary in Louisville, Ky., dedicated its gymnasium in 1897 to support its efforts to prepare ministers who were physically fit and active.

By the 1920s, southern churches started to organize sports teams and leagues. One of the most distinct was in Paducah, Ky., where Baptist ministers organized their own bowling league. And later that decade, an award-winning Sunday school class, the "Fearless Flyers," was established for the football and basketball players at Mars Hill College in North Carolina. The players also made a habit of taking their Bibles with them to games as a way of preparing to give their testimony. During the same years, the *Baptist Student* featured a series of articles on Christian athletes such as the University of Tennessee's Gene "the Bristol Blizzard" McEver, who led the nation in scoring and who taught a boys' Sunday school class.

In the South the appeal of muscular Christianity (an evangelical movement that promoted physical manliness as a means to uplift Christian morals and expand the Christian gospel) was signaled in Billy Graham's first evangelistic crusade, held in Charlotte, N.C., in 1947. In order to promote attendance at the revival services, Graham enlisted the participation of the premier American miler, Gil Dodds. Before giving his testimony, Dodds competed in an exhibition run against an athlete from the University of North Carolina and displayed his speed in winning a six-lap race around the audience. Although the Charlotte crusade was so successful that Graham sought celebrity athletes to appear in his subsequent revival meetings, other southern religious leaders challenged the purpose of blending professional sports with evangelism. In the same year as the Charlotte crusade, the president of Asbury College in Wilmore, Ky., issued a manifesto about the college's opposition to intercollegiate athletics. He claimed that intercollegiate sports tend to become professional because they direct excessive resources to a few athletes and their emphasis on winning tends to deflect attention away from the development of Christian leadership skills. In contrast, he endorsed intramural sports that promote participation, emphasize physical exercise, and cultivate a spirit of cooperation.

In the latter half of the 20th century, church recreation programs throughout the South expanded their facilities, staff, and organization, forming interchurch leagues for youth, men's, and women's basketball and softball teams and conducting regional and state championship tournaments for the most competitive teams. By the turn of the 21st century, many church recreational programs throughout the South had developed into comprehensive sports ministries, especially at larger churches. At the Alamo City Christian Fellowship in San Antonio, Tex., the sports ministry program featured teams and leagues in basketball, football, soccer, softball, T-ball, and cheerleading; and at the Calvary Church in Charlotte, N.C., the sports ministry also included karate classes, aerobics programs, and a golf tournament, while plans were being developed to add tennis tournaments, distance races, Frisbee events, and fantasy sports. To train staff members for leading such ministries, several religious colleges began to offer undergraduate majors in sports ministry. At Campbellsville University in Kentucky, the program of study was started by the School of Theology, while at Belhaven College in Jackson, Miss., the major was offered through the Sports Applications Department, which also supervised the college's programs in sports administration and exercise science. Taking the concept of sports ministry beyond the local community, the Second Baptist Church in Richmond, Va., sponsored mission trips to Eastern Europe and Brazil that featured the church's basketball team. Reporting on this "Sports Evangelism," the Virginia *Religious Herald* commended the ways that basketball, as a kind of universal language, created opportunities for sharing the gospel with non-English speakers.

From the colonial period to the 21st century, southern religious leaders, groups, and institutions have transitioned through several distinct attitudes regarding the role of sports, at first in society and more recently in the church itself. Initially, religious leaders condemned sports because their play was thought to desecrate the Sabbath, foster gambling, and induce riotous behavior, such as drinking alcohol and using profanity. Following the rise of the muscular Christianity phenomenon in the North and Midwest, southern religious leaders and organizations began to accommodate sports, allowing some physical activities in order to increase their appeal, most often to males. Finally, with the growth of sports programs in southern churches and religious schools, religious leaders have begun to use sports to enhance evangelistic efforts.

JOSEPH L. PRICE
Whittier College

Allen Guttmann, *A Whole New Ball Game: An Interpretation of American Sports* (1988); Tony Ladd and James A. Mathisen, *Muscular Christianity: Evangelical Protestants and the Development of American Sport* (1999); Ted Ownby, *Subduing Satan: Religion, Recreation, and Manhood in the Rural South, 1865–1920* (1990); Joseph L. Price, ed., *From Season to Season: Sports as American Religion* (2001).

Theological Orthodoxy

The term "orthodoxy," meaning right belief, has functioned in southern religion mainly as a polemical self-designation. While numerous groups have claimed to be orthodox, often as a way of contrasting themselves to groups presumed unorthodox, the term has never had a uniform meaning.

In the South, the term has most often been used by Protestants to designate belief in the infallibility of the Bible, the biblical miracles, the divinity of Christ, and the doctrine that Christ's death on the cross satisfied the conditions for eternal salvation in a heavenly afterlife for the faithful. For 19th-century southern Catholics, however, orthodoxy required adherence to the councils and creeds of the church, which meant respect for the authority of the Catholic Church's doctrinal tradition as well as Scripture. For the confessional Lutheran party led by Paul and David Henkel in 19th-century Virginia, orthodoxy required acceptance of the 16th-century Augsburg Confession and Formula of Concord. For the high-church Episcopalians led by John Ravenscroft in 19th-century North Carolina, it meant fidelity to the creeds and practices of the first five centuries of the church. For many in the 20th century, orthodoxy was also assumed to require a belief in God's continuing miraculous intervention in human life, a doctrine rejected by a good number of the Protestant theologians who defined orthodoxy for their denominations in the 19th century and who insisted that the age of miracles ended with the close of the apostolic era.

The insistence on biblical infallibility followed a pattern set by the Protestant theologians of 17th-century Europe, who emphasized the inerrancy of the Bible as a counterweight against the Catholic defense of the authority of the church and against the first stirrings of a rudimentary historical criticism of the biblical text. One seminal source for the spread of inerrancy views in the South was the Westminster Confession (1646) of the English Puritans, a doctrinal summary that deeply influenced the confessional standards of the region's Presbyterians and Baptists. Well into the second half of the 19th century, moreover, educated clergy from those two groups read the works of 17th-century European Protestant scholastic theologians, like Francis Turretin of Geneva, who had defined infallibility with ever more subtle care. With the emergence of the historical criticism of the Bible, which made its way into southern colleges and seminaries in the early 20th century, the critics of "liberalism" staked their case on the infallibility of Scripture, which became a cardinal theme of southern fundamentalism.

Belief in biblical infallibility, however, never produced doctrinal consensus, and indeed its proponents acknowledged that no interpretation of the Bible could be infallible. Traditionalist Presbyterians and most Baptists found in the

A Blessing From North Carolina . . .
For God so loved the world, that he gave his only begotten Son, that whosoever believeth in him shall not perish but have everlasting life.
JOHN 3:16

Stained-glass Jesus as seen in Wheat Street Baptist Church, Atlanta, Ga. (Charles Reagan Wilson Collection, Center for the Study of Southern Culture, University of Mississippi)

Bible the warrants for a Calvinist theology that limited salvation to the elect. Most Catholics, Lutherans, Episcopalians, Methodists, and Disciples of Christ, along with other groups, read the Bible as teaching that every human being had a capacity, made possible by God's assisting grace, to accept the divine offer of salvation. Yet these groups also differed among themselves about the nature of the church, the meaning of the sacraments, the proper understanding of "justification" (God's forgiveness of sin), and the right view of "sanctification" (the renewal of the forgiven person). Differing views of salvation, for example, stood behind the emergence in the late 19th century of separate Holiness churches that maintained the earlier Methodist confidence in an experience of "entire sanctification"—a specifiable moment in which the Christian experienced perfect love. Similar differences informed the emergence of Pentecostal groups that sought a baptism of the Holy Spirit evidenced in speaking in tongues. Each of these groups claimed to be orthodox, but fundamentalists long remained suspicious of Pentecostals, and the Holiness and Pentecostal traditions also eyed each other warily.

For some of these groups, a specific "orthopraxy," right practice, became fully as important as orthodoxy, and the normative practices on which they insisted also frequently had roots in the 17th century. In particular, the emphasis on a specifiable experience of conversion, an identifiable and datable moment of rebirth, originated during that period among the Pietists of Germany and Holland and the Puritans, who promoted a conversionist spirituality in England. For revivalist Presbyterians and Baptists, as well as for early southern Methodists and the later Holiness and Pentecostal traditions that flowed partly from Methodist backgrounds, an emphasis on a particular kind of religious experience became a necessary condition of faithful membership. Some of these groups tended, as well, to associate right practice with certain cultural virtues, ranging from sobriety of dress to abstention from the consumption of alcohol. For many, belief in a Pietist and Puritan understanding of rebirth became itself a feature of orthodoxy.

Among more educated 19th-century southern clergy, orthodoxy was always as "rational," in a specific sense, as it was biblical. They argued that reason served as the means for the preparation, validation, and interpretation of the biblical revelation. To prepare the mind to accept revealed truth, the theologian could assemble all the traditional rational arguments for the existence of God based on the harmony of the natural order, the mutual adaptation of its parts, its complexity, the necessity of a sufficient cause for its existence, and the universality of religious belief. In constructing such a "natural theology," the clergy depended heavily on the Scottish Common Sense philosophy of the 18th-century Enlightenment. Having prepared the mind through natural theology to recognize the elementary truths of religion, reason could then validate a biblical revelation that stood above reason. For this task, the theologians employed the traditional "evidences of revelation," external and internal. The external evidences included validation of the biblical miracles and prophecies, which were supposed to demonstrate the divine status of the biblical message. The internal evidences included claims that the truths of the Bible were internally coherent as well as consistent with human need, an elevated ethic, and modern science. Reason, in short, could determine that the Bible was the authentic Word of God, and in that sense, reason had a place of authority in an orthodox theology. And finally, all agreed that the interpretation of Scripture required the exercise of human understanding, which enabled theologians to reinterpret biblical narratives—such as the creation narrative—in the light of modern science. Despite their claim to rely on Scripture alone, southern Christians who defined themselves as orthodox have almost always depended implicitly on a certain kind of rationalism.

Claims of orthodoxy have functioned to maintain group identity and solidarity, but they have also generated continuing divisiveness among southern Christians. Attempts to replicate the belief and practice of the 1st-century Christian churches, for instance, led to repeated divisions. Primitive Baptists broke off from other Baptists in the 1820s because of a belief that missionary agencies were unorthodox. Alexander Campbell led in the formation of the Disciples of Christ in 1832, drawing members from Baptist and Presbyterian churches with the claim that reliance on Scripture alone could restore primitive Christian truth. By 1906 the Churches of Christ had broken away from Campbell's movement, claiming that it no longer followed Scripture alone. By the 1920s assertions of a unique claim to orthodoxy drove the southern Fundamentalist movement, which helped give rise to such separatist groups as the American Baptist Association (1905) and the Presbyterian Church in America (1973). Beginning in 1979, fundamentalist Baptists engineered a takeover of the Southern Baptist Convention and purged the denomination's institutions in the interests of orthodoxy as they understood it.

In the 20th century, such divisions occurred partly because southern denominations gradually became more internally diverse, with varying interpretations of appropriate belief and practice. By the beginning of the 21st century, it became increasingly clear that no single orthodoxy would prevail among southern Christians.

E. BROOKS HOLIFIELD
Emory University

John B. Boles, *The Great Revival, 1787–1805: The Origins of the Southern Evangelical Mind* (1972); Theodore Dwight Bozeman, *Protestants in an Age of Science: The Baconian Ideal and Antebellum American Religious Thought* (1977); E. Brooks Holifield, *The Gentlemen Theologians: American Theology in Southern Culture, 1795–1860* (1978), *Theology in America: Christian Thought from the Age of the Puritans to the Civil War* (2003); Richard T. Hughes and C. Leonard Allen, *Illusions of Innocence: Protestant Primitivism in America, 1630–1875* (1988); George M. Marsden, *Fundamentalism and American Culture* (1980); Grant Wacker, *Heaven Below: Early Pentecostals and American Culture* (2001).

Urban Religion

Cities have served the South as religious centers and as sites of religious diversity. Along the South's periphery, in such cities as Baltimore, Miami, New Orleans, and El Paso, Roman Catholics constitute a majority of those people with religious affiliations. Although Baptists, Methodists, Presbyterians, and Disciples of Christ collectively account for most church members in interior cities, Episcopalians and Lutherans as well as Catholics and Jews constitute notable minorities. Usually worshipping in biracial or separate churches in the antebellum period, African Americans increasingly established their own denominational structures after the Civil War and created mostly Baptist and Methodist congregations. Less numerous than other groups, the Churches of Christ, Unitarians, Seventh-day Adventists, Christian Scientists, and Holiness congregations have contributed to the religious diversity of southern cities. With southern antecedents dating from 1768 in St. Augustine, Fla., members of the Greek Orthodox Church have formed significant congregations in some cities in the 20th century.

Among Protestants, cities have accommodated ministers and educators with theological views ranging from modernism to fundamentalism. In the early 20th century, black and white Protestant churches grew dramatically as they often used citywide revivals, robust Sunday school programs, and celebrated preachers to recruit new members, many of whom had recently arrived from rural areas. Baltimore was the scene of the 1784 Christmas conference that created the Methodist Episcopal Church, and in 1789 the same city became the first Catholic see in the United States. Catholic churches have experienced ethnically based differences with successive arrivals of immigrants from France, Ireland, Germany, Italy, and Latin America. In the early 1800s Charleston counted the largest Jewish community in the United States. Although Sephardic Jews often settled first in southern cities, they were followed by those from Germany and were later joined by Jews from eastern Europe. Orthodox Jewish congregations were well established in southern cities prior to the Civil War, and Reform and Conservative congregations grew in number in the late 19th and early 20th centuries.

After World War II large numbers of Catholics and Jews migrated from the North, and a massive influx of Cubans transformed the religious landscape of Miami. Occasions of interfaith cooperation have been numerous, but anti-Catholic sentiment was particularly evident in the Know-Nothing political movement of the 1850s and the Ku Klux Klan activities of the 1920s. Anti-Semitism generally appeared in social settings but potently manifested itself in the lynching of Atlanta's Leo Frank in 1915 and in a temple bombing in Atlanta and an attempted temple bombing in Birmingham in 1958.

The urban South's places of worship have varied and changed across time. Early religious gatherings occurred in individual homes, but congregations later constructed buildings of wood, stucco, stone, and brick. Churches and temples initially featured Greek Revival architecture, but from the mid-19th century Gothic Revival, Romanesque, and neocolonial styles of architecture grew in popularity. Charleston's Robert Mills designed a number of exceptional edifices, including the circular Congregational church in his hometown and

St. Louis Cathedral, New Orleans, La., 2003 (Frank J. Methe, photographer, Clarion Herald)

Richmond's Monumental Episcopal Church, erected on the site of a deadly 1811 theater fire. Steeples long dominated many city skylines. The 185-foot steeple of Charleston's St. Michael's Episcopal served as a city watchtower, and the church's chimes sounded alarms. Rebuilt and remodeled several times, St. Louis Cathedral has continued to occupy a central location in New Orleans and has continued to bear the imprint of Spanish, French, and American architects. During the Civil War, some places of worship were damaged by bombardments and by Union troops who used them as barracks and stables. Led by women's groups, churches beautified their interiors in the late 19th century and added stained-glass windows, some of which commemorated Confederate leaders. In the early 20th century, congregations increasingly purchased powerful organs and assembled vested choirs for services that became increasingly elaborate. New Sunday school annexes and recreational facilities reflected growing attention to young people. Built to accommodate revival crowds and morally uplifting events, Nashville's Union Gospel Tabernacle hosted evangelists Sam Jones,

Dwight L. Moody, and Billy Sunday but was renamed Ryman Auditorium for its major benefactor and served as a city cultural center. The final decades of the century witnessed the emergence of megachurches, such as Houston's Second Baptist, which boasts 30,000 members.

Southern cities have functioned as centers of religious education. In addition to schools, denominations have established colleges, universities, seminaries, and schools for layworkers. The Atlanta area, for example, houses Emory University with its Candler School of Theology, Morehouse College, Spelman College, Clark Atlanta University, Agnes Scott College, Atlanta Christian College, Columbia Theological Seminary, and the Interdenominational Theology Center. Similarly, cities have operated as centers for the production and distribution of religious publications, including weekly newspapers, tracts, devotional booklets, magazines, hymnals, books, and Sunday school resources. As the home to publishing houses of half a dozen major denominations, Nashville has earned the label of "the Protestant Vatican." That phrase also refers to the city's institutions of higher learning as well as to the many denominational offices maintained there. Other cities have served as headquarters for various denominational commissions, boards, and state organizations and hosted annual meetings of state and national religious bodies.

Urban Christians and Jews have long engaged in benevolent activities. In the antebellum period, religious groups created societies to aid the poor and the sick of their communities. Mobile established several interdenominational boardinghouses providing seamen with inexpensive food and lodging. Beginning in the early 19th century, religious organizations built orphanages and homes for the elderly. Church-related societies formed by African Americans raised funds for the needy and the homeless as well as for orphans and widows. During devastating epidemics of cholera and yellow fever, ministers, priests, and nuns cared for victims in cities from Norfolk to New Orleans. In 1918 Richmond churches assembled large soup kitchens to aid those suffering from the Spanish flu. In the late 19th century various denominations constructed hospitals, nursing schools, and medical schools, and Houston's Methodist Hospital and Baylor University School of Medicine earned national acclaim in the 20th century. In working-class neighborhoods settlement houses sponsored by Christians and by Jews provided residents with kindergartens, evening classes, playgrounds, and medical care. In the early 20th century, working women found inexpensive lodging at church-supported boardinghouses as well as at the interdenominational facilities of the Young Women's Christian Association (YWCA).

Urban religious leaders have frequently engaged in social activism. In efforts to guard community morals, ministers have repeatedly promoted Sabbath observance laws and antigambling measures. In antebellum Charleston and Savannah antidueling societies relied on the support of churchgoers. Pious women participated in temperance and prohibition organizations of the 19th and early 20th centuries. In the 1920s preachers condemned allegedly lewd dances, fashions, and movies. Other religious leaders tried to reform southern cities. In the 1830s Baltimore's evangelical journeymen contributed to the trade union movement and workingmen's political activities. In the Progressive era ministers, rabbis, and laypeople often formed the vanguard for local and state organizations committed to improved public schools, better public health, systematic public welfare, and prison reforms. Laywomen Lila Meade Valentine and Mary-Cooke Branch Munford stood at the forefront of numerous reform campaigns in Richmond. As rector of St. John's Episcopal Church in Montgomery, Edgar Gardner Murphy played a pivotal role in the Alabama Child Labor Association and the National Child Labor Association, headed by Charlotte minister Alexander McKelway. Religious women often led the Equal Suffrage movement, and urban clergy and laity signed the 1927 "Appeal to the Industrial Leaders of the South." After World War II, black churches served as organizing points for voter registration drives and furnished important leaders such as Dr. Martin Luther King Jr., the Reverend Ralph David Abernathy, and the Reverend Fred Shuttlesworth to the civil rights movement. African American congregations also contributed numerous clergymen and members who led and participated in demonstrations. As the key meeting place for the Montgomery bus boycott, Holt Street Baptist Church earned a large place in history. So, too, did Birmingham's 16th Street Baptist Church for its role as an assembly point for the 1963 demonstrations, a role that led to its subsequent bombing.

Only a few urban whites have taken stands for racial justice. In the antebellum period, clergymen and laymen generally endorsed or accepted the institution of slavery, and some held slaves. After the Civil War religious leaders rarely protested Jim Crow laws, and Birmingham preachers boosted the Ku Klux Klan of the 1920s. Still, ministers in other cities denounced the Klan, and some joined laypeople in local chapters of the Commission on Interracial Cooperation led by the Reverend Will W. Alexander from its headquarters in Atlanta. In the 1950s urban Catholic schools often desegregated, and white ministers and rabbis in Atlanta and Miami called for support of public schools and racial justice. Yet Dallas ministers concurred with First Baptist's W. A. Criswell, who stood firmly behind segregation. In the 1960s and 1970s, numerous white congregations split over the issue of admitting African Americans as members. Since the 1980s Strategies to Elevate People (STEP) has fostered interracial, ecumenical cooperation with programs enhancing educational, housing, and job opportunities in a number of southern cities. Arenas of diversity and, at times, conflict, southern cities have operated as dynamic centers of regional religion.

SAMUEL C. SHEPHERD JR.
Centenary College of Louisiana

Don H. Doyle, *Nashville in the New South, 1880–1930* (1985), *Nashville since the 1920s* (1985); Wayne Flynt, *Alabama Baptists: Southern Baptists in the Heart of Dixie* (1998); Samuel S. Hill, ed., *Religion in the Southern States* (1983); Randall M. Miller and Jon L. Wakelyn, eds., *Catholics in the Old South: Essays on Church and Culture* (1983); Samuel C. Shepherd Jr., *Avenues of Faith: Shaping the Urban Religious Culture of Richmond, Virginia, 1900–1929* (2001); William R. Sutton, *Journeymen for Jesus: Evangelical Artisans Confront Capitalism in Jacksonian Baltimore* (1998); Elizabeth Hayes Turner, *Women, Culture, and Community: Religion and Reform in Galveston, 1880–1920* (1997); Peter W. Williams, *Houses of God: Region, Religion, and Architecture in the United States* (1997).

Women and Religion

Three factors help explain the place of women in religious movements and institutions in the American South. The first is the overwhelming dominance of evangelical Protestantism among whites since the turn of the 19th century and among blacks since emancipation. Second, the white South is more ethnically homogeneous than other regions. Third, the South has been slower to abandon the traditional family structure, which is reflected in the patriarchal nature of all southern institutions.

The distinctive religious history of the South began with the two Great Awakenings. Although the revivals of the mid-18th century had some small impact on the seaboard South, the religious fervor inspired by the camp meetings around the turn of the 19th century changed the spiritual topography of the South for all time. Evangelical Protestantism, with its emphasis on the individual conversion experience, came to dominate the region by the 1850s. Finding its institutional expression primarily in the Methodist and Baptist churches, the movement had a twofold impact on white women. Evangelical religion was family-oriented. Women and children were as lost in sin as were the family patriarchs, and however steadfastly the fathers were able to dominate the institutions of the South, they could not control the souls of their womenfolk.

Conversion was not a gender-specific experience. Women were free to give their souls to Jesus, whatever the men did with theirs, and give they did. They outnumbered the men in church membership, and although they were denied positions of authority in the institutional structure, their prayerful presence and domestic support for a largely itinerant ministry were critical to a sense of successful mission.

The nature of evangelical religion also encouraged the gathering together of women and their families for religious services. Out of this gathering rapidly grew societies of women working together to pursue certain spiritual goals, missionary work, religious education of children, and various aid societies. Joint religious activities have been central to the organized social life of southern white women since that time.

Where African Americans, slave or free, were Christian, they tended to follow the same pattern as white evangelicals. Black women were not permitted to take roles of institutional leadership but had the same freedom of religious expression as did white women, although the circumscribed nature of their social lives did not permit them to form as extensive a network of female societies. In the folk religion of the South, on the other hand, some black women held positions of power. On the plantations they often acted as spiritual leaders— prophetesses or witches—called on for assistance by blacks and whites alike. Black women often took the lead in organized voodoo activities, particularly in New Orleans, where the two Marie Laveaus, mother and daughter, were widely celebrated priestesses during a 50-year period in the middle of the 19th century.

The continued dominance of evangelical Protestantism after the Civil War and the failure of people with strikingly different religious orientations to migrate into the South tended to reinforce patterns established earlier. Institutional religious leadership would go to the men; the women would find their role in the ladies' auxiliary. As the South became increasingly middle class, the women sought ways in which they could spend their increased leisure time in projects allowing them to use their intelligence and energy in the service of others. The church organizations provided that opportunity.

The women in the largest white denominations organized their activities along similar lines. Baptist, Methodist, and Presbyterian women all developed missionary societies. The task of these organizations was to create support, both financial and spiritual, for foreign missionaries. Although women were barred from the clergy of these major religious groups, they were encouraged to become foreign missionaries. Many unmarried women went abroad under the auspices of the missionary societies. Wives were also commissioned along with their husbands in missionary activities — not as clergy but as nurses, teachers, social service workers, and, above all, witnesses to Christ's saving grace. There was probably no role available to southern women that so enabled them to use their courage, intelligence, initiative, and resourcefulness as that of spinster missionary. One of the most widely known religious figures among Southern Baptists is Charlotte "Lottie" Moon, a genuine cultural heroine, who served as a missionary in China for many years and whose exemplary life is used by Baptists to symbolize the entire missionary enterprise.

Unlike the Baptist women, who focused almost exclusively on foreign missions, the Methodists began to look closer to home as well for fields of service. As Methodist women began to seek and be denied positions of leadership in the denomination, they developed progressive societies to address the evils in the culture around them. They organized social settlements and a variety of services for poor and working women. It was Methodist women's organizations that represented the social gospel movement in the South. These women also formed a vanguard in the struggle to establish some basis for racial cooperation.

Even before the Civil War the evangelical denominations provided education for their women. These women, after all, managed the homes in which the next generation of evangelicals would be raised. After the war, in both white and black denominational schools and colleges, women were given an education that sometimes led them to reject the principle on which the education was based. Many of those black and white women who challenged the religious, social, and political status quo got their inspiration from the very tradition they opposed.

Recent work on postbellum African American churchwomen has identified preaching women like Jerera Lee and Julia Foote, in the African Methodist Episcopal Church, but it has also shown ways the male-dominated church leadership created roles, such as stewardess and deaconess, to contain their influence. Still, women exercised much influence using the new forums available to them. The uninstitutionalized role of "church mothers" also proved significant, representing collective wisdom and experience to the community. Black Baptist women were especially significant in representing ideals of uplift and respectability in middle-class churches.

In recent years, as women have increasingly insisted that they be allowed to provide ministerial leadership in their churches, the South has continued to lag behind the rest of the nation in ordaining women. The Southern Baptist Convention (SBC) has aggressively led in limiting women's leadership roles in the past decade. In 2001 the SBC changed its doctrinal standards to state explicitly that women pastors are unbiblical and officially unsanctioned. Another organization, the Council on Biblical Manhood and Womanhood, based in Louisville, Ky., campaigns through churches and elsewhere to preserve traditional gender roles. Molly Marshall, the first tenured woman at the Southern Baptist Theological Seminary, was forced to resign in 2004 because she supported women in ministry, a story chronicled in a documentary film, *Battle for the Minds*. Women nevertheless are becoming more numerous in the ministry in certain denominations. The largest number of female clergy in the South is in the Pentecostal churches. As of 1998, Episcopal dioceses in the South had 368 women priests. The United Methodist Church and the Presbyterian Church in the United States of America also ordain women, and each has close to 20 percent female clergy. Women continue to be active in the "parallel church," a term used to describe the network of church agencies and organizations led by women.

Roman Catholic women have long made contributions through religious orders working in the South. The Sisters of Loretto at the Foot of the Cross were organized in Kentucky in 1812, for example, and the Sisters of Mercy worked in Mississippi beginning in the early 19th century. Nuns have made important contributions through ministries in education, health, and social welfare.

Whereas women have been influential in founding new religious movements in other parts of the United States, rarely, if ever, has a woman been instrumental in the formation of such a movement in the South. The religious homogeneity of the region, as well as the patriarchal emphasis of the culture, has tended to restrict religious innovation of any kind. Southern women have channeled their spiritual energies into the traditional religious structure. Those who have been unable to fit into the cultural mold have either left the region or turned inward upon themselves and nurtured their spiritual lives. The stifling of southern women's spiritual insights has led some of these women to seek self-fulfillment in areas outside the life of the churches, an enterprise that only today is meeting with any degree of success.

THOMAS R. FRAZIER
Baruch College

Charta M. Haywood, *Prophesying Daughters: Black Women Preachers and the Word, 1823–1913* (2003); Christine Leigh Heyrman, *Southern Cross: The Beginnings of the Bible Belt* (1997); Evelyn Brooks Higginbotham, *Righteous Discontent: The Women's Movement in the Black Baptist Church, 1880–1920* (1993); Samuel S. Hill, *The South and the North in American Religion* (1980); Donald Mathews, *Religion in the Old South* (1977); Albert J. Raboteau, *Slave Religion: The "Invisible Institution" in the Antebellum South* (1978); Dana Robert, ed., *Gospel Bearers, Gender Barriers: Mission-*

ary Women in the 20th Century (2002); Anne Firor Scott, *The Southern Lady: From Pedestal to Politics, 1830–1930* (1970); Noreen Dunn Tatum, *Crown of Service: A Story of Woman's Work in the Methodist Episcopal Church, South, from 1878 to 1940* (1960).

Zion, South as

The 17th century saw the crumbling of the old feudal and manorial systems that had dominated the geographic and economic landscape of Europe and had held the landless peasant in virtual bondage, but the modern institutions that replaced the old systems did little to elevate the least elements of the general populace. Capitalism was more beneficial to the neophyte capitalists than to the laborers; population pressures, worn-out soil, and problems associated with the displacement abounded; unsatisfactory religious conditions paralleled economic woes. Princes in central Europe demanded that their subjects adhere to the religion of their political leaders, and religious dissent was not countenanced. When England's King James I promised to "harry them out of the land," he was referring to dissenters to the Church of England who were experiencing both economic hardship and religious intolerance.

Given these Old World conditions, the New World beckoned people from the British Isles and mainland Europe. Explorers reported the wonders of the Western Hemisphere, painting America as a land of milk and honey. Dissatisfaction with conditions in Europe combined with the advantages of America —both real and fancied—resulted in countless people migrating to the New World. The first English people to settle in Virginia came for multiple reasons: a higher standard of living, a permanent home, a place to worship. These immigrants viewed Virginia and the colonies to the south as a paradise, a utopia, a new Zion. They thought of themselves as descendants of God's chosen people and of America as the new Promised Land.

The Puritans who settled New England attempted to establish a utopian "city upon a hill," but New Englanders did not have a monopoly on religious idealism. It inspired the southern colonists as well. As historian Perry Miller pointed out, southern settlers came from an English culture that reflected a religious worldview. The Great Awakening, at a later time, affected all the colonies. As British and other Europeans swarmed into the southern colonies, they worked to reap the fruits of the boundless land, at the same time thanking God for their harvests and for the freedom they enjoyed.

As people along the seaboard moved westward, religion and religious ideas permeated southern colonial culture. Geographic and demographic conditions kept early southerners from joining churches in large numbers, but this fact did not negate the religiosity of the South. The Second Awakening of the early

SHILOH BATTLEFIELD · TENNESSEE

PRAYING HANDS

A Card That GLOWS IN THE DARK
Recharges Itself Daily In A Light Room #25

Glow-in-the-dark postcard from Shiloh Battlefield, Tenn.
(Charles Reagan Wilson Collection, Center for the
Study of Southern Culture, University of Mississippi)

19th century both grew out of and reinforced this religiosity. Also, it increased church membership statistics, especially those of the Baptists, Methodists, and Presbyterians. By the mid-19th century, southerners had begun to identify religion and culture so closely that they could not be separated.

The southern religious experience became intertwined with the South's political ideology, both essential elements in what became the southern way of life. Throughout the middle period of American history, when economics, states' rights views, westward expansion, the abolition movement, and a host of other tangible conditions and intangible forces drove wedges between North and South, southerners took umbrage at those who criticized their region and its institutions. The South's intellectual and emotional defense of itself and its ideals, its myths and its realities, were to some extent an outgrowth of the impact of religious zeal. When the great sectional crisis reached its climax, the South defended its way of life with fervor imbued with religious convictions. From the southern point of view, the Civil War was a fight between right and wrong, a religious crusade, a holy war, a defense of a beloved Zion. Southerners who died for the cause saw themselves as being like the religious warriors of an earlier era who defended the Holy Land from the attacks of the infidels.

Once the Civil War was over, southerners surrounded themselves with both old and new myths, as they idealized a society gone with the wind and orated about the glories of the Lost Cause. In the latter years of the 19th century and into the 20th, when powerful social and economic forces racked American society, southerners turned to religion for solace. The church in both hamlet and city was a solid rock in an unstable world. Religious revivals stemming from the frontier camp meeting tradition reaped a great harvest of souls. Baptists and Methodists together constituted as much as 90 percent of the churchgoing population in some states within a region recognized as the most religious in the nation. Religion continued to infiltrate politics, society, and culture, and— despite the Baptists' belief in the doctrine of separation of church and state— the two largest Protestant denominations in the South became essentially the established churches of the region. In the 20th century, when denominations like the Southern Baptists and Methodists epitomized and defended the status quo, much of the southern religious commitment continued to be the result of firmly held beliefs (rightly or wrongly) that the South contained the most desirable conditions in the nation. Whatever its shortcomings, for southerners the South continued to be the American Zion.

MONROE BILLINGTON
New Mexico State University

Kenneth K. Bailey, *Southern White Protestantism in the 20th Century* (1964); Edwin S. Gaustad, *Religion in America: History and Historiography* (1973); Charles A. Johnson, *The Frontier Camp Meeting: Religion's Harvest Time* (1955); George M. Marsden, *Religion and American Culture* (1990); Martin E. Marty, *Pilgrims in Their Own Land: 500 Years of Religion in America* (1984); Rufus B. Spain, *At Ease in Zion: Social History of the Southern Baptists, 1865–1900* (1967); Donald C. Swift, *Religion and the American Experience: A Social and Cultural History, 1765–1997* (1998).

African Methodist Episcopal Churches

The African Methodist Episcopal (AME) Church and the African Methodist Episcopal Zion (AME Zion) Church have never been distinctively "southern" churches, but they have been two of the most popular and powerful religious denominations among southern blacks. Both groups originated in northern cities — Philadelphia and New York City, respectively — in the late 18th century. Blacks were among early converts to Methodism in North America, but segregated church services and discrimination in the ritual of communion led to the withdrawal of black Methodists. Richard Allen, Absalom Jones, and William White were early founders of the AME Church, while William Brown, Francis Jacobs, and Peter Williams had incorporated the precursor of the AME Zion Church in New York City by 1801. Before the Civil War, the two denominations had established congregations in such border-South cities as Louisville, Washington, and Baltimore, and the AME Church had even appeared in New Orleans. Both denominations opposed slavery and were therefore closely watched in these locations. Daniel Payne and Morris Brown, both born and reared in Charleston, S.C., became the most prominent antebellum southerners in either denomination, serving as AME Church bishops.

The AME churches assumed a new significance in the South with the Civil War and emancipation. Membership expanded as ministers and missionaries came south to work with the freedmen. At the end of the war, the AME

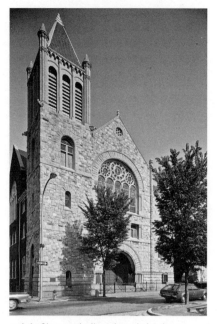

Bethel African Methodist Episcopal Church, 419 South Sixth Street, Philadelphia, Pa., 1973 (Jack Boucher, photographer, Library of Congress [HABS, PA,51-PHILA,288-2], Washington, D.C.)

Zion Church, led by bishop J. J. Clinton of the Southern Conference, worked vigorously in Alabama, Florida, Louisiana, and, perhaps most effectively, North Carolina. Such colleges and schools of technology as Fayetteville State, Winston-Salem State, and Hood Theological Seminary were formed in this era. Leaders of the AME Church organized a state conference in 1865 in South Carolina, and from there ministers expanded throughout the Deep South and into the Southwest. South Carolinian Henry McNeal Turner was among the prominent leaders of the postbellum AME Church. He served as bishop of the Georgia Conference from 1880 to 1892 and played a key role in introducing Methodism to Africa. Both

AME denominations are currently active in Africa and the Caribbean as well as the United States.

CHARLES REAGAN WILSON
University of Mississippi

Lewis V. Baldwin, *"Invisible" Strands in African Methodism: A History of the African Union Methodist Protestant and Union American Methodist Episcopal Churches, 1805–1980* (1983); David M. Bradley, *A History of the A.M.E. Zion Church*, 2 vols. (1956–70); James T. Campbell, *Songs of Zion: The African Methodist Episcopal Church in the United States and South Africa* (1995); Harry V. Richardson, *Dark Salvation: The Story of Methodism As It Developed among Blacks in America* (1976); Clarence E. Walker, *A Rock in a Weary Land: The African Methodist Episcopal Church during the Civil War and Reconstruction* (1982); William J. Walls, *The African Methodist Episcopal Zion Church: Reality of the Black Church* (1974).

Asbury, Francis

(1745–1816) MINISTER.

Francis Asbury was born four miles from Birmingham, England, 20 or 21 August 1745. As early as age 15, he began to preach, and in 1766 he became one of John Wesley's traveling ministers in the "Methodist" connection. Five years later he volunteered to become a Wesleyan missionary to the colonies. There the greatest interest in the evangelical movement existed in the South, where Asbury took charge of the Baltimore district in 1773. As the only missionary to remain during the Revolution, he became superintendent of the evangelical enterprise throughout the nation. In the first years of the Revolution he began to attract the suspicion of the authorities, who questioned his loyalty to the Revolutionary cause, and he found himself restricted to preach in Delaware. Such suspicions declined, and by 1779 Asbury had begun to resume control of the American evangelical movement.

Asbury attempted to maintain discipline among the lay preachers, especially the increasingly rebellious southerners, and at the same time he implored Wesley to provide greater support for the American enterprise. Finally, in 1784, Wesley sent representatives who met with Asbury and most of the lay ministers at the "Christmas Conference" in Baltimore, at that point the center of evangelical Anglicanism. Although Thomas Coke, Wesley's main representative, was officially in charge of the meeting, Asbury in fact controlled the events. The members voted to create a new denomination, the Methodist Episcopal Church, and, at Asbury's insistence, they voted to invest him with the office of superintendent, a position Wesley had intended to give him without the advice or consent of the American clergy. Again showing his conscious independence of Wesley, Asbury began to call himself "bishop."

As leader of the new denomination, Asbury traveled great distances on horseback and focused most of his attention on the South and Southwest, where the greatest numbers of Methodists remained during his lifetime. He continually fought minor bureaucratic battles and often ran the denomination with a strong, some said dictatorial, style. He weathered the great crisis of the early years of the denomination, James O'Kelley's movement to democratize Methodism, and only in the last years of his life yielded power to his hand-chosen successor, William McKendree. Never in particularly robust health, Asbury nevertheless continued to travel until his death on 31 March 1816.

Francis Asbury never received acclaim as a great preacher; nor was he a scholarly man. Strongly committed to the necessity of sinless behavior, he vigorously opposed slavery during much of his life, yielding only toward the end of his travels to moderation on the issue. Asbury's greatest strength, and the one that made him one of the most exceptional men in American religious history, was organizational. He had a keen instinct for church politics, managed church expansion with intelligence and remarkable intuition, and built a denomination that became central to 19th-century southern religion.

DAVID T. BAILEY
Michigan State University

Herbert Asbury, *A Methodist Saint: The Life of Bishop Asbury* (1927); Elmer T. Clark, ed., *The Journal and Letters of Francis Asbury* (1958).

Bible Belt

"Bible Belt" is a term coined by H. L. Mencken in the 1920s to describe areas of the nation dominated by belief in the literal authenticity of the Bible and accompanying puritanical mores. He did not give the term a specific location, but he did associate it with rural areas of the Midwest and, especially, the "Baptist backwaters of the South." He used the term as one of derision,

King James Version Scripture on church fan (*Charles Reagan Wilson Collection, Center for the Study of Southern Culture, University of Mississippi*)

referring, for example, to "the Bible and Hookworm Belt" and calling Jackson, Miss., "the heart of the Bible and Lynching Belt."

The term has been used by scholars as well. In mapping the geographic range of the Churches of Christ, Edwin Gaustad commented that the denomination's influence represented "perhaps more a Bible Belt than any other region can offer." A 1952 survey, by John L. Thomas in *Religion and the American People* (1963), concluded that, based on the prevalence of Bible reading, the Bible Belt was primarily in the West South Central, East South Central, and South Atlantic U.S. Census areas. Cultural geographer James R. Shortridge analyzed 1971 denominational membership figures and mapped a Bible Belt region of "conservative churches" extending in influence from the Atlantic seaboard through Texas and eastern New Mexico; its northern boundary was the upper state lines of Virginia, Kentucky, Missouri, and Oklahoma, extending into southern Illinois. "Jackson, Mississippi, could perhaps be called the 'buckle' of the Bible Belt, but Oklahoma City is definitely marginal, and Kansas is not in it," he wrote. Stephen W. Tweedie's study "Viewing the Bible Belt" analyzed the viewership of evangelical, fundamentalist religious television programming and concluded that "the Baptist South certainly is a major part of this Bible Belt, but areas of strength also include parts of the Methodist dominated Midwest as well as portions of the predominantly Lutheran Dakotas." These modern studies seem, then, to confirm Mencken's use of the term, although now it is used proudly by those in the Bible Belt to describe their commitments.

"Bible Belt" is a particularly useful term to describe the importance of the Scriptures in the South. When Haze Motes in Flannery O'Connor's *Wise Blood* left his hometown of Eastrod, Tenn., he took with him only a black Bible and a pair of glasses belonging to his mother. At his little country school, he "had learned to read and write but that it was wiser not to: the Bible was the only book he read." He was perhaps typical of many southern true believers. On the early frontier and in rural areas throughout southern history, the Bible has been a main source of reading material and intellectual stimulation.

Preachers took it as their only text for preaching. Politicians used a campaign language spiced with references to biblical stories and quotes to illustrate their political points, and two favorite southern pastimes—storytelling and conversation—were often filled with biblical references. Writers such as O'Connor and Faulkner used biblical symbols and motifs, artists painted biblical heroes and heroines in their works, and quilters even stitched the stories as themes for their works. Historian Kenneth K. Bailey noted of the South in 1900 that "few Southerners doubted the literal authenticity of the Scriptures or the ever-presence of God in man's affairs," and sociologist John Shelton Reed's studies of southern attitudes in contemporary times suggest the Bible Belt is still literally that.

CHARLES REAGAN WILSON
University of Mississippi

Kenneth K. Bailey, *Southern White Protestantism in the 20th Century* (1964); H. L. Mencken, *Prejudices: Sixth Series* (1927); John Shelton Reed, *The Enduring South: Subcultural Persistence in Mass Society* (1972); James R. Shortridge, *The Geographical Review* (October 1976); Stephen W. Tweedie, *Journal of Popular Culture* (Spring 1978).

Blue Laws

Considered reverential by some, overly puritanical by others, blue laws, or Sunday closing laws, exist in most of the southern states. Based on an English statute passed in 1678 during the reign of Charles II and carried piously into the colonies, blue laws prohibit worldly business and diversion—except when deemed necessary or charitable—on the traditional day of rest.

The term "blue laws" comes from the blue paper used in binding the Massachusetts statutes on moral behavior in the 1600s. The first American colonial law regulating Sabbath activities was passed in Virginia in 1610, requiring Sunday church attendance, and other southern colonies followed suit. In the 19th century Sabbath laws did not require church attendance but did regulate public activities on that day.

Fearing growing secularization after the Civil War, religious groups such as the Baptists, Methodists, and Presbyterians urged their members to refrain from participating in public entertainment, social activities, and recreational travel on Sundays, and eventually they successfully pressured for greater enforcement of blue laws, especially in small towns and rural communities.

Today, stores are closed or merchandising is restricted in honor of holy observance. Realistically, the laws assure merchants of at least one noncompetitive day a week.

The result of such laws, passed by state and local governments, is a chaotic canon of "dos and don'ts." Hence, the merit of the legislation is challenged constantly. For example, Arkansas's blue law—which permitted the sale on Sunday of film and flashbulbs but not cameras—was deemed unconstitutional in 1982.

In Louisiana there are only a handful of businesses—including icehouses, bookstores, funeral parlors, and steamboats—that can operate legally on Sundays. In South Carolina most commercial endeavors are illegal on Sunday. Exceptions include sanctioned steeplechases, annual harness races, and the sale of fish bait, seeds, swimwear, and ice cream. These anomalous statutes appear on many a code of ordinances, but most communities wink at the law. Enforcement is haphazard and sporadic.

Though probably an endangered species, blue laws linger on most local lawbooks. The one sabbatical restriction that most southern officials insist on is the prohibition of the sale of alcohol—except in large cities, in resort areas, and at private clubs. Because of the irreconcilable differences between whiskey and worship, Sundays in the rural South will be dry for a long time to come.

LINTON WEEKS
Washington Post

Neil J. Dilloff, *Maryland Law Review* (no. 4, 1980); Warren L. Johns, *Dateline Sunday, USA: The Story of Three and a Half Centuries of Sunday-Law Battles in America* (1967); Richard E. Morgan, *The Supreme Court and Religion* (1972).

Campbell, Alexander

(1788–1866) MINISTER.

Campbell was a major figure in a religious movement that came into being on the American frontier in the early 19th century and continues to thrive in the modern South. Its purpose was to restore the unity of the church on the basis of the Scriptures. Campbell, Thomas Campbell (his father), Barton W. Stone, and Walter Scott were the founders of a movement whose congregations today call themselves Churches of Christ, Christian Churches, and Christian Church (Disciples of Christ). The movement had great appeal to individuals in Virginia, North and South Carolina, Georgia, Tennessee, and Kentucky.

Campbell was born in northern Ireland. His father was a minister in the Anti-Burgher Seceder Presbyterian Church. Accepting the teachings of the Scottish school of Common Sense philosophy, the Campbells were influenced by the evangelical movement led by such men as James and Alexander Haldane, Roland Hill, and John Walker.

Disturbed by the conflict between Protestants and Catholics in northern Ireland, Alexander Campbell's father came to America in 1807. His wife and family, led by young Alexander, followed in 1809. When the family reunited in America, both father and son had broken with the Presbyterian tradition. Practicing believer's baptism by immersion, the Campbells were in fellowship with the Baptists of western Pennsylvania and northern Virginia between 1815 and 1830, but they soon parted over doctrinal questions.

Alexander Campbell was giving leadership to a growing group of followers, generated in part by a series of debates with such figures as Robert Owen, Bishop John Purcell, and Nathan Rice and William Maccalla of Kentucky. By means of his publications, *The Christian Baptist* and its successor, *The Millennial Harbinger*, Campbell's views were spread throughout the South. In 1829 Campbell served as a delegate to the Virginia Constitutional Convention.

To prepare young men for the minis-try, Campbell founded Bethany College in 1840. Located in Brooke County, Va. (now West Virginia), the college was unique in that it was the first college to teach the Bible as a subject along with other studies. Students came to Bethany from most of the southern states but especially from Alabama, Georgia, and Mississippi.

As the slavery controversy grew more heated in the 1850s, Campbell was called on to take a stand. Always popular with southern audiences, he temporized saying "slavery is a matter of opinion," meaning that it was not central to Christian faith. This position satisfied neither audiences of the North nor those of the South.

Campbell lived near the college, serving as president and teaching several generations of preachers until his death in 1866.

LESTER G. MCALLISTER
Christian Theological Seminary

Lester G. McAllister, *Thomas Campbell: Man of the Book* (1954), with William Tucker, *Journey in Faith: A History of the Christian Church* (1975); Robert Richardson, *Memoirs of Alexander Campbell* (1868).

Campbell, Will D.

(b. 1924) MINISTER, WRITER, CIVIL RIGHTS ACTIVIST.

In December 2000 when Will D. Campbell received the National Medal for the Humanities, President Clinton referenced the New Testament in his introduction: "Scripture says 'be doers of the word and not hearers only'; Will Campbell is a doer of the word."

Campbell's life bears ample testimony. Born 18 July 1924 in the piney

Will Campbell, a leader of the Committee of Southern Churchmen, 1990s (Peachtree Publishers, Atlanta, Georgia)

woods of southwestern Mississippi, Campbell spent his early life centered on family and faith. The primordial forces of blood, spirit, and water brought Campbell into the fold of Christian faith at seven and into the gospel ministry at sixteen.

Louisiana College was Campbell's introduction to the wider world. His ministerial studies there (1941–43) were interrupted by military service as an army medic in the South Pacific (1943–45). Reading Howard Fast's novel *Freedom Road* transformed Campbell's vision of the South, a view that intensified as he regarded the disparity toward blacks in the army.

After the war, in 1946, Campbell and Brenda Fisher, his college sweetheart, married and moved to North Carolina, where Campbell completed his studies at Wake Forest College (B.A., 1948). Campbell's decision to attend Yale Divinity School was a momentous one. He embraced both the study and the lifestyle of an Ivy League graduate student in the early 1950s.

In 1952 Will and Brenda Campbell returned to the South as the "first family" of the Taylor (La.) Baptist Church. Campbell's parish ministry lasted 18 months, long enough for him to become acquainted with the vocational realities of his calling. Although he believed the gospel sympathetically addressed the rights of local mill workers, congregational problems arose when Campbell attended union meetings.

Convinced that he would find more freedom in a university setting, Campbell became the director of Religious Life at the University of Mississippi just as the 1954 *Brown v. Board of Education* decision was handed down by the U.S. Supreme Court. Two tense, troubling years later, he left the university to accept a job with the liberal National Council of Churches. In 1956 Campbell became the director of the council's Southern Office of the Department of Racial and Cultural Relations in Nashville, Tenn. During the next several years he was the "trouble shooter" for the council, traveling around the South to witness the tremendous racial upheaval in southern communities.

Campbell's role in the civil rights movement is well known. He was one of the few who escorted black children to school in Little Rock in 1957. Campbell is also often identified as the only white man allowed to participate in the formation of the Southern Christian Leadership Conference. And he was present at many of the events enshrined today as marker points in the civil rights movement, including sit-ins in Greensboro, N.C., and demonstrations in Birmingham and Nashville.

But by 1963 the exigencies of vocational life within the National Council led Campbell to resign. Experiences within the parish, the university, and the council persuaded him that securing institutional viability is always the bottom line. He became the director of the Committee of Southern Churchmen, a liberal, loosely organized group of Christians. The committee's journal, *Katallagete*, provided a venue for Campbell to develop his writing.

The publication of *Brother to a Dragonfly* (1977) brought Campbell national exposure as a writer and a National Book Award nomination. Campbell portrays the tragic death of his brother, Joe, within the context of the nation's struggle with the legacy of slavery. However, Campbell's first book, *Race and the Renewal of the Church* (1962), remains his best seller and establishes the biblical and theological foundation for later writings.

Arguably the most well known passage of Campbell's writings is found in *Brother to a Dragonfly*. He speaks of his "conversion" to faith, led by two of the "most troubled men I have ever known," his brother, Joe, and a friend, P. D. East. Prodded by East, Campbell realized that he had rejected his own people in his work. Far more significantly, the theological failure of his own beliefs came into focus. His concept of God as loving and accepting disenfranchised blacks had not allowed for God's love and acceptance of poor whites, Klansmen, or "rednecks."

Now nearing 80, Campbell and his wife live on a farm in Mt. Juliet, Tenn. From his log cabin office, Campbell continues his pastoral and priestly duties, baptizing, marrying, burying, and offering shelter for body and soul. He has written 15 volumes, including four children's books. Exploring a wide range of topics anchored in southern life, Campbell's work includes *And Also with You* (1997), the story of Episcopal bishop Duncan Gray and his role in James Meredith's arrival at Ole Miss; *Providence* (1992), which deals with the forced removal of Native Americans from their tribal lands in Mississippi; *Cecelia's Sin* (1983) and *The Glad River* (1982), which explore faith and community; *The Convention*, a "parable" of a denomination confronting the calling of women to ministry (1988); and, most recently, *Robert G. Clark: Journey to the House: A Black Politician's Story* (2003). The recipient of five honorary doctorates and numerous prestigious literary awards, Campbell remains active as a writer and speaker and, as always, a preacher.

LYNDA WEAVER-WILLIAMS
Virginia Commonwealth University

Thomas L. Connelly, *Will Campbell and the Soul of the South* (1982); Merrill M. Hawkins Jr., *Will Campbell, Radical Prophet of the South* (1997); Susan Ketchin, *The Christ-Haunted Landscape: Faith and Doubt in Southern Fiction* (1994); Mike Letcher, director, *God's Will* (video), University of Alabama Center for Public Television and Radio (1999).

Camps and Retreats

Each of the South's three largest denominations — Baptist, Methodist, and Presbyterian — maintains some kind of camp or conference center in the mountains of western North Carolina. The Presbyterians operate the Montreat Conference Center, the Methodists support Lake Junaluska, and the Southern Baptists have Ridgecrest Assembly.

The South was relatively slow to start special church camps. The builders of one of the first camps, Montreat in North Carolina (1897), were northern religious leaders who modeled the new camp on the Ocean Grove retreat in New Jersey. Beginning in the 1920s and 1930s, many southern church groups first started camping in state parks and then moved on to establish camps and retreats in the mountains or near beaches.

In some ways, the camps and retreats uphold church traditions, and in some ways they represent modern innovations. The decision to retreat into the woods for a special time of worship clearly recalls camp meetings. Advertisements for the camps consistently state that their goal is to isolate campers from distractions so they can concentrate on spiritual matters, and the location helps campers have what some refer to as a "mountaintop experience."

On the other hand, the camps are very modern institutions. Like many Sunbelt institutions, church camps advertise organized opportunities for sports and recreation. While people throughout much of southern history have lived on or near farms, camps now provide opportunities for people who live in cities and towns to enjoy themselves in a natural environment.

Church camps also represent a modern innovation in their ability to offer a full range of services to their congregations. Many denominations have used camps and retreats as places for seminars for singles, for men, for women, for married people, for people interested in missionary work or Sunday school teaching or church music. Some groups, especially the Methodists, have used camps for experimenting with interracial and international friendships and shared activities.

In the mid-20th century, the camps emerged as particular attractions for children. They offer Christian play, acquaintances, leaders, and lessons, with plenty of chances for both Bible study and swimming. Many camps offer what one could call a Christian primitivism, with fascinations with American Indian lore. For years at the Southern Baptists' Camp Ridgecrest, boys participated in Council Ring ceremonies, in which those who had learned enough Indian lore gained Indian names and were inducted into an imaginary Indian nation. Girls at the adjoining Camp Crestridge went through a series of steps to work toward another ideal — the Belle.

Especially because parents are sending their children into the care of church leaders, different camps make clear their differences in theology. Reports and advertisements for many evangelical church camps routinely state the number of people who have conversion experiences or dedicate their lives to Christian service. Many

Pentecostals take note of special experiences. An Assembly of God newspaper reported that at an Arkansas church camp in 1973, "Let us shout a big 'Praise the Lord' for the 91 saved and the 157 that were filled with the Holy Spirit." On the other end of evangelical theology, some leaders of Church of Christ camps worry that children might be persuaded by emotion, so they caution camp counselors against appeals not grounded in clear biblical reasoning. An Episcopalian writer argued in 2001 that church camps "are extremely successful at instilling in the hearts and minds of the young the basic stuff of the faith" by surrounding them with other Episcopalians outside what he called "a sea of Bible-belt fundamentalism or hierarchical authoritarianism."

James Cannon, minister and organizer of the Virginia Anti-Saloon League (Westerville Public Library, Westerville, Ohio)

TED OWNBY
University of Mississippi

Ted Ownby, *Beyond Bubba: White Manhood in the Recent South*, ed. Trent Watts (forthcoming).

Cannon, James, Jr.

(1864–1944) MINISTER.
Cannon entered the ministry of the Methodist Episcopal Church, South, after a religious conversion experienced while attending Randolph-Macon College. He received training at Princeton Theological Seminary and was given his first charge in 1888 in the Virginia Conference.

Cannon's multifaceted career included educational, editorial, and interdenominational work. He twice served as principal of Blackstone Female Institute in Virginia, substantially adding to that school's funding and enrollment. As the first superintendent of the Junaluska Methodist Assembly in North Carolina, he further demonstrated his administrative talents.

From the beginning of his ministry Cannon was active in ecclesiastical affairs and participated in the annual state and general conferences of his denomination. Cannon's work outside the confines of his church included semiautonomous editorial positions with church newspapers in Virginia and organizational activity with the Federal Council of Churches and Near East Relief. Like many other southern progressives, he adopted prohibition as his primary reform ideal. Helping organize the Virginia Anti-Saloon League in 1901, he also founded a dry publication, the *Richmond Virginian*. Cannon fought against the wet Democratic machine in Virginia, got a wet-dry referendum on the ballot, and then led the state's prohibition forces to victory in 1916. As chairman of the legislative committee of the Anti-Saloon League, he successfully lobbied in Washington for passage of prohibition legislation culminating in the 18th Amendment.

In 1918 the General Conference elected Cannon bishop, a position he held for the next 20 years. His original district included most of the Southwest and part of the Deep South. He also accepted responsibility for Methodist mission fields and made extensive inspection tours of the Belgian Congo, Mexico, and South American countries.

During the 1920s Cannon became chief spokesperson for prohibition enforcement. In the tumultuous presidential campaign of 1928, he broke with the Democratic Party for the first time and organized the Anti-Smith Democrats. Always a combative personality in both speech and print, Cannon continuously had to answer charges of anti-Catholicism.

Not long after the defeat of Al Smith, Cannon came under relentless attack from the Hearst press and other enemies he had accumulated over the years. The charges against him included wartime hoarding, stock market gambling, misappropriation of campaign funds, and adultery. Much of the early 1930s he spent in seemingly endless legal battles and investigations. On one occasion he shocked the nation by walking out of a congressional hearing. Although he was never found guilty of any wrongdoing by either court or church tribunal, his image suffered irre-parable damage. He spent the remainder of his life after 1938 in retirement but never relinquished his passion for prohibition.

Perhaps no one in public life exemplified southern mores in the 1920s better than did Cannon. The fall of national prohibition in 1933 was a watershed for the type of leadership he provided. No southern minister would be as influential until Martin Luther King Jr. emerged as a civil rights leader in the mid-1950s.

WILLIAM ELLIS
Eastern Kentucky University

Virginius Dabney, *Dry Messiah: The Life of Bishop Cannon* (1949); Robert A. Hohner, *Prohibition and Politics: The Life of Bishop James Cannon Jr.* (1999); Richard L. Watson Jr., ed., *Bishop Cannon's Own Story: Life As I Have Seen It* (1955).

Christian Broadcasting Network

The Christian Broadcasting Network (CBN) was founded in 1960 by M. G. (Pat) Robertson and began broadcasting from one-kilowatt station WYAH-TV in Portsmouth, Va., on 1 October 1961. From this modest beginning, CBN grew by the early 1980s to become the largest religious broadcaster and the fourth largest cable network in the United States. In 1984 its programs appeared by syndication on approximately 200 television stations in the United States and on CBN Cable Network transmitted via satellite to more than 4,000 cable systems. The Christian Broadcasting Network owns and operates television stations in three major markets and has 80 radio affiliates.

Satellite delivery systems permit 24-

Pat Robertson, Christian Broadcasting Network founder, 2004 (Christian Broadcasting Network)

hour global transmitting capability, and CBN programs, through World Reach Broadcasts, are seen or heard in approximately 200 nations and produced in 70 languages. A CBN-owned and -operated television station in Lebanon transmits to much of the Middle East.

The flagship program of CBN is the *700 Club*, a 90-minute talk, news, and political commentary show, hosted by Robertson and seen in 95 percent of the television markets in the country. The program took its name from a telethon in 1967 during which participants pleaded for 700 people to pledge $10 a month to meet the network's budget. From this inauspicious start, the total annual budget for CBN operations by the mid-1980s had reached approximately $100 million.

The Christian Broadcasting Network has initiated a number of religious programs. The most successful to date has been *Another Life*, a soap opera with a

Christian outlook. The network conducts a counseling ministry, which is tied to the *700 Club*. In 1983 the network had 79 domestic and 40 international counseling centers, and 2004 the 700 Club Prayer Counseling Center had 150 phone counselors who responded to more than 1.5 million requests per year. These centers also administer a program called "Operation Blessing," which provides material assistance for people in need.

The headquarters of CBN are in Virginia Beach, Va., on a 700-acre site that also includes Regent University, which opened in 1978 with 77 students and focuses on graduate education. Student enrollment grew to 2,600 in 2004. The CBN master plan calls for 14 schools eventually and projects a student body of 6,000.

Born in Lexington, Va., in 1930, Robertson is the son of the late U.S. senator A. Willis Robertson. Pat Robertson earned a degree in law at Yale University (1955) and is an ordained Southern Baptist clergyman (1961). He has used the *700 Club* as a platform for his conservative political, as well as religious, views, was a Republican presidential candidate in 1988, and continues as one of the key leaders of the Christian Right.

JEFFREY K. HADDEN
University of Virginia

Dick Dabney, *Harper's* (August 1980); Alec Forge, *The Empire God Built: Inside Pat Robertson's Media Machine* (1996); Jeffrey K. Hadden and Charles E. Swann, *Prime Time Preachers: The Rising Power of Televangelism* (1981).

Dabbs, James McBride

(1896–1970) MINISTER, WRITER, AND REFORMER.

Dabbs was born in 1896 in Sumter County, S.C. He died there in 1970. In the course of his life he was a teacher, a farmer, a poet and essayist, and a symbol of both the past and future. Educated at the University of South Carolina, Clark University (Massachusetts), and Columbia University, he taught English at the University of South Carolina (1921–24) and Coker College (1925–37). In 1937 he returned to the family home, where he farmed with an intensity unknown to the academics of the time, who extolled the virtues of the agrarian way but remained in the scholarly world.

As a poet, Dabbs was often published, but his mark was made as an essayist. He addressed issues of agrarianism, industrialism, and change in the South. His themes were often similar to those of the Vanderbilt Agrarians, but while he knew the personalities and their work, his relationship to them was not intimate. More significant, his writing began to address religious issues in the 1940s, and he had become by 1950 a dissenting voice in South Carolina. He tended his garden while the postwar world convulsed. Eventually the convulsions reached Sumter County; the black citizens there and across the South began to march. Dabbs's learning and resulting worldview, his religious insights and commitment to the Presbyterian Church, and, most important, his love for the South made him a formidable spokesperson for change. He found his voice in journals such as the *Christian Century* and in organizations like the South Carolina Council on Human Relations and eventually the Southern Regional Council. As president of the Southern Regional Council (1957–63), Dabbs was a spokesperson for the view that the South of the future would be integrated.

In his books he reworked themes addressed in his most widely read book, *The Southern Heritage* (1958). He argued that those standing in the mainstream of southern history were the blacks demanding recognition and a place in the body politic. His influence was subtle and far reaching. He spoke to a generation of young southerners who felt caught between their love of the region and the reality of the postcolonial world. As historian-folklorist Charles Joyner noted, "He was not so much a liberalizing force, but he was a means of reconciling the alienation from the South which I then felt as a result of my hostility to racism. Earlier I had drawn a circle leaving the black folks out, later replacing it with a circle replacing the blacks with the red-necks. Dabbs opened the circle." Representing as he did the revered influences of the region, the church, the university, and the land, Dabbs prepared the way for an era of reconciliation. His other books included *The Road Home* (1960), *Who Speaks for the South?* (1964), *Civil Rights in Recent Southern Fiction* (1969), and *Haunted by God* (1972).

ROBERT M. RANDOLPH
Massachusetts Institute of Technology

John Egerton, *New South* (Winter 1969); Richard H. King, in *Perspectives on the*

American South, vol. 2, ed. Merle Black and John Shelton Reed (1984); Robert M. Randolph, in *From the Old South to the New: Essays on the Transitional South*, ed. Walter J. Fraser Jr. and Winifred B. Moore Jr. (1981).

England, John

(1786–1842)

ROMAN CATHOLIC BISHOP.

Born in Cork, Ireland, John England won fame there as a preacher, writer, editor, and political agitator against the proposal to allow the British king a veto in the selection of Catholic bishops. When he came to the United States in 1820, he found in his diocese 5,000 Catholics scattered over 140,000 square miles. Most were Irish immigrants or refugees from revolution in Santo Domingo. He had responsibility for Catholics in Georgia and the Carolinas from 1820 to 1842.

England was an active bishop, establishing congregations headed by catechists in the three southern states, where priests visited periodically to say mass. Religious education was his major concern. He wrote a catechism and translated the Roman missal into English for lay use. In 1822 he founded the first Catholic newspaper in the United States, the *United States Catholic Miscellany*, and in 1825 opened the first Roman Catholic seminary in the South. By 1842, 20 priests had been ordained. England founded an orphanage and organized two communities of teaching sisters for the education of whites and free blacks and for the religious instruction of slaves. His effort to establish a school for blacks was blocked. In 1833 he became the first American to serve in the papal diplomatic corps as apostolic delegate to Haiti.

On the national church scene, England was instrumental in persuading Catholic bishops to meet in the series of national councils that began at Baltimore in 1829. A similar collegial sense of the need for shared responsibility in church affairs led him to frame a diocesan constitution and to organize in each parish a lay vestry to share in management of temporal affairs. Organizations representing clergy and laity met in each state and in a general convention of the diocese. In shaping diocesan government England paid explicit attention to the polity of other Christian churches and to the democratic atmosphere of the country, which he tried to integrate with traditional Roman Catholic structures. He opposed John C. Calhoun's nullification doctrine—an extreme version of states' rights—but had an ambivalent approach to slavery. He was "not friendly to the existence or continuation of slavery" but was hostile to abolitionists and in an 1840 exchange with Secretary of State John Forsyth stated that Pope Gregory XVI's condemnation of the slave trade the previous year did not apply to American domestic slavery. In American Roman Catholic annals, John England stands as one of the two or three greatest bishops.

JAMES HENNESEY
Boston College

Peter Guilday, *The Life and Times of John England, First Bishop of Charleston, 1786–1842*, 2 vols. (1927, 1969); Sebastian G.

Messmer et al., eds., *The Works of the Right Reverend John England*, 7 vols. (1908); Ignatius A. Reynolds, ed., *The Works of the Right Reverend John England, First Bishop of Charleston*, 5 vols. (1849, 1978).

Falwell, Jerry

(b. 1933) MINISTER.

Born on 11 August 1933 in Lynchburg, Va., Jerry Falwell is the son of a successful businessman and a pious Baptist mother. Falwell did not regularly attend church as a youth, but on Sunday mornings his mother turned on a radio broadcast called the *Old Fashioned Revival Hour*, a pioneering religious broadcast from southern California. His born-again conversion occurred at a Lynchburg Baptist church on 20 January 1952. Two months later, after intensive study of the Bible, he decided to become a minister. Falwell entered Lynchburg College in 1950 as an engineering student, but after his conversion experience he transferred to the Baptist Bible College in Springfield, Mo., earning a Th.G. degree in 1956. He returned to Lynchburg that year and founded the Thomas Road Baptist Church. His ministry soon included a daily radio program, and in late 1956 he launched the *Old-Time Gospel Hour*, a weekly television broadcast of the Sunday morning worship services at his Lynchburg church that is still on the air.

In 1971 Falwell began Lynchburg Baptist College, now called Liberty University, and a new campus was built in 1977. During the American Bicentennial of 1976, Falwell staged a series of "I Love America" rallies throughout the nation, after which he became increas-

Jerry Falwell, founder of Moral Majority, 1980s (Thomas Road Baptist Church, Lynchburg, Va.)

ingly involved in conservative politics. He held "Clean Up America" campaigns in 1978 and 1979 and in the latter year founded the Moral Majority, a group that advocated a political agenda focusing on such issues as prayer in school, abortion, homosexuality, and pornography. His 1980 book *Listen, America!* urged that "a coalition of God-fearing moral Americans" reform society. Moral Majority was credited with helping to defeat several liberal senators and to elect Ronald Reagan in the election of 1980. Falwell called that November election "my finest hour," and since 1980 he has been an influential spokesperson in New Right politics.

Falwell is the epitome of a middle-class, business-oriented fundamentalist minister in the contemporary South. Dressed in his three-piece suit, Falwell substitutes upbeat lectures for the traditional fire-and-brimstone sermons, even when talking about the coming judgment of the Lord. Like other "tele-vangelists," though, Falwell has been accused of financial mismanagement. In 1973 the Securities and Exchange Commission, for example, filed charges against his church for "fraud and de-ceit" and "gross insolvency," but a fed-eral judge later dismissed the charges. Due to the increasing competition of other electronic churches in the 1980s the average viewing audience for his television broadcast declined from 889,000 households in 1977 to 438,000 in November 1986. "Gospel Hour" con-tributions fell from $52.6 million in 1983 to $44.3 million in 1986. In early 1987 Falwell replaced Jim Bakker as director of the PTL television network follow-ing Bakker's admission of a sexual indiscretion. Falwell's control of the PTL network's vast broadcast facili-ties greatly increased his influence and public visibility.

Moral Majority disbanded in 1989, unable to advance its agenda into law and facing increasing financial diffi-culties. Since then Falwell has devoted attention to the Thomas Road Baptist Church, Liberty University, and his television ministry.

CHARLES REAGAN WILSON
University of Mississippi

Frances FitzGerald, *Cities on a Hill: Jour-neys through Contemporary American Cultures* (1986); Julie B. Hairston, *Southline* (6 May 1987); Susan F. Harding, *The Book of Jerry Falwell: Fundamentalist Language and Politics* (2000); Charles Moritz, ed., *Current Biography* (1981); Jerry Strober and Ruth Tomczak, *Jerry Falwell: Aflame for God* (1979).

Fatalism

There is an outlook distinctive to the South in which history is viewed as having a predestined outcome. This dark outlook has shaped southern so-cial institutions, literature, and politics, and it has inhibited social reform. In such a view, time and history are not the arena of grand visions and idealistic reconstruction à la Thoreau and Emer-son. Rather, as Faulkner had Quentin Compson's grandfather say while giving him his pocket watch in *The Sound and the Fury*, time is "the mausoleum of all hope and desire." The battles with time "are not even fought. The field only reveals to man his own folly and despair, and victory is an illusion of philosophers and fools."

Fatalism is manifest in the Stoic romanticism that W. J. Cash saw rooted in the "neo-Catholicism" and "neo-medievalism" of both William Alexan-der Percy and the Vanderbilt Agrari-ans. It is evident in Faulkner's sense of doom as the sins of the fathers are visited on the third and fourth genera-tions in *Absalom, Absalom!* It is present in the Calvinistic ordaining of blacks, women, and laborers to their place in the social order (W. J. Cash said the God of the southern mind was "a Calvinist Jehovah"). It is a part of the populist rage, down to George Wallace, that sees the courts and the national media consign the South to a loser status. Journalist Gerald W. Johnson saw a positive side to this outlook in the "sober realism" of southern poli-tics; indeed, Senators Sam Ervin and J. W. Fulbright were good examples of this impulse to resist grand schemes of political salvation.

Stoic fatalism was very much a part of Robert E. Lee's consciousness—as it was for William Alexander Percy. It accented resignation before the forces of fate and death, rather than a struggle with guilt and social responsibility. Percy's melancholy Stoicism led him to write his "Sideshow Gotterdammerung" in 1941 (*Lanterns on the Levee*): "A tarnish has fallen over the bright world . . . my own strong people are turned lotus-eaters: defeat is here again, the last, the most abhorrent."

The Stoic notion of "harmony" was often invoked during the civil rights struggle as a counter to the call for "justice." A deep and continuing conflict abides in the soul of the South between Stoic resignation to fate and death and Christian reconciliation to sin and guilt. The struggle is seen in the fiction of Walker Percy and Flannery O'Connor and is at its height in Faulkner's *Absalom, Absalom!*, where Sutpen plays out his tragic role while "behind him Fate, destiny, retribution, irony—the stage manager—was already striking the set." Faulkner portrays the failure of the Stoic tradition in Sutpen. For Faulkner, the human problem is seen as guilt, and when things go wrong, the responsibility is humankind's.

In addition to the Stoic and Calvinist contributions to the sense of fatalism in the South, there is the compounding imprint of history. The Great Defeat, restrictive freight rates, punitive federal legislation, the caricatures portrayed through the media—all hung over the South like "a promissory note" in which all southerners had to pay for their past and "fate or luck or chance, can foreclose on you without warning" (Faulkner, *Requiem for a Nun*).

The primary forces working in southern history to counter this sense of fatalism have been Christian affirmations of reconciling hope, liberal idealism that argued history could be bent in more humane and realizable directions, and, more recently, the forces of technological development and capital formation, which suggest the Sunbelt may be the land of fateful promise, rather than defeat and guilt.

ROBERT L. JOHNSON
Cornell University

William Faulkner, *Absalom, Absalom!* (1936); John W. Hunt, *William Faulkner: Art in Theological Tension* (1965); William Alexander Percy, *Lanterns on the Levee* (1941).

Graham, Billy

(b. 1918) EVANGELIST.

Born 7 November 1918 near Charlotte, N.C., William Franklin Graham Jr. was the firstborn of a fundamentalist Presbyterian couple. His rise to national fame as an evangelist came during the prime of McCarthyism and the early fear of atomic warfare. Graham exploited these two sensations by proclaiming a brand of Christian Americanism that promised to give the United States victory over both internal subversion and external Soviet threat. He perceived the United States as the chosen nation after the order of ancient Israel, with himself as Jehovah's

Billy Graham, the modern South's best-known evangelist, 1980s (Billy Graham Evangelistic Association, Minneapolis, Minn.)

and organizational sophistication in transforming the Billy Graham Evangelistic Association into an efficient corporation for exporting southern fundamentalism. Paradoxically, long-range, this-worldly planning for this soul-winning corporation was mingled with the typically southern preoccupation with the apocalypse macabre. His 1983 book *Approaching Hoofbeats: The Four Horsemen of the Apocalypse* represents a throwback to southern revivalism's characteristic preoccupation with "prophecy," including sensational, if not obscene, scenarios of the fate of those outside the circle of the saved. Throughout his ministry Graham struggled to balance his lurid and explicit premillennial apocalyptic vision with his implicit postmillennial drive to transform the United States into a latter-day Christocracy.

In the early 1950s Graham and his fellow southerners in the organization were faced with a consistency crisis. Could they preach to integrated audiences north of the Mason-Dixon line and to segregated audiences in the South and Southwest? In 1953, a year before the U.S. Supreme Court struck its monumental blow against segregation, in *Brown v. the Board of Education*, Graham had elected to preach only to integrated audiences in the South, beginning with the crusade to Chattanooga, a city made infamous by an earlier race riot. Graham chose, however, to make a weak witness against segregation, which he regarded as much less wicked than either sexual lust or failure to regard Jesus as the Messiah.

The seeds of the New Religious

prophet to help save America from spiritual, military, and economic ruin. His favorite Old Testament personality was Daniel, a prophet involved with politicians and politics. Graham befriended presidents and saw himself as their spiritual adviser. He encouraged both Eisenhower and Nixon to run for office, and during the Nixon and Kennedy presidential campaign of 1960, he wrote a magazine article portraying Nixon as a Christian, moral leader. At the last minute, Graham withdrew the article from publication.

The Billy Graham Evangelistic Association represents one of the earliest phases of entrepreneurial religion of the modern South. Despite his rural, small-town upbringing, Graham quickly utilized the most advanced technology

Right of the 1980s are found in Graham's early preaching. He denounced the Supreme Court for removing God from the public schools and called for an American "Christocracy." To date, no other Christian in the world has preached to more people than has Billy Graham. His 1982 trip to preach in the Soviet Union drew considerable fire and misinterpretation from both civil libertarians and fundamentalists. Captured by the vision of proclaiming his evangelical gospel inside the Soviet Union (where communism was the official religion), Graham took the risk of criticism, knowing in advance that he would be falsely accused of becoming a tool of Soviet propaganda regarding religious liberty there. In the early 1980s Graham modified his premillennial apocalyptic views sufficiently to entertain plans of nuclear disarmament. Since the 1990s, Graham has continued large-scale evangelistic crusades, including trips to Russia and China. He has been plagued by ill health, though, and his son Franklin has emerged as a prominent evangelist who is continuing Billy Graham's legacy into the future. One of Billy Graham's most dramatic appearances was at the service in the National Cathedral in Washington, D.C., on the National Day of Prayer and Remembrance after the 11 September 2001 terrorist attack.

JOE E. BARNHART
North Texas State University

Joe E. Barnhart, *The Billy Graham Religion* (1972); Marshal Frady, *Billy Graham: A Parable of American Righteousness* (1979); Billy Graham, *Just As I Am: The Autobiography of Billy Graham* (1997); John C. Pollock, *Billy Graham: The Authorized Biography* (1966).

Great Revival

This series of religious revivals that swept across the southern states between 1800 and 1805 is sometimes called the Second Great Awakening in the South. The movement was more accurately the South's first great awakening. It changed the religious landscape of the region, ensuring a Protestant evangelical dominance that continues today.

Small outbreaks of intense religious activity had occurred previously in the South, but these earlier small revivals had been confined to specific locales and to one denomination. Examples of these were the Presbyterian revival centered in Hanover County, Va., in the 1740s, the Separate Baptist revival beginning in North Carolina in 1755 and soon spreading to Virginia, and the Methodist awakening beginning in Virginia and North Carolina in the 1760s. These smaller awakenings slowly built up a popular evangelical belief system and a network of churches and ministers. Although these are prerequisites for a larger revival, a sense of cultural-religious crisis was required to weld the separate denominations together into common concern and action.

Westward migration in the late 1780s and 1790s, political controversies, and the worrisome news about the radical, deistic tendencies of the French Revolution contributed to a widespread perception of religious crisis in the 1790s. As clerics tried to understand their dilemma, they began to believe that it was a punishment sent by God for their preoccupation with worldly affairs. Recognition of this cause and a willingness to ask God for "deliverance" would, it was argued, end the religious "declension." Through such a religious defense the depressed clergy of the 1790s found reason to expect a miraculous recovery of religious vitality. This sense of expectancy led them to interpret an intensely emotional religious service led by James McGready in Logan County, Ky., in June 1800 as visible evidence that God was ushering in a new season of religious vitality, a second Pentecost. This feeling of heady optimism quickly spread across the South, facilitated by the adoption of camp meetings — huge, outdoor revivals.

In area after area church membership increased markedly, new churches were established, and many young male converts decided to enter the ministry as thousands of laypeople either joined churches for the first time or revived their dormant faith. The resulting religious energy greatly strengthened the popular denominations (especially the Baptists and Methodists) and led to almost a complete dominance in the South by 1830 of evangelical Protestantism, a dominance that included blacks as well as whites.

JOHN B. BOLES
Rice University

John B. Boles, *The Great Revival, 1787–1805: The Origins of the Southern Evangelical Mind* (1972), in *Religion in the South*, ed. Charles Reagan Wilson (1985); Dickson D. Bruce Jr., *And They All Sang Hallelujah: Plain-Folk Camp-Meeting Religion, 1800–1845* (1974).

Hays, Brooks

(1898–1981) POLITICIAN AND
RELIGIOUS LEADER.
Brooks Hays personified, during his more than 50 years in public service, the Christian layperson in politics. Born 9 August 1898 near Russellville, Ark., to Sallie Butler and Steele Hays, he graduated from the University of Arkansas (B.A., 1919) and George Washington University (LL.D., 1922). After serving in World War I, he married in 1922, the year he was admitted to the bar.

Hays was an assistant attorney general of Arkansas and twice an unsuccessful reform candidate for governor of that state and once for Congress before he went to Washington as an attorney for the U.S. Department of Agriculture in 1935. A prominent member of the Southern Baptist Convention, he became an influential religious leader during his years as a member of Congress from Arkansas (1943–59). Washington, D.C., ministers chose him as their Layman of the Year in 1951, and he was later named Churchman of the Year by the Religious Heritage Foundation. He served on the Southern Baptist Christian Life Commission for 15 years and was its chairman in 1957 and 1958. He was president of the Southern Baptist Convention from 1957 through 1959.

His long-standing and widely publicized support of civil rights for southern blacks involved him in his congressional district's 1957 controversy over the integration of Little Rock Central High School. Attempting to moderate the passions on all sides, he was the victim of what was most likely an illegal write-in vote that stripped him of his seat in Congress at the height of the passionate battle in 1958.

The following year, as his prestige grew through what was considered a "political martyrdom," Hays became a director of the Tennessee Valley Authority. With the return of Democrats to the White House in 1961, he became special assistant to President Kennedy and then to President Johnson for "congressional relations, international relations, federal-state relations, and church-state relations." In this capacity he carried his appeal for Christian brotherhood throughout the nation and around the world from 1961 to 1964.

Between 1964 and 1974 Hays taught government at Rutgers University and the University of Massachusetts, ran unsuccessfully for governor of Arkansas, directed the first Baptist Ecumenical Institute at North Carolina's Wake Forest University, and ran unsuccessfully for Congress from North Carolina. He died at his home in Chevy Chase, Md., 12 October 1981.

> JAMES T. BAKER
> *Western Kentucky University*

James Baker, *Brooks Hays* (1989); Brooks Hays, *A Hotbed of Tranquility* (1968), *Politics Is My Parish* (1981), *A Southern Moderate Speaks* (1959), *This World: A Christian's Workshop* (1958).

King, Martin Luther, Jr.

(1929–1968) MINISTER, THEOLOGIAN, SOCIAL ACTIVIST.

Martin Luther King Jr. was a clergyman, intellectual, and civil leader with deep roots in southern black Baptist Protestantism. The son, grandson, and great-

Church fan depicting civil rights leader Martin Luther King Jr. (Charles Reagan Wilson Collection, Center for the Study of Southern Culture, University of Mississippi)

grandson of Baptist preachers, he was born in Atlanta, Ga., on 15 January 1929 and was exposed throughout his youth to the restrictions of Jim Crow. While a student at Atlanta's Morehouse College (B.A., 1948), he fell under the influence of black preacher-intellectuals such as Benjamin E. Mays and George D. Kelsey, and he himself chose a career in ministry. He then studied liberal Christian ethics at Crozer Theological Seminary (B.D., 1951) in Chester, Penn., and later completed graduate work in philosophical theology at Boston University (Ph.D., 1955).

In 1954 King was called to the pastorate of the Dexter Avenue Baptist Church in Montgomery, Ala. A year later he was catapulted to national and international fame as the president of the Montgomery Improvement Association (MIA) and the leader of the Montgomery bus boycott (1955–56). During this first effort at social protest King developed his philosophy and method of nonviolent direct action to achieve social change. In 1957 he assumed the lead in expanding the MIA into a Southwide organization known as the Southern Christian Leadership Conference (SCLC). For the next 11 years, he epitomized the African American freedom struggle in the South as he brought to his leadership role spiritual and ethical values that were heavily grounded in his extended family and black church background. Combining social analysis with biblical piety and theological liberalism, King employed creative nonviolence and civil disobedience as he and his followers challenged the structures of racial and economic injustice in Albany, Birmingham, Selma, St. Augustine, Memphis, and other southern cities. His vision during these campaigns centered largely around the achievement of what he termed "the New South."

A pivotal point in King's career came during the celebrated March on Washington on 28 August 1963, when he delivered his "I Have a Dream" speech and dramatized the civil rights cause before the nation. In 1964 he received the Nobel Peace Prize, an achievement that led him to increasingly address the interrelated issues of racial oppression, class exploitation, and wars of aggression in an international context. After the passage of the landmark Civil Rights Act of 1964 and the Voting Rights Act of 1965, King turned his attention to the North as he and his SCLC staff challenged unsuccessfully the slum conditions in Chicago. He also spoke with mounting intensity against the United States' involvement in the war in Vietnam, an issue brilliantly raised in his "A Time to Break Silence," an address given at Riverside Church in New York City on 4 April 1967.

King's tendency to relate the problem of poverty in the United States to what he called the nation's "misguided adventure in Vietnam" exposed him to criticism from both supporters and opponents, and financial contributions to his SCLC sharply declined. Even so, he never wavered in his conviction that the civil rights movement in the American South was inseparable from the anticolonial crusades in Africa, Asia, and other parts of the Third World. The interplay between South, nation, and world was captured most poignantly in King's ideal of "the world house," by which he meant a completely integrated society and world based on the *agape* love principle.

In 1967 and early 1968 King became increasingly unpopular as he combined his antiwar proclamations with a trenchant critique of capitalism and calls for a radical redistribution of economic power. Despite the scrutiny of the FBI, which was concerned about him and his associates, King devoted his final days to the planning of the Poor People's Campaign, which has been labeled his "last crusade." He was assassinated on 4 April 1968 while participating in the Memphis Sanitation Strike in Tennessee.

Worldwide recognition of King has increased significantly since his death. His birthday is celebrated in some 100 countries. Monuments to his memory exist throughout the United States, and perhaps the greatest tribute to him occurred on 19 October 1983, when the U.S. Senate voted overwhelmingly to designate the third Monday in January a federal holiday in his honor. King's incorporation into southern public symbolism is most evident in the existence of the Martin Luther King Jr. Center for Nonviolent Social Change Inc. in Atlanta and in the recent erection of a National Civil Rights Museum on the site where King was murdered in Memphis.

LEWIS V. BALDWIN
Vanderbilt University

Lewis V. Baldwin, *There Is a Balm in Gilead: The Cultural Roots of Martin Luther King Jr.* (1991), *To Make the Wounded Whole: The Cultural Legacy of Martin Luther King Jr.* (1992); Vincent Harding, *Martin Luther King: The Inconvenient Hero* (1996); Martin Luther King Jr., *Where Do We Go from Here: Chaos or Community?* (1968); Gerald D. McKnight, *The Last Crusade: Martin Luther King, Jr., the FBI, and the Poor People's Campaign* (1998); James M. Washington, ed., *A Testament of Hope: The Essential Writings and Speeches of Martin Luther King Jr.* (1986).

Merton, Thomas

(1915–1968) RELIGIOUS FIGURE
AND WRITER.

Thomas Merton was born in Prades, France, the son of Owen Merton, a New Zealand painter, and Ruth Jenkins Merton, an American artist. Merton settled in the United States in 1935 to study at Columbia University after a tumultuous youth on the Continent and in England, where he studied after the death of his parents. Converted to the Catholic Church while at Columbia, he entered the Cistercian (Trappist) monastery of Our Lady of Gethsemani near Bardstown, Ky., in 1941. His spiritual autobiography, *The Seven Storey Mountain* (1948), was an immense success. He followed that work with a torrent of books, essays, reviews, and poems on a range of subjects that ran from monastic history and spirituality to social commentary and literary criticism. He died an accidental death on 10 December 1968 in Bangkok, Thailand, while attending a monastic conference. His best-known books include *New Seeds of Contemplation* (1949; rev. 1961), *The Sign of Jonas* (1952), and *Conjectures of a Guilty Bystander* (1966), as well as the posthumous *Zen and the Birds of Appetite* and *Collected Poems* (1977) and *The Literary Essays of Thomas Merton* (1981). Five volumes of his letters and seven of his journals have also been posthumously published.

Merton rarely left his Kentucky monastery, but his connections with the South are not merely geographic. He was a contributor to the *Sewanee Review* and in the final year of his life edited a small literary journal, *Monk's Pond*. He published studies of the fiction of William Faulkner, Flannery O'Connor, and other southern writers. From his student days he showed a keen interest in questions of racism and social justice. Given his longtime admiration for Gandhi, it is not surprising that he was an admirer of the nonviolent work of Martin Luther King Jr. Influenced partly by his reading of James Baldwin and John Howard Griffin, he championed civil rights to a sometimes skeptical and reluctant church public. His interest in social justice led him to be a natural ally of southern church people of a similar mind. He was a contributor to *Katallagete* and through his association with Will Campbell came to know the work of Walker Percy.

Merton lived his life in the solitude of a monastery in Kentucky's knob country, but his immense intelligence and compassion led him to both love and criticize his fellow southerners from the singular angle of the contemplative monk.

LAWRENCE S. CUNNINGHAM
The University of Notre Dame

Lawrence S. Cunningham, *Thomas Merton and the Monastic Vision* (1999); Patrick Hart and Jonathan Montaldo, eds., *The Intimate Merton* (1999); Michael Mott, *The Seven Mountains of Thomas Merton* (1984); William H. Shannon et al., eds., *The Thomas Merton Encyclopedia* (2002).

Methodist Episcopal Church, South

Methodists first entered the South in the 1760s, and by the 1780s most American Methodists were concentrated there. The movement grew dramatically after the revivals of the early 1800s. The Methodist Episcopal Church, South, existed from 1845 until 1939, with most of its membership in the southern states, but with a few churches in the border states and in the West. The precipitating cause of its formation was the slave ownership of one of the bishops of the Methodist Episcopal Church, James O. Andrews, an involvement that led to the division of the church into predominantly northern and southern parts. The church enthusiastically supported the Confederacy, providing chaplains and missionaries and distributing Bibles and religious literature. Methodist leaders such as Atticus G. Haygood later became advocates of a New South.

The Methodist Episcopal Church, South, whose membership was almost three million in 1939, reflected a distinctive kind of Methodism. It emphasized the Bible and religious experience more than its northern counterpart did. Both branches of Methodism were led by bishops; but, following the southern paternalistic tradition, southern Methodists gave their bishops virtually unlimited power, so that the 58 men who filled the episcopal chairs dominated the life of the southern church, appointing the preachers, presiding over various conferences, and serving as leaders of most of the important boards and agencies.

Southern Methodists limited the mission of the church to the saving of souls, steering clear of most social issues. Bishop James Cannon Jr., however, led many Methodists in support of prohibition. Entering vigorously into missionary work in Africa, Latin America, and the Far East, southern Methodists confined their work in these areas, as at home, to evangelism, education, and medical care. A notable exception to this understanding of the

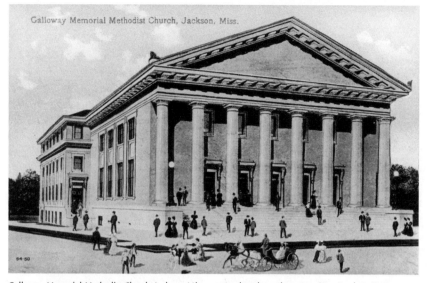

Galloway Memorial Methodist Church, Jackson, Miss., postcard, early 20th century (Ann Rayburn Paper Americana Collection, Archives and Special Collections, University of Mississippi Library, Oxford)

mission of the church was the women's home and foreign missionary movement, which, catching a vision of a social gospel, worked to improve the lot of blacks, immigrants, and women and sought to secure world peace.

In many ways, the southern church lagged behind the northern branch of Methodism, not establishing a theological seminary until the 1870s, more than 30 years after northern Methodists had taken the same step, and not admitting women to the General Conference until the 1920s, 20 years after this had been done in the North. Southern Methodists were busy, like northern Methodists, maintaining schools, colleges, and universities, but the southern institutions often lacked both support and academic distinction and generally served as bastions of the white southern way of life. The church established Vanderbilt University in 1873 but

withdrew support in 1914. Southern Methodist, Emory, and Duke became prominent Methodist universities.

Having begun its existence with a large number of black members, the Methodist Episcopal Church, South, after the Civil War, pushed most of these free blacks into their own ecclesiastical organization and became an institution devoted primarily to the welfare of white southerners.

Thus, the Methodist Episcopal Church, South, represented an almost perfect example of Richard Niebuhr's "Christ of Culture" Christianity — usually not just following its proclaimed Lord, Jesus Christ, but taking its values from the white South that had helped create it and that it in turn sustained.

F. JOSEPH MITCHELL
Troy State University

John Patrick McDowell, *The Social Gospel in the South: The Woman's Home Mission Movement in the Methodist Episcopal Church, South, 1886–1939* (1982); Frederick A. Norwood, *The Story of American Methodism: A History of the United Methodists and Their Relations* (1974).

Moon, Charlotte Digges "Lottie"

(1840–1912) SOUTHERN BAPTIST MISSIONARY.

For four decades Lottie Moon was a pioneer China missionary of the Southern Baptist Convention (SBC). Her life is skillfully celebrated by denominational literature, which has described her as the most famous individual in Southern Baptist history, as well as the human symbol of her church's ongoing commitment to overseas missionary work.

Charlotte Digges "Lottie" Moon, Southern Baptist missionary, 1840–1912 (© International Mission Board)

Growing up on a plantation near Charlottesville, Va., Lottie Moon developed marked interests in religion and in the study of foreign languages and cultures. Following the Civil War she taught school in Kentucky and Georgia until 1873, when deepening spiritual concerns led her to enter missionary service. From that point until her death 40 years later Moon worked as an evangelist and teacher at Tengchow (known today as Penglai) and at other Southern Baptist stations in Shandong Province, northeastern China. In addition to demonstrating compassion for the Chinese and skill in adapting to their culture, she displayed considerable courage and professional resourcefulness. All these qualities were particularly evident in her life during the late 1880s at Pingdu, an isolated city in the Shandong interior. Working alone under difficult circumstances, Moon initiated at Pingdu a successful mission at a time when Baptist efforts in northern China were otherwise near collapse.

Moon's unique reputation among Southern Baptists, however, is a product of the Lottie Moon Christmas Offering for Foreign Missions. Inspired by an 1888 effort to raise money in the United States to help her work at Pingdu, the Christmas Offering became a churchwide institution and in 1918 was named specifically for her. An extensive promotional literature developed, which over the years has idealized Moon in books, poems, pamphlets, motion pictures and film strips, portraits, photo albums, tape cassettes, dramatic scripts and impersonations, greeting cards, Web site features, and even a Lottie Moon cookbook. The Christmas Offering, with annual collections now well over $100 million, has long provided more than 40 percent of the annual funding of the SBC's Foreign Mission Board (redesignated the International Mission Board [IMB] in 1995) and is indispensable to American Protestantism's largest foreign missionary program.

Any explanation of Lottie Moon's status among Southern Baptists is inevitably subjective and arguable. Her story as historically promoted by the SBC, however, contains at least two themes interesting in terms of southern culture. One is a traditional theme that W. J. Cash called southern gyneolatry or the "pitiful Mother of God" image, centering on white women of intelligence, courage, and high capacity for self-sacrifice. The other theme, also strongly present, is of Lottie Moon as an undeclared feminist — single, self-reliant, wiser and stronger than male associates, pushing in "her own way" (the title of one of her SBC biographies) to advance the Kingdom of God and the status of women both in China and within the Southern Baptist Convention. Rather than being mutually exclusive, these contrasting themes seem instead to have extended Lottie Moon's range and enduring influence.

Within the SBC Lottie Moon has always been linked particularly to the Woman's Missionary Union (WMU), the denomination's most important organization for women and for broad support of mission work. New scholarship by Regina D. Sullivan details how in the 19th century Lottie Moon's story tied into the birth of the WMU as a women's movement within the male-dominated SBC and how, a century later in the 1990s, control of Moon's image became part of a new struggle between SBC moderates, represented by the WMU, and a conservative denominational leadership represented by the IMB. Reshaped to fit changing needs and times, the Lottie Moon story is shown by Sullivan to be "endlessly malleable" and a *lieu de memoire*, or memory site, where Southern Baptists continue to define their identity and future.

IRWIN T. HYATT JR.
Emory University

Catherine B. Allen, *The New Lottie Moon Story* (2nd ed., 1997); Irwin T. Hyatt Jr., *Our Ordered Lives Confess: Three Nineteenth-Century American Missionaries in East Shantung* (1976); Una Roberts Lawrence, *Lottie Moon* (1927); Regina D. Sullivan, "Woman with a Mission: Remembering Lottie Moon and the Woman's Missionary Union" (Ph.D. dissertation, University of North Carolina, 2002).

Moral Majority

The Moral Majority was an educational, lobbying, and fund-raising organization dedicated to conservative Christian causes. Founded in 1979 with the assistance of "New Right" leaders, the Moral Majority was led by Jerry Falwell, pastor of the 18,000-member Thomas Road Baptist Church in Lynchburg, Va.

Nationally, Moral Majority maintained a legislative office near the Capitol in Washington, D.C., monitored legislation, issued regular appeals to its members for political action through letter writing, lobbied Congress on behalf of specific legislation, and published the *Moral Majority Report*, a small monthly newspaper. Legally, Moral Majority was composed of three separate organizations: Moral Majority, a lobby; the Moral Majority Foundation, an educational foundation; and the Moral Majority Legal Defense Foundation, an organization that offered legal assistance and funds to various conservative religious groups such as Christian schools that regularly did battle with secular authorities.

Moral Majority operated a "Political Action Committee" during the 1980 national campaign but abandoned it after spending only $20,000. The national organization was loosely replicated at state and local levels by Moral Majority chapters variously centered in election districts, counties, or major population centers. Lobbying, publication of voting records and newsletters, and organized action were also undertaken at the local level. The national Moral Majority was active in establishing local chapters and in training their leaders, often by sponsoring regional training programs in conjunction with the Committee for the Survival of a Free Congress. Voter registration, involving participation of local churches, was also a major concern at all levels.

Although the basic source of support for Moral Majority was independent fundamentalist churches, often Baptist, the organization saw its agenda as moral, not religious. It welcomed and cooperated with all who shared its views regardless of their religious orientation. Moral Majority sought to "return the nation to moral sanity," to revitalize those values "which made America great." It opposed abortion, homosexuality, pornography, the exclusive teaching of evolution, feminism, the welfare state, and secularism in general. Issues supported included prayer in public schools, state support for private (particularly religious) education, recognition of parents' and churches' rights to educate children without outside interference, a strong national defense coupled with an aggressively anti-Communist foreign policy, and a laissez-faire capitalism at home that subordinated itself to the national interest abroad.

Geographically, Moral Majority drew its major support from the South and Midwest and its most effective leadership from the South. It represents a "going public" and an attainment of national influence on the part of southern religion. Moral Majority's political activism constituted a significant revision of the traditionally separatist and nonworldly tendencies of its supporting churches, but not necessarily a reversal or a sharp break. Moral Majority perpetuated a southern Protestant tradition of selective social activism on a narrow range of issues centered on personal morality. In so doing, it reflected fundamentalism's Holiness roots and the conviction that social well-being is born of individual purity. The call for national repentance as a cure for impending disaster (God's rejection of America) coupled with its Manichaean sense of rigid good and evil in all matters, religious, social, or political, reflected a tradition of revivalism that moved its converts from total depravity to thorough regeneration.

Moral Majority represented a wedding of fundamentalist religion with a "chosen people" style of civil religion, which represented a major tie between religion and mythology in the region. It was convinced that America's success as a nation depended on its people rendering obedience to God's law as understood in a fundamentalist reading of the Bible. Moral Majority supporters regarded themselves as a saving remnant, calling the nation back to faithfulness, to its covenant with the biblical God who, although once so close to rightfully forsaking America, awaited a sign of repentance that would again allow him to bless that bastion of true religion and return it to its rightful, dominant place in world affairs. Two of Jerry Falwell's books, *How You Can Help Clean Up America* (1978) and *Listen, America!* (1980), give a summary of the Moral Majority's aims and its "action programs for decency" in the nation.

Moral Majority had failed by the late 1980s to gain key legislation to support its agenda, and Falwell dissolved the organization in 1989. After that, Pat Robertson supplemented Falwell as leader of the Christian Right, and the Christian Coalition emerged in the 1990s to advance many of the moral and family values that Moral Majority had championed.

DENNIS E. OWEN
University of Florida

Gabriel Fackre, *The Religious Right and the Christian Faith* (1982); Samuel S. Hill and Dennis E. Owen, *The New Religious Political Right in America* (1982); William Martin, *With God on Our Side: The Rise of Religious Right in America* (1996); Peggy Shriver, *The Bible Vote: Religion and the New Right* (1981).

Moravians

The Moravians are a Protestant religious group, known also as the Unitas Fratrum, that was founded in the 15th century by followers of John Hus, a Bohemian reformer and martyr. The movement spread to America, and today the headquarters of the Southern Province of the Moravian Church in America are located in Winston-Salem, N.C. Although not representative of predominant southern religious evangelicalism, the Moravians have contributed a distinctive history and aesthetic tradition to the South's culture.

To serve as missionaries to the American Indians, as well as to escape German intolerance of their beliefs, a small group of Moravians left Europe and settled in Georgia in 1735. Their settlement was brief, for in 1740, when pressured to fight the Spanish, they moved to Pennsylvania. After the church purchased a 98,985-acre tract of land in the Piedmont of North Carolina, members of the sect again traveled to the South to settle. They called the tract Wachau (Wachovia) and settled the villages of Bethabara (1753) and Bethania (1759) before founding, in 1766, Salem, the town that became the governmental and economic center of the settlement.

The ambitious settlers established in a wilderness a carefully planned, organized community—a theocracy, in which the church was the governing body and their religion a way of life. To ensure the survival of the community and its ideals, the church kept strict control during those early years. Residents did not buy land but leased it from the church, until the lease system was abolished in 1856. Church members were divided according to age, gender, and marital status into choirs, each group having its own officers, living quarters, and burial sites in the congregation cemetery. Trade competition was restricted in favor of a system of monopolies so that each member had opportunity to earn a living.

As a self-sufficient commercial center, Salem, along with the smaller Moravian communities, had skilled craftsmen, trained doctors, fine musicians, and dedicated schoolteachers. The Moravians stressed education, and their female academy at Salem, opened to non-Moravians in 1802, quickly gained prominence and operates today as Salem Academy and College. Moravian aesthetic tastes became well known, too, as Moravian craftsmen often produced distinctive work that dominated their cultural region. Fine pottery, needlework, furniture, paintings, metalwork, and architecture remain as evidence of their talents.

Believing that they should, in all endeavors, serve the Lord, early Moravians worked and lived to that end, and in the process they made significant contributions to the ethnic, material, and religious culture of the South. Their unique music is central to church programs, love feasts, and Easter sunrise services that are celebrated by Moravians and non-Moravians alike. The rigid structure of the early Moravian communities dissolved years ago, but the church remains active and dedicated to its missionary efforts.

JESSICA FOY
Cooperstown Graduate Program
Cooperstown, New York

John Bivins and Paula Welshimer, *Moravian Decorative Arts in North Carolina* (1981); Adelaide Fries, K. G. Hamilton, D. L. Rights, and M. J. Smith, eds., *The Records of the Moravians in North Carolina*, 11 vols. (1922–69); Kenneth G. Hamilton, *North Carolina Historical Review* (April 1967); John F. Sensbach, *A Separate Canaan: The Making of an Afro-Moravian World in North Carolina* (1998); Daniel P. Thorp, *The Moravian Community in Colonial North Carolina: Pluralism on the Southern Frontier* (1989).

National Baptists

The National Baptist Convention, U.S.A., Inc., the unincorporated National Baptist Convention of America, and the Progressive National Baptist Convention have a combined membership of 12 million people in more than 50,000 congregations and together form a historical tradition that has dominated southern black Baptist life since the late 19th century. Black Baptists had worshipped in independent congregations and as part of biracial churches before the Civil War, but emancipation quickly brought the establishment of separate black denominations.

Church fan from Standard Burial Association,
Natchez, Miss., 1960s (Charles Reagan Wilson
Collection, Center for the Study of Southern
Culture, University of Mississippi)

From 1865 to 1895 black Baptists
worked to achieve a separate religious
identity. The Consolidated American
Baptist Missionary Convention tried
unsuccessfully to unify black Baptists,
but it collapsed from internal social
divisions in 1879. Black unity received
a boost in 1895 with the formation in
Atlanta of the National Baptist Convention, U.S.A., Inc. The year 1915 brought
division, however, as a dispute over
control of the National Baptists' publishing house led to the withdrawal
of supporters of Robert H. Boyd, the
corresponding secretary of the publications board, and the establishment
of the unincorporated National Baptist
Convention of America. The Progressive National Baptist Convention, led
by L. Venchael Booth, split off from
the "incorporated" National Baptists in
1961 as the result of a controversy concerning the process of electing church
leaders.

The South has served as institutional center for the National Baptist
churches. The National Baptist Convention, U.S.A., Inc., built a $12 million
World Center in Nashville in the mid-
1990s as its headquarters, and the
denominations maintain publishing
houses in Nashville as well.

Black Baptist churches represent a
vital social, as well as religious, force
in the South. The mainstream has been
dominated by the ideals of, in James M.
Washington's typology, "bourgeois
black Baptists." The middle-class ethos
of the mainstream has been supplemented by "prophetic black Baptists"
who have sought progressive political
change. "Black Baptist folk culture" is
still a third representation of the faith,
stressing the distinctive use of music,
prayers, oral testifying, and African
rhythms in worship.

CHARLES REAGAN WILSON
University of Mississippi

William D. Booth, *The Progressive Story:
New Baptist Roots* (1981); Joseph H. Jack-
son, *A Story of Christian Activism: The
History of the National Baptist Convention,
U.S.A., Inc.* (1980); Owen D. Pelt and Ralph
Lee Smith, *The Story of the National Baptists*
(1960); James M. Washington, *Frustrated
Fellowship: The Black Baptist Quest for
Social Power* (1986).

O'Connor and Religion

Flannery O'Connor's contribution to
the literature of the English-speaking
world is widely known. Equally impor-

tant is her contribution to the knowledge of religion in the South and to contemporary understanding of the Christian faith grounded in southern experience. As a native of Georgia, she knew intimately the dominant Protestant faith of the area and was especially fascinated by the untutored practices and convictions of backwoods religious folk. She often found their religious convictions skewed and desperate and their practice crude; yet she found among them, by her own accounting, a surprising pattern of true Christianity that encompassed the pattern of her own Catholic faith. A Hazel Motes (*Wise Blood*) and a Tarwater (*The Violent Bear It Away*) are eccentric, but through their rough circuitous route they find and claim the Christian God missed by countless reasonable and progressive people.

At an artistic level, O'Connor investigates the concrete, regional scene (a possessed evangelist, a manipulative grandmother, a Bible salesman) in order to touch a deeper, wider reality. The plot of each story therefore climactically focuses on some revealing action or gesture (a blinding of oneself, a reaching out toward one's killer, the theft of an artificial limb) that penetrates the essentials of character and circumstance.

The religious level of her work follows readily on the artistic because of her sensitivity to the region: "While the South is hardly Christ-centered, it is most certainly Christ-haunted," she stated in a 1960 lecture. Yet a theologically discerning southern writer can disclose, through Christ-haunted chaos, moments that are surprisingly Christ-centered. True revelation occurs even amid distortion. The result is pointedly ecumenical: the author's Catholic doctrine comes alive in the actions of backcountry Protestants. Her stories are thereby full of irony and humor, the ultimate comedy of the one true God, who uses outlandish servants in order to reveal himself. As Christian evangel, O'Connor therefore jolts her readers with cultural and Christian reality, sharply distinguished in her work from the conventional and benign Christianity of custom.

WILLIAM MALLARD
Emory University

Robert H. Brinkmeyer Jr., *The Art and Vision of Flannery O'Connor* (1989); David Eggenschwiler, *The Christian Humanism of Flannery O'Connor* (1972); Paul Elie, *The Life You Save Might Be Your Own: An American Pilgrimage* (2003); James A Grimshaw Jr., *The Flannery O'Connor Companion* (1981); Ralph C. Wood, *Flannery O'Connor and the Christ-Haunted South* (2004).

Presbyterian Church in the United States (PCUS)

Initially known as the Presbyterian Church in the Confederate States of America (PCCSA), the denomination originated as a result of the Civil War. It was organized at Augusta, Ga., in 1861 and remained separated from the Presbyterian Church in the United States of America (PCUSA) until 1983, when it reunited with the parent body, which had become the United Presbyterian Church in the United States of America (UPCUSA). The PCUS thus no longer has a separate existence, but it was an institutional embodiment of a distinctly regional religious identity. The PCCSA supported slavery and secession, and it continued to exist as the PCUS after the war because of southern concern about an unbiblical and unnatural involvement in political life by the PCUSA, a concern aggravated by the bitterness of the war and Reconstruction. The PCUS established itself in border states, the Southeast, and Texas.

Theologically, the PCUS affirmed with Protestant Christians the belief that the Bible of the Old and New Testaments is the only "rule of faith and practice," and it endorsed the Trinitarian and Christological decrees of the early Christian councils. In addition, the denomination adopted and its officials subscribed to *The Westminster Confession of Faith* (1646) and the Larger and Shorter Catechisms of the 17th century as subordinate standards to the Scriptures. Nineteenth-century theologians James Henley Thornwell (1812–62) and Robert Lewis Dabney (1820–98) shaped a southern Presbyterian mind. James Woodrow (1828–1907), although disciplined by the denomination, nevertheless helped the South adjust to the evolution hypothesis. Church historian Ernest Trice Thompson (1894–1985) and biblical critic John Bright (1908–1995) led the denomination in facing recent intellectual ferment. Some leaders attempted to modify the theological stand in recent years with the writing of "A Declaration of Faith." This attempt was defeated by the presbyteries of the church, but the "Declara-

tion" was widely used throughout the church.

Presbyterians in the PCUS believed themselves part of the "one holy catholic and apostolic church." Structurally, however, the PCUS was Presbyterian, governed by a representative system with a graded court structure, provisions for the form and discipline of which were found in *The Book of Church Order*. Congregations elected pastors, in cooperation with the presbytery, and also elders and deacons, all ordained in the name of the Trinity by the laying on of hands. Pastors were ordained to the ministry of word and sacrament; elders, to assist in governance; and deacons, to assist in service. Congregations formed presbyteries of pastors and elders, and presbyteries were organized in synods and a General Assembly. At first the PCUS controlled its various programs through committees of the various courts and then in 1949 organized education and publishing, domestic and foreign missions, and the pension system under boards. Pastors Stuart Robinson (1814–81), Benjamin M. Palmer (1818–1902), and Moses Drury Hoge (1818–99) and laymen Woodrow Wilson (1856–1924), John J. Eagan (1870–1924), and Francis Pickens Miller (1895–1978) gave unusual leadership to the church. After 1963 women were ordained to all the offices of the church. Rachel Henderlite (b. 1905) was the first woman ordained.

Liturgically, members of the PCUS used *The Directory of Worship* of the Westminster Assembly, modified through the centuries, which provided a guide for the public and family worship of God. They were suspicious of fixed forms, a suspicion reinforced by the revivalist spirit prevalent in the South. They placed an emphasis on worship (biblically sound, simple, intelligible, and spiritually satisfying) with a focus on reading and interpreting the Bible and the administration of the two sacraments, baptism of children and adults in the name of the Trinity and by sprinkling, and the Lord's Supper, celebrated at least four times a year and sometimes more often. In 1932 the PCUS followed the PCUSA in allowing the "voluntary use" of the *Book of Common Worship* (adopted by the PCUSA in 1903), a collection of services and prayer designed to enrich the worship of congregations. Although Presbyterians were at first Psalms singers only, throughout the years they broadened their use of hymns of "human composure." *The Hymnbook* (1955) became the most widely used hymnal.

From the beginning the PCUS engaged in the support of education and missions, domestic and foreign, and also showed its social concerns. Four seminaries (Union, Richmond, Va., 1812; Columbia, Decatur, Ga., 1828; Louisville, 1901; Austin, 1902) and numerous liberal arts colleges (such as Hampden-Sydney, 1776; Davidson, 1836; Stillman, 1876; Agnes Scott, 1889; and the Presbyterian School of Christian Education, 1914) served the church, as did the *Presbyterian Outlook* (1911), the *Journal of Presbyterian History*, the *Presbyterian Survey* (1911), and the John Knox Press. Presbyterians adopted the Sunday school movement and in 1963

experimented with a graded Covenant Life Curriculum in cooperation with other denominations and under the leadership of educator Lewis Sherrill (1882–1957). After the Civil War the PCUS developed mission work among blacks and Native Americans and established churches in China, Japan, Korea, Colombia, Brazil, Mexico, Africa, Greece, and Italy. Although the denomination thought it had a special mission to preserve the "spirituality" of the church, with the prodding of such individuals as Walter L. Lingle (1868–1956), president of Davidson College, and E. T. Thompson, Presbyterians took more responsibility for dealing with social, racial, economic, and international problems. A Committee on Moral and Social Welfare was organized in 1934 to care for the moral nurture of Christians.

Although at first not ecumenically inclined, gradually the PCUS emerged from its regionalism to participate in the World Alliance of Reformed Churches (1876–77), the Federal Council of Churches (1912), the National Council of Churches (1950), and the World Council of Churches (1948). In 1982, before the reunion with the UPCUSA, the PCUS embraced in its constituency 821,008 communicant members, 4,250 churches, and 6,077 ministers.

JAMES H. SMYLIE
Union Theological Seminary
Richmond, Virginia

A Digest of the Acts and Proceedings of the
General Assembly of the Presbyterian Church

in the United States, 1861–1965 (1966); James H. Smylie, *A Brief History of the Presbyterians* (2003); Ernest Trice Thompson, *Presbyterians in the South*, 3 vols. (1963–73).

Prohibition

Although closely identified with the southern ethos in the 20th century, the movement to limit the sale and use of alcoholic beverages has never been an exclusively southern endeavor. The first areas touched by this effort were in the East and Midwest in the antebellum period. Prohibition, as an ideal, originated in the voluntarism of the early temperance movement. After the Civil War more advocates adopted the policy of abstinence, or "teetotalism," and followed the legislative example of the state of Maine. Such groups as the Woman's Christian Temperance Union and the Anti-Saloon League of America organized for the fight.

In the first decade of this century dry sentiment gained momentum in the South as Georgia enacted statewide prohibition. By 1910 more than two-thirds of southern counties were dry. Nationally, the economic exigencies of World War I combined with the denouement of Progressivism to bring about the passage of the 18th Amendment and the start of the prohibition period (1920–33), during which the manufacture and sale of alcoholic beverages were forbidden.

Various interpretations have been offered for this monumental struggle against liquor. Until the early 1970s liberal historiography scorned prohibitionists in general, and the southern variety in particular, as misguided provincials who eschewed genuine reform, advocating prohibition instead as a panacea for their fears about a changing America.

Recent scholarship has been more sympathetic to the prohibitionist cause, finding a greater degree of diversity among its adherents. For example, not all members of the liturgical churches opposed prohibition. Patrick Henry Callahan, a leading southern Catholic layman, actively supported prohibition. Moreover, studies of individual psychological crises of the late 19th and early 20th centuries indicate that alcohol abuse did, indeed, cause severe economic and social distress. Alcoholism particularly attacked the prevalent middle-class ideal of family autonomy. In effect, the methods now used to study the drug subculture are being applied to alcoholism, past and present.

The presidential election of 1928 solidified the southern consensus favoring prohibition. Many southerners voted against Al Smith because of his lack of support for prohibition, though their votes were read as anti-Catholic. After the repeal of national prohibition in 1933, the South became the bastion of dry support in the nation. While Mississippi opted for statewide prohibition, other southern states adopted some form of local option and allowed municipalities and counties, even precincts, to decide the issue. Will Rogers once commented that "southerners will vote dry as long as they can stagger to the polls." In the present decade, more southerners live in areas of strict alcohol control than any other region of the United States.

Consequently, the bootlegger and moonshiner have continued to ply their trades, often with the full cooperation of local authorities. Most southern communities have legends about the classic confrontations between moonshiner and revenue agent.

With the development of the Sunbelt South and urbanization, legalization of liquor without restriction has become more common. However, conservative and fundamentalist Christian groups oppose such change in southern mores and often still muster enough votes to win local wet-dry elections.

WILLIAM ELLIS
Eastern Kentucky University

Jack S. Blocker Jr., *American Temperance Movements: Cycles of Reform* (1989); Paul A. Carter, *Another Part of the Twenties* (1977); Norman H. Clark, *Deliver Us from Evil: An Interpretation of American Prohibition* (1976); James H. Timberlake, *Prohibition and the Progressive Movement, 1900–1920* (1963).

Protestant Episcopal Church

The earliest English settlers at Jamestown brought their Anglican religion with them. With the American Revolution, though, the Church of England became the Episcopal Church and lost its position as the established church of the South. The recovery of the Episcopal Church in the South from its near extinction after the Revolution was brought about through the work of strong leaders, many of them southerners, such as Richard Channing Moore, the second bishop of Virginia, who was a New Yorker, and the second and third bishops of South Carolina, Theodore Dehon and Nathaniel Bowen, who were New Englanders. Stark Ravenscroft, the first bishop of North Carolina, was born in Virginia but educated in Scotland and England.

The degree to which Episcopalians in the South felt isolated from their northern brethren by cultural factors before the late 1830s is difficult to discern. The American Colonization Society, whose aim was to colonize parts of West Africa with freed black slaves, received active support from such Episcopalians as William Meade, later third bishop of Virginia. The existence of slavery was recognized as a factor of southern culture that the church, per se, was unable to eliminate. The church thus aimed to convert blacks and to influence owners and other whites to treat slaves humanely.

Many southern Episcopalians sent their sons to eastern colleges in the antebellum era but became irritated about the prevalence of antislavery sentiments there. This strengthened the felt need for a first-class collegiate institution under the control of the Episcopal Church. Leonidas Polk, bishop of Louisiana, took the lead in promoting the founding of such a college. The site chosen was on Sewanee Mountain in Tennessee, and the name chosen was the "University of the South." Some temporary buildings were erected, and the cornerstone of the proposed main building was laid just before the outbreak of the Civil War, which brought all activity to a close.

St. Mark's Episcopal Church, Mississippi City, Miss., postcard, early 20th century (Ann Rayburn Paper Americana Collection, Archives and Special Collections, University of Mississippi Library, Oxford)

Southern Episcopalians were not of one mind regarding secession. Polk so strongly supported secession that he accepted a commission as a Confederate general. Bishop Nicholas H. Cobbs of Alabama was strongly opposed, as was Bishop James Hervey Otey of Tennessee, the first chancellor of the university. Some of the clergy strongly opposed to secession left the South, but others stayed. The Protestant Episcopal Church in the Confederate States was organized after the outbreak of hostilities on the principle that the church follows nationality. No desire was expressed to end relations with the church in the North. There was little friction between the churches, and after the surrender of the Confederate forces the church in the South resumed affiliation with the church in the North, beginning with the appearance of southern representatives at the General Convention of 1865. There were problems encountered in this reunion, but resolutions condemning the actions of southern Episcopalians were defeated, and the fellowship of the church was restored. Sewanee was revived and became an important resource for the southern dioceses.

One of the urgent problems of the Episcopal Church in the postbellum South was the situation of its black membership. After emancipation, many blacks left the church. The need for clergy of their own race was acute. Undergraduate study was afforded in several schools supported by the church's Freedman's Commission, including St. Augustine College, St. Paul Normal and Industrial School, and Voorhees College. In Virginia the Bishop Payne Divinity School was established at Petersburg and provided theological instruction to black candi-

Grace Episcopal Church, St. Francisville, La., erected in 1858 (Louisiana State Board of Tourism)

South by 1900. In 1985 there were 22 more dioceses in the South than there were in 1865. Along with multiplication of dioceses came increasing differences in social, cultural, theological, and ritualistic emphases and a diminution of consultation and agreement about them. Migrants from the great urban centers of the North and East have diluted the southern mind-set, so that the sense of southern identity in the southern Episcopal Church has been muted. In the past decade the southern dioceses have faced the divisive issue of ordination of women and gay priests and bishops, a challenge facing the worldwide Anglican connection.

LAWRENCE L. BROWN
Episcopal Theological Seminary of the Southwest

Lawrence Lord Brown, *Historical Magazine of the Protestant Episcopal Church* (March 1966); Arthur Benjamin Chitty, *Reconstruction at Sewanee: The Founding of the University of the South and Its First Administration, 1857–1872* (1954); William Wilson Manross, *A History of the American Episcopal Church* (1935); Joseph H. Parks, *General Leonidas Polk, C.S.A.: The Fighting Bishop* (1962); Charles S. Sydnor, *The Development of Southern Sectionalism, 1819–1848* (1948).

dates. The commission later became the American Church Institute for Negroes and gained backing nationwide. Separate convocations for the black churches were established under the jurisdiction of the diocesan bishop, and the creation of a racial episcopate was proposed but rejected by General Convention several times.

Several dioceses founded missions in outlying areas, attracting children of working-class families lacking transportation to the mother church. Galveston, Dallas, San Antonio, and Houston in Texas furnish examples of such missions. Growing numbers of churches demanded more supervision than bishops of the older dioceses could give, so new jurisdictions were created. The Eastern Shore of Maryland was the first, in 1868; northern Texas and western Texas were set apart as missionary jurisdictions in 1874. Later divisions had added 11 new jurisdictions in the

Roberts, Oral

(b. 1918) MINISTER.

Oral Roberts was born in 1918 in Pontotoc County, Okla., the son of Ellis Melvin Roberts and Claudius Irwin. His father, a minister in the Pentecostal Holiness Church, spent most of his life pastoring small churches in the South. Oral Roberts received the Pentecostal

Oral Roberts, Pentecostal and Methodist minister, 1980s (Oral Roberts University, Tulsa, Okla.)

baptism of the Holy Spirit in 1936 and joined his father in the ministry.

A defining spiritual crisis in Roberts's early life occurred in July 1935, when he experienced what he believed was a miraculous healing from tuberculosis and stuttering during a tent meeting in Ada, Okla. Roberts believed that after his healing God called him to take healing to his generation.

In 1938 Roberts married Evelyn Lutman Fahnestock, a bright and sensible young schoolteacher whose common sense provided stability for the Roberts family and good advice for her husband throughout their lives. The two had a strong marriage, and no hint of moral scandal ever surfaced in the Oral Roberts ministry. The couple had four children; their youngest son, Richard Lee, joined the Oral Roberts minis-

try in 1968, and in 1993 he succeeded his father as president of Oral Roberts University.

In 1947, sensing that something exceptional was afoot in the post–World War II Pentecostal subculture, Roberts resigned his secure position as a local church pastor, moved to Tulsa, and launched an independent itinerant ministry. In the early 1950s the Roberts ministry boomed; he conducted healing campaigns all over the United States and in more than 50 foreign countries. Huge audiences crowded into his tents, which steadily grew in size, reaching a capacity of more than 12,500. By Pentecostal standards, Roberts's meetings were models of decorum, featuring long, Scripture-filled sermons followed by an altar call; conspicuously absent were public manifestations of the gifts of the spirit. Each service ended with Roberts praying for the sick. By the time he stopped holding campaigns in 1968, an estimated one million people had passed through his healing line, and millions more had witnessed one of his healing revivals, heard his sermons, answered his altar calls, and become financial "partners for deliverance."

In contrast to many of the less sophisticated evangelists who participated in the American healing revival, Roberts was an excellent organizer and businessman. As his ministry mushroomed, he built an efficient staff in Tulsa to handle the growing volume of mail that brought in floods of contributions and prayer requests from his partners. Within five years, Roberts had pieced together a radio network of more than 500 stations. In 1947 he began publishing a monthly magazine, *Healing Waters* (which went through a series of name changes before becoming *Abundant Life* in 1956), to keep his partners informed about his crusades and to present them with financial challenges. At the peak of his career Roberts's mailing list contained well over a million names.

Like Billy Graham, Oral Roberts grasped the enormous potential of television in the early 1950s. In 1955 he launched weekly telecasts of his crusades. The programs shocked many Americans, but they thrilled the Pentecostals, who supported Roberts's healing campaigns. At first, he was ridiculed by the press as a "fake healer," but by the late 1950s he had put together a large network of stations that blanketed the country and made him one of the most recognizable religious leaders in the world.

The healing revival of the 1950s that spawned the Roberts ministry and scores of smaller ones was supported largely by Pentecostals. In the early 1950s, Pentecostal denominations began withdrawing support from independent healing ministers whose financial appeals and healing claims grew more and more extreme. In the 1960s Roberts became a key figure in taking the Pentecostal message beyond the borders of the old-line Pentecostal denominations, and his crusades and television programs did much to lay the foundation for the charismatic movement that grew in the last quarter of the century.

In 1965 Oral Roberts University opened in Tulsa with Roberts as its president. It became the most pres-tigious Pentecostal private school in America; its futuristic campus was a showpiece for the Oral Roberts ministry. At the end of the 20th century, the university boasted a student population of more than 5,000 and was one of the fastest growing and most respected private schools in the Southwest.

In 1968 Roberts made a series of high-risk decisions that shocked many of his closest advisers. First, he stopped holding crusades and discontinued his television program. Then he resigned his ordination in the Pentecostal Holiness Church to become a Methodist minister and a member of the prestigious Boston Avenue Methodist Church in Tulsa. Roberts insisted that he had changed none of his convictions, but he believed that the charismatic message had broadened its appeal to other traditions.

Then, in 1969, Roberts returned to television in primetime with a series of hour-long specials. Slickly produced by Hollywood producer Dick Ross, the programs featured the talented World Action singers from Oral Roberts University and a stream of well-known show business personalities. The shows were stunning financial and programming successes, attracting viewing audiences as large as 64 million. Roberts proved that well-produced religious programs could compete with secular programming, launching the modern entertainment-based electronic church. A 1980 Gallup Poll revealed that 84 percent of the American public recognized the name Oral Roberts.

By the mid-1970s Oral Roberts had done much to improve his public image and escape the stigma of being a "faith healer." But he entered a new period of controversy when he announced in 1975 that Oral Roberts University would add a School of Medicine and that his ministry would erect a huge "City of Faith" medical complex. This venture placed unbearable financial strains on the ministry, and he was forced to abandon the scheme in 1990.

During the years when the City of Faith was being constructed, Roberts resorted to some of the most high-pressure fund-raising techniques ever employed by television evangelists, once again raising thunderous objections from critics. Coincidentally, Roberts's extreme appeals for funding came at the same time that a media frenzy focused on sexual and financial scandals involving evangelists Jim Bakker and Jimmy Swaggart. Although no hint of financial or moral wrongdoing ever surfaced in Roberts's life or ministry, in the public mind Roberts's appeals to build the City of Faith were seen as a part of a pattern of irresponsibility in independent ministries.

While not a theologian, Oral Roberts thought seriously about the basic tenets of his belief in miracles, healing, and the gifts of the Holy Spirit. Perhaps more than any other single person, he has been responsible for adding the "prosperity message" to Pentecostal theology, a concept that gave divine approval to success and money. In the final analysis, Roberts's most significant contribution to the Pentecostal/charismatic movement has been his ability to popularize the content of the theology. He has summa-rized his message in phrases repeated thousands of times on television and in print: "Something good is going to happen to you"; "God is a good God"; "Expect a miracle"; "He that is in you is greater than he that is in the world."

Oral Roberts has been a consummate subjective personality who has believed that his feelings are nothing less than the voice of God. When he felt strongly that God was leading him, his determination to obey has been virtually unmovable, even if God's instructions were fraught with difficulties and dangers. During his long career he has made many critical decisions that left his imprint on healing revivalism, religious television, Pentecostal theology, Christian education, and the spread of the charismatic movement around the world.

DAVID EDWIN HARRELL JR.
Auburn University

David Edwin Harrell Jr., *All Things Are Possible: The Healing and Charismatic Revivals in Modern America* (1975), *Oral Roberts: An American Life* (1985); Evelyn Roberts, *His Darling Wife, Evelyn* (1976); Oral Roberts, *Expect a Miracle: My Life and Ministry* (1995); Wayne A. Robinson, *Oral: The Warm, Intimate, Unauthorized Portrait of a Man of God* (1976).

Sacred Places

Does the religious life of the South, centering in evangelical Protestantism, really acknowledge specific sites to which some kind of sacred significance is attached? Not so, of course, if the question assumes a classic catholic frame of reference. In several other respects, however, it does. In the South, the dominance of center to left-wing Protestantism dictates the particular terms on which certain places are recognized as very special, even sacred.

Sacred places fall into four categories (examples are given below). The first is places where denominations had their American start or where momentous events have occurred in their history. The second is locales where indigenous denominations or movements originated. The third is religious "capital cities," that is, headquarters of denominations or clusters of religious institutions. The fourth is major conference or retreat centers. There are many other notable places in the image-life and actual practice of the southern faithful, not least among them churches, rural and urban, to which people return for annual homecomings and the cemeteries that sometimes adjoin them.

(1) Jamestown, Va., is a notable place for Episcopalians because of the Church of England's placement there in 1607; Sewanee, Tenn., home of the University of the South, is the church's modern "capital." Similarly, Bardstown, Ky., for Roman Catholics, reflects on their forebears' settlement in the West, and of course St. Augustine, Fla., dates from 1565. Methodists point with pride to Lovely Lane Chapel in Baltimore, where their church in the United States was officially launched in 1784, and to Frederica and Savannah in Georgia, the initial stopping point for John Wesley on his visit to the colonial South in 1733. Several groups claim Savannah and Charleston, including Jews, who established early settlements in both

places; Unitarians in the latter case; and black Catholics in the former. Black Baptists revere Silver Bluff Church near Augusta, the first black church in North America, founded around 1773, and Gillfield Church in Petersburg, Va., which dates from the 18th century and was notable for controlling its internal affairs throughout the slavery era.

(2) The Stone-Campbell Tradition (Disciples of Christ, Churches of Christ), which is a part of restorationist Christianity, celebrates Bethany, W.Va., and Cane Ridge near Paris, Ky., co-originating places for that movement. Pentecostalists, a rather diverse family, all take pleasure in memories of Dunn, N.C., Franklin Springs, Ga., and Hot Springs, Ark.

(3) Nashville outranks all other religious "capital cities." Baptists and Methodists have major installations there, especially in the publishing industry. Probably more church people visit Nashville than any other sacred place. Springfield, Mo., in the border South, is a headquarters for fundamentalist Baptists and Pentecostalists.

(4) In western North Carolina, Presbyterians summer at Montreat, Methodists confer at Lake Junaluska, and Southern Baptists throng to Ridgecrest. Most denominations sponsor regional and state conference and retreat centers across the region.

Pilgrimages, shrines, and holy places as such are not part of southern evangelicalism's outlook. The general religious climate does not provoke their creation or acknowledgment. Yet in ways that accord with the regional cul-

Serpent handlers of eastern Kentucky, 1946 (National Archives, Washington, D.C.)

ture, the South has its share of "sacred places."

SAMUEL S. HILL
University of Florida

Samuel S. Hill, ed., *Encyclopedia of Religion in the South* (1984).

Serpent Handlers

These religious people are members of various independent Pentecostal Holiness churches who interpret Mark 16:18 ("They shall take up serpents") as an injunction to use poisonous snakes in religious services. At least two nights every week they gather in their one-room frame houses of worship and, to the accompaniment of loud rhythmic music, handle rattlesnakes, copper-heads, and other venomous snakes with complete abandon. Sometimes they place the snakes on top of their head, wrap them around their neck, tread on them with bare feet, or toss them to other worshippers. Bites are surprisingly infrequent and are generally seen as evidence that the victim experienced a wavering of faith or failed to follow the Holy Ghost. Most devotees refuse to consider medical treatment for a bite, preferring to trust the Lord for their healing. Since the start of the snake-handling movement in 1913, at least 80 men and women have died from snake-bites suffered in religious meetings. The movement's early leader was George W. Hensley, an illiterate preacher from eastern Tennessee. It began in the coal-mining areas of the Appalachians, at a time when the region was beginning the process of economic modernization.

The great majority of snake handlers live in the southern highlands, in ordinary towns, hamlets, and hollows scattered throughout the region. With very few exceptions they are whites, descendants of English and Scots-Irish pioneers who settled in the mountains in the period between 1780 and 1840. Their daily lives differ in no essential respects from those of neighboring unbelievers. The men work in the mines, mills, and factories, while the women attend to domestic chores. Snake handlers are people of limited formal education. Some of the older members can neither read nor write.

It would be an error to see the snake-handling religion as a gross aberration in southern religious life. The roots of the snake-handling movement lie deep in the religious heritage of the South—in the Methodism of John Wesley and the frontier revivals and backwoods camp meetings of the early 19th century. Moreover, with the exception of the practices of snake handling, fire handling, and strychnine drinking, there is no element of ritual or belief in the snake-handling religion that is not found in conventional Pentecostal Holiness churches throughout the South. And even these dangerous ritual practices are, after all, based on a literal interpretation of Scripture and on the idea (common to Pentecostal people in the South and everywhere else) that the spirit of God can "move upon" believers and empower them to perform extraordinary and unusual acts.

Despite state and municipal laws prohibiting handling of poisonous snakes, and despite the ever increasing number of snakebite fatalities, snake handlers remain firm in the conviction that they are "doing the will of the Lord." Their religion continues to draw new adherents even today. Most of these people are sons and daughters of veteran followers of the movement. Some families can claim three and even four generations of followers in the faith.

STEVEN M. KANE
University of Rhode Island

Fred Brown and Jeanne McDonald, *The Serpent Handlers: Three Families and Their Faiths* (2000); Thomas Burton, *Serpent-Handling Believers* (1993); Steven M. Kane, *Appalachian Journal* (Spring 1974), *Journal of American Folklore* (October–December 1974), *Ethos* 10 (1982), in *Encyclopedia of Religion in the South*, ed. Samuel S. Hill (1984), in *Perspectives on the American South*, vol. 4, ed. James C. Cobb and Charles R. Wilson (1987); David L. Kimbrough, *Taking Up Serpents: Snake Handlers of Eastern Kentucky* (1995); Weston La Barre, *They Shall Take Up Serpents* (1962); Scott Schwartz, *Faith, Serpents, and Fire: Images of Kentucky Holiness Believers* (1999).

Shakers

The people who took the name of United Society of Believers in Christ's Second Appearing began as a dissenting group among English Quakers. Mother Ann Lee and her followers came to America and founded a settlement in New York in 1774. The Shakers—short for "shaking Quakers"—received their name from the spiritually ecstatic, fre-

Members of the Pleasant Hill Shaker village going to worship meeting, 1890 (Collection of Shaker Museum at South Union, Ky.)

netic whirling and dancing of their religious meetings. They founded the agricultural community of Pleasant Hill in the bluegrass country of Kentucky in 1805 and the South Union community soon after near the Tennessee border with Kentucky. Shaker settlements believed in equality among blacks and whites, women and men; cooperative living; celibacy; nonviolence; and simplicity in living. They depended for continuity on recruiting new members and on raising orphans who one day would become adult members of the group. Members lived in groups of 30 to 100 people called families, each with its own residence, barns, workshops, and industries.

The Shaker communities were the most successful utopian settlements of the antebellum South. They ran well-operated farms. Pleasant Hill pioneered in establishing nurseries and orchards in Kentucky, new crops, the silk industry, experimentation with new seed varieties, and the importation of new breeds of sheep and hogs. They were inventive and not afraid of new technology. They made distinctive pottery, quilts, rugs, bonnets, silk scarves, brooms, cedar pails, and churns. They were noted for an aesthetic tradition favoring simplicity and functionality in design. Shaker furniture was of clean, wooden construction. Northeastern Shakers used pine, but those in Kentucky primarily worked with cherry, walnut, and, to a lesser degree, oak. Architecture stressed solid buildings, of brick and stone, with little embellishment and arranged in symmetrical patterns. Shaker music was an important part of their culture. Hymns were passed along from member to member by letter until the first hymnal appeared in 1813.

The Shaker communities of the South suffered physical and financial damage during the Civil War, as these pacifists cared for both Union and Confederate soldiers. After the war their decline continued, as the Shakers were increasingly unable to recruit new members. Pleasant Hill closed in 1910 and South Union in 1922. Restoration efforts at Pleasant Hill began in 1961, and the restored farm reopened for public tours in 1968.

CHARLES REAGAN WILSON
University of Mississippi

Thomas D. Clark and Gerald Ham, *Pleasant Hill and Its Shakers* (1968); Julia Neal, *The Kentucky Shakers* (1982); Mary Richmond, *Shaker Literature: A Bibliography*, 2 vols. (1976).

Southern Baptist Convention

No other major denomination has shaped white southern religion and culture as powerfully or as long as has the Southern Baptist Convention (SBC). Organized in 1845 as a result of disagreement with northern Baptists over slavery and sectionalism, the SBC became the official "established" church of the South and America's largest Protestant denomination. While retaining a traditional Baptist emphasis on local church autonomy, freedom of conscience, and individualistic conversion, the SBC united a fiercely independent constituency around southern culture, denominational programs, and missional zeal. White southern culture provided a core of values, myths, and symbols that enhanced denominational stability; the denomination itself reinforced them. By sanctioning the southern white way of life—economics, politics, morality, race—Southern Baptists helped preserve regional unity among whites following the Civil War and validated their own continued existence as a distinct Baptist denomination.

The denomination was the means by which a defeated people sought to reclaim their region and to distinguish themselves from their northern counterparts and other "independent" Baptists in the South. Southerners rejected the northern Baptist "society" approach to denominational endeavors for a more centralized "convention" system, which coordinated activities of all agencies. Autonomous local churches united in order to accomplish broader evangelical tasks than their individual resources could facilitate.

While general theological consensus prevails, Southern Baptist churches are heirs of diverse theological traditions. Some represent a Regular Baptist tradition incorporating Calvinism, orderly worship, and a strong commitment to education. Others reflect a Separate Baptist heritage of modified Calvinism, revivalistic worship, and an antieducational bias. Still other segments reveal fundamentalist, Arminian, sectarian, and moderately liberal perspectives. Denominational solidarity and southern cultural stability long provided a sense of "Southern-Baptistness" that held theological diversity in check.

Southern Baptist evangelical zeal has focused primarily on individual conversion and personal morality, often ignoring the corporate sins of southern society. In so doing, the denomination has witnessed significant numerical growth while perpetuating the prevailing mores of white southern culture. Preachers utilized the rhetoric of southern Populism and evangelical revivalism to awaken sinners to Christian and white southern values. The denomination sought to dominate southern culture, often without changing it.

This unity of culture and denomination protected the SBC from the doctrinal schisms that divided many Protestant denominations during the 20th century. As pluralism has overtaken their culture and their denomination, Southern Baptists have experienced a significant identity crisis. Unity and diversity, once protected by cul-

tural and denominational uniformity, have become increasingly difficult to maintain.

Beginning in the late 1970s, fundamentalists and moderates fought a bitter battle for control of the SBC. Fundamentalists had long attacked Southern Baptist seminaries as hotbeds of liberalism, with much of the conflict over the doctrine of biblical inerrancy, which is the belief that the Bible is without error in any aspect of its content, from faith to history to anthropology. Fundamentalists insisted that all SBC denominational employees should endorse inerrantist dogmas. Moderates affirmed biblical authority but rejected the absolute inerrancy of the Scriptures.

With the election of Memphian Adrian Rogers as president of the SBC in 1979, fundamentalists began a systematic and well-planned takeover of the denomination that led to their complete control, to bitter conflict with moderates, and to deep divisions among Southern Baptists. Fundamentalists have dominated the elections of presidents since then, and their presidents have used their appointive powers of the office to place those who believe in the inerrancy of the Bible on every trustee board and agency of the denomination. Those boards and agencies soon instituted doctrinal tests for employment, which led to a major exodus of those unhappy with the new rigid expectations of faith. The fundamentalists were less successful in dominating state Baptist conventions in the South, with Virginia and Texas, in particular, dominated by moderates. As a result of the controversy, new moderate Baptist organizations emerged, providing new connections for missionary work, education, publication, and fellowship. Among these new groups are the Alliance of Baptists (1986), the Cooperative Baptist Fellowship (1991), and Texas Baptists Committed (1991). Each group drew individuals and churches previously a part of the SBC.

BILL J. LEONARD
Southeastern Seminary
Wake Forest University

John Lee Eighmy, *Churches in Cultural Captivity: A History of the Social Attitudes of Southern Baptists* (1972); Bill J. Leonard, *Baptist Quarterly* (June 1985); Walter B. Shurden, *The Struggle for the Control of the Southern Baptist Convention* (1993); Rufus B. Spain, *At Ease in Zion: A Social History of Southern Baptists* (1961).

Sunday Schools

Sunday schools have played an important role in the South, especially in the decades following the Civil War. Initially a secular institution whose modern origins date from late 18th-century England, Sunday schools had been established in some southern towns and cities by the post-Revolutionary period. The Sunday school became increasingly religious in focus as church officials recognized the importance of establishing a place for children within the church and of guiding their spiritual and moral development. Statistics showed over time that most conversions occurred as a result of children's Sunday school involvement, and denominational leaders saw them as the best means to recruit new church members.

Northern religious organizations played a role in establishing southern Sunday schools by sending agents to organize them and encourage children to dedicate their lives to God. After the Civil War, the American Sunday School Union and other northern organizations made even greater efforts to uplift what they viewed as a religiously destitute region and enhance the spiritual lives of its youngsters. Gradually southern denominations began to compete for the souls of children by founding their own schools. With modernization and expansion came increased bureaucratization of the institution as Sunday school committees and state and regional boards took charge. Yet to ensure an appeal to children, hymn singing, competitive games, and Sunday school picnics and parades became well integrated into the curriculum. Adult Sunday schools became popular by the early 20th century as a means to ensure Sunday school growth, enhance family religion, and expose grownups to important spiritual and moral lessons.

Like most southern churches, Sunday schools were segregated. African Americans saw the Sunday school as a place to uplift youngsters, instill middle-class values and good manners, teach children to read, and strengthen members' commitment to the church and the race. White Sunday schools emphasized fine manners, sound morals, punctuality, generous giving, and memorizing Scripture.

Both men and women played an important role in what became known as the Sunday school movement by the

It's RALLY DAY at Sunday School next Sunday, postcard (Charles Reagan Wilson Collection, Center for the Study of Southern Culture, University of Mississippi)

late 19th century; gender defined their participation. Women volunteered as teachers; men usually served as superintendents and officials. By the turn of the century, most major black and white denominations in the South had established or expanded their church publishing houses to produce a stream of literature for classroom and home consumption and earn profits for the church.

While responsible for much of the growth of southern churches before World War I and appealing to most Protestants, Catholics, and Jews, Sunday schools encountered opposition from a few fundamentalist sects such as Primitive Baptists. Traditionalists questioned an institution that supplanted the central role of the church, the fact that the Bible failed to mention its existence, and its secular lessons. Nevertheless, Sunday schools continued

to expand throughout the early 20th century in most southern churches and synagogues.

Today, the Sunday school attracts less attention than it did a century ago and has experienced a decline in attendance. Yet in many southern churches and families, Sunday classes for both children and adults remain important, reflecting the region's deep concern for religion and family.

SALLY G. MCMILLEN
Davidson College

James D. Anderson, *The Education of Blacks in the South, 1865–1935* (1988); Anne M. Boylan, *Sunday School: The Formation of an American Institution, 1790–1880* (1988); Sally G. McMillen, *To Raise Up the South: Sunday School in Black and White Christianity, 1865–1915* (2002).

Thornwell, James Henley

(1812–1862) PRESBYTERIAN
CLERGYMAN AND THEOLOGIAN.
Religious educator, editor, and author,
James Henley Thornwell was born in
Marlboro District, S.C.; graduated from
South Carolina College in 1831; studied
at Andover Theological Seminary, Har-
vard, and Presbyterian Theological
Seminary (Columbia, S.C.); and was
licensed to preach in 1834. He served
several churches for short periods of
time and took part in the affairs of
the Presbyterian Church in the United
States of America (PCUSA; Old School)
beginning in 1837 when he attended his
first General Assembly, being elected
moderator in 1847. He was elected professor of metaphysics at South Carolina
College in 1837 and taught at that institution until 1855, serving as president
after 1851. In 1855 he became professor
of didactic and polemic theology at the
Presbyterian Theological Seminary, a
position he held until his death.

Thornwell was known as a careful
logician, for his biblicism, and for his
Calvinist orthodoxy because of his defense of the Westminster Confession
of Faith with ideas of Francis Bacon
and the aid of the Scottish philosophy
of the 18th-century Enlightenment. As
churchman, he held to a strict interpretation of doctrine and structure. He
opposed, for example, the development
of boards for furthering the church's
work because they did not conform to
biblical or doctrinal standards of ecclesiastical accountability. As educator he
supported the teaching of new scientific
knowledge, confident of the harmony
of Christian faith and God's created
order. He also supported public education in the state of South Carolina. He
edited the *Southern Quarterly Review*
and the *Southern Presbyterian Review*
for a time.

Referred to as the Calhoun of the
church, Thornwell used his skills as an
author to support the institution of
slavery on biblical and natural grounds,
calling not for the condemnation of
the master-slave relationship but for
its regulation. When the Civil War
erupted, he defended the South and
accused the General Assembly of the
PCUSA of unbiblical and unnatural
meddling in the affairs of state and
of thus violating the true "spiritual"
character of the church. He encouraged the Synod of South Carolina to
endorse political as well as ecclesiastical
secession and took part in the organization of the Presbyterian Church in the
Confederate States of America, which
became the Presbyterian Church in the
United States after the war. His pam-
phlet "The State of the Country" was
widely circulated, and he was the principal author of the new denomination's
"Address to All the Churches of Jesus
Christ throughout the Earth" in 1861.
Although he did not write or publish a
systematic theology, *The Collected Writings of J. H. Thornwell* (4 vols., 1871–73)
was edited and published by J. B. Adger
and J. L. Gireadeau, assuring his continued influence among Presbyterians
and in the South.

JAMES H. SMYLIE
*Union Theological Seminary
Richmond, Virginia*

Theodore Dwight Bozeman, "A 19th Century Baconian Theology: James Henley Thornwell, an Enlightenment Theologian" (T.M. thesis, Union Theological Seminary, Richmond, Va., 1970), *Journal of Presbyterian History* (Winter 1972); James O. Farmer Jr., *The Metaphysical Confederacy: James Henley Thornwell and the Synthesis of Southern Values* (1986); E. Brooks Holifield, *The Gentleman Theologians: American Theology in Southern Culture, 1795–1860* (1978); Benjamin M. Palmer, *The Life and Letters of J. H. Thornwell* (1875).

INDEX OF CONTRIBUTORS

Page numbers in boldface refer to articles.

Christadelphians, 59
Christian academies, 58
Christian Baptist, 127, 174
Christian Broadcasting Network (CBN),
41, **179–80**
Christian Century, 181
Christian Church, 126, 174
Christian Coalition, 113, 124, 197
Christian Index, 147
Christianity Today, 79
Christian Purities Fellowship, 59
Christian Right, 180, 197
Christian Scientists, 156
Christian Union, 23
Christ's Sanctified Holy Church, 59
Church Dogmatics (Barth), 47
Church mothers, 162
Church of Christ, 22, 50, 126, 128, 155, 171,
173, 177, 210
Church of England, 69, 111, 164, 204
Church of God (Anderson, Ind.), 23
Church of God (Cleveland, Tenn.), 62, 110,
126, 131
Church of God in Christ (Memphis,
Tenn.), 109, 110, 131
Church of God Mountain Assembly
(Jellico, Tenn.), 23
Church of God of Prophecy (Cleveland,
Tenn.), 23, 109
Church of Jesus Christ of Latter-day
Saints, 62, 126
Church of the Covenant (Houston, Tex.),
143
Church of the Nazarene, 23
Church sports leagues, 150
Churches, country, xviii, **49–54**; music
of, 50; political causes of, 50; and sec-
tarianism, 50; origins of, 51; power of,
51; and Rural Life movement, 51; black,
52; and Country Life Commission, 52;
pastors' salaries in, 52; within Southern
Baptist Convention, 52; problems with,
52–53; consolidation of, 53; membership statistics of, 53; proposed solutions
for, 53; Sunday schools and youth

groups in, 53; and women's programs,
53; resistance to change, 54
Church Women United, 56, 57
City of Faith (Oral Roberts University),
209
Civil rights, **54–58**; and freedom singing,
54; leadership of, 54, 56; and Martin
Luther King Jr., 54; music inspired by,
54; roles of women in, 56; seculariza-
tion of movement, 56; white church
response to, 56, 57, 58; and politics, 112
Civil Rights Act of 1964, 190
Civil Rights in Recent Southern Fiction
(Dabbs), 181
Civil War, 166; and black religion, 37;
and Calvinism, 48; as "Holy War," 48,
166; missionary activities during,
95
Clark Atlanta University (Ga.), 158
Clark University (Worcester, Mass.), 181
"Clean up America" campaign, 183
Clements, William M., 65
Clergy, black, 37, 54
Cleveland, Tenn., 62, 109
Clinton, Bill, 42
Clinton, J. J., 169
Cobbs, Nicholas H., 205
Cockfighting, 147, 148, 149
Coke, Thomas, 170
Coker, Daniel, 37
Coker College (Hartsville, S.C.), 181
Collected Poems (Merton), 191
Collected Writings of J. H. Thornwell, 218
Colleges and universities, black, 37
Colored Methodist Episcopal Church, 37
Color Purple, The (Walker), 93
Columbia, S.C., 29
Columbia Presbyterian Seminary (De-
catur, Ga.), 98, 202
Columbia Theological Seminary (Atlanta,
Ga.), 47, 158
Columbia University (New York, N.Y.),
181, 191
Commission on Interracial Cooperation,
57, 140, 159

Committee for the Survival of a Free
  Congress, 196
Committee of Southern Churchmen, 176
Committee on Moral and Social Welfare,
  202
Communion, 1, 6, 8–9
Compromise of 1850, 85
Cone, James, 38
Congregational Church (Charleston,
  S.C.), 156
Congregationalist Church, 26, 47, 64
Congress of Racial Equality, 140
Conjectures of a Guilty Bystander (Mer-
  ton), 191
Conjure, 35, 37
Conservative Jewish movement, 84
Consolidated American Baptist Mission-
  ary Convention, 199
Continental Lutheranism, 64
Convention, The (Campbell), 176
Conversion, 154
Cooperative Baptist Fellowship, 216
Copeland, Kenneth, 43
Coral Ridge Hour, The (television pro-
  gram), 42
Coral Ridge Presbyterian Church (Fort
  Lauderdale, Fla.), 42
Cotton-Patch Gospels (Jordan), 140
Council on Biblical Manhood and
  Womanhood, 163
Councils on Human Relations, 56
Counterculture, religious, 42
Country Life Commission, 52
Covenant Life Curriculum, 202
Covington, Dennis, 94
Craig, Lewis, 71
Cram, Ralph Adams, 26
Creeks, 72, 102, 103
Crescent City, Fla., 75
Cristero Revolution, 86
Criswell, W. A., 159
Crozer Theological Seminary (Chester,
  Pa.), 189
Cuban Catholic Church, 86, 87
Cuban Revolution, 86

"Culture wars," 42
Cumberland Presbyterians, 22, 57, 71, 72
Curanderismo, 86, 87
Curry, Connie, 57

Dabbs, James McBride, 48, **181**
Dabney, Robert Lewis, 47, 48, 201
Dallas, Tex., 27, 33
Dallas Theological Seminary (Tex.), 77,
  79
Dalton, Ga., 61
Darrow, Clarence, 76
Davidian Seventh-day Adventists, 59
Davidson College (Davidson, N.C.), 202
Dayton, Amos Cooper, 130
Dayton, Tenn., 76
De Hann, Richard, 43
DeBose, Bishop, 99
"Declaration of Faith" (Presbyterian
  Church), 201
Deep South Regional Humanities Center
  (Tulane University), xiii
Dehon, Theodore, 204
Deism, 71, 128
Delta Insight Group (Memphis, Tenn.),
  29, 31
Democratic Party, 111, 140
Denny, Bishop, 99
Department of Racial and Cultural Rela-
  tions (Nashville, Tenn.), 175
Devil, the, 91
Dexter Avenue Baptist Church (Mont-
  gomery, Ala.), 189
Dharma, 31
Dharma Bums (Kerouac), 31
Dharma Memphis, 29
Dillard University (New Orleans, La.), 37
Directory of Worship, 201
"Dirty South," xii
Disciples of Christ, 71, 153, 155, 174, 210
Diversity, religious, xvii, xviii, **58–62**;
  of blacks, 59, 60; and civil rights, 59;
  and ethnicity, 59; impact of geography
  on, 59; race as a factor of, 59; and im-
  migration, 60; national trends of, 61;

and Wicca, 61; of Protestantism, 121; in urban areas, 156

Divorce, 137

Dixon, Amzi C., 74

Dodds, Gil, 150

Dogmatics (Brunner), 47

Dombrowski, James, 57

Dow, Lorenzo, 128

Dowie, John Alexander, 107

Dresung Loseling Institute (Emory University), 32

Drew University (Madison, N.J.), 140

Dubois, W. E. B., 38

Duke Chapel (Duke University), 26, 193

Duke University (Durham, N.C.), 26, 99

Dunkers, 62, 70

Dunn, N.C., 210

Durham, N.C., 26, 69

Durham, William, 109

Eagan, John J., 201

East, P. D., 176

Eckankar meditation movement, 145

Edgerton, Clyde, 94

Edict of Nantes, 62

Egerton, John, 140

Eisenhower, Dwight, 186

Ellison, Ralph, 93

El Paso, Tex., 24

Emmanuel College (Greensboro, N.C.), 64

Emory University (Atlanta, Ga.), 34, 98, 158, 193; chapel of, 27

England, John, **182**

Enlightenment, the, 47, 154, 218

Episcopal Church. *See* Protestant Episcopal Church

Ervin, Sam, 184

Ethnic Protestantism, **62–65**; roots in backcountry, 62

European American Studies Association, xiii

Evangelical Protestantism, xvii, 35; in Africa, 37; in rural areas, 49, 50, 51; diversity of, 61; as dominant religion, 61; within folk church, 66

Evil, 91, 92

Evolution, Darwinian, 74, 98, 112, 196; in public schools, 75, 99, 112; crusade against by Fundamentalists, 75, 76, 99; at Baylor University, 76

Fahnestock, Evelyn Lutman, 207

Faith and Life Community (University of Texas), 140

Faiths Together (Houston, Tex.), 29

Falcon, N.C., 109

Falwell, Jerry, 42, 43, 76, 77, 113, 140, 142, **183–84**, 197; as creator of Moral Majority, 42, 195; and opposition to political action, 42, 112

Family values, 124

Fanning, Tolbert, 128

Fard, Master, 80

Farmer, James, 140

Fast, Howard, 175

Fatalism, **184–85**

Faulkner, William, 89, 90, 92, 93, 172, 191; Calvinist influences on, 49; religious symbols in works of, 49; Baptist characters of, 91; black preachers in the work of, 117; and Fatalism, 184, 185

Fayetteville State University (Fayetteville, N.C.), 169

Federal Council of Churches, 178, 202

Fellowship of Southern Churchmen, 56, 57, 112, 140

Fellowship of the Concerned, 140

Feminism, 196

Fence Rail, The, 74

Ferris, William, xvi, 66

Festival of Faiths (Memphis, Tenn.), 29

Few, William Preston, 100

Fifth Avenue Methodist Church (Wilmington, N.C.), 96

"Fire and Cloud" (Wright), 93

Fire Baptized Holiness Church, 131

Fire handling, 212

First Baptist Church (Austin, Tex.), 27

First Baptist Church (Charleston, S.C.), 94

First Baptist Church (Dallas, Tex.), 159

First Baptist Church (Fort Worth, Tex.), 74, 76

Fisk University (Nashville, Tenn.), 37

Florida, 75, 147; Catholic churches in, 27; Sikhs in, 33; Cuban immigrants to, 60, 86; New Age religion in, 105

Florida Southern College (Lakeland), 27

Flush Times of Alabama and Mississippi, The (Baldwin), 72

Folk medicine, 68

Folk religion, **65–69**; as "unofficial religion," 65; and emphasis on evangelism, 66; informality of, 66; isolation of, 66; music of, 66, 68; and orientation toward the past, 66; preachers of, 66, 68; and Providence, 66; and scriptural literalism, 66; and sectarianism, 66; worship services of, 66; and Calvinism, 68; and faith healing, 68; familialism of, 68; and folktale sermons, 68; international, 68; and lack of hierarchy, 68; in literature, 68; vestiges of in mainline churches, 68

Foote, Julia, 162

Ford Foundation, xv

Foreign Mission Board, 96, 195

Formula of Concord, 152

Forsyth, John, 182

Fort Lauderdale, Fla., 42

Four Horsemen of the Apocalypse, The (Graham), 186

Franciscan Friars (St. Augustine, Fla.), 146

Frank, Leo, 156

Franklin, C. L., 117

Franklin, Sam, 57

Franklin Springs, Ga., 210

Frederica, Ga., 210

Freedom Rides, 140

Freedom Road (Fast), 175

Freedom Singers, 54

Free Will Baptist Church, 22

French Church (Charleston, S.C.), 63

Frontier Baptists, 95

Frontier religion, **69–73**, 187; in colonial frontier, 69; phases of, 69; Bap-

tist, 70; and dissent within Anglican Church, 70; and Great Awakening, 70; and Presbyterian Church, 70; of trans-Appalachian West, 70; and Great Revival, 71; in Kentucky and Tennessee frontier, 71; lack of piety of, 71; conditions of, 72; in Deep South, 72; and expulsion of Indians, 72; preaching styles in, 72; segregation of, 72; slaves in, 72; Jewish, 84; Restorationist, 126

Fulbright, J. W., 184

Full Gospel Businessmen, 68

Fundamentalism, **73–79**, 215; and Darwinism, 73, 74; and liberal theology, 73; northern origins of, 73, 79; and secular trends, 73; after World War II, 73; and Bible conferences, 74; and creed of theological concerns, 74; and Niagara Bible Conference, 74; Northern, 74; southern conduits of, 74; efforts to curtail liberalism, 75; links with evangelicals, 75; after World War I, 75; after Scopes Trial, 76; and independent Bible churches, 77; interdenominational, 77; moderate, 77; political agenda of, 78, 112; in politics, 77, 78; and rejection of separatism, 77; and Republican Party, 78; and rise of neoevangelicalism, 77; and theological orthodoxy, 153

Fundamentals, The, 74

Furman, Richard, 94, 95

Gambling, 113, 147, 148, 149

Gandhi, Arun, 29, 33

Gandhi, Mohondas K., 29, 33, 191–92

Gantry, Elmer, 68

Gaustad, Edwin, 171

Geertz, Clifford, xv

General Assembly and Church of the Firstborn, 59

General Association of Landmark Baptists, 130

General Council of the Assemblies of God, 131

81; acceptance of, 82; anti-Semitism, 82, 83, 84; colonial migration of, 82; American Reform Judaism, 83, 84, 156; European, 83; gender roles of, 83; gentile tolerance of, 83; and Haskalah (Jewish Enlightenment), 83; modification of practices of, 83, 84; Orthodox, 83, 84, 156; and anti-Zionism, 84; Conservative Jewish movement, 84, 156; frontier, 84; kashruth laws, 84; practices, customs, and traditions of, 84; schools of, 84; and Second Great Awakening, 84; secularization of, 84; third migration, 84; urban, 84, 85, 156; dissipating congregations of, 85; portrayed in literature, 94; politics of, 113; spirituality of, 144; sacred places of, 210

Jim Crow statutes, 37, 103, 112, 159

John Knox Press, 202

Johns Hopkins University (Baltimore, Md.), 98

Johnson, James Weldon, 38

Johnson, Lyndon, 189

Jones, Absalom, 169

Jones, Bob, Jr., 76, 77

Jones, Bob, Sr., 76, 77

Jones, Charles (activist), 57

Jones, Charles (sea captain), 96

Jones, Charles Price (church leader), 109

Jones, Fay, 27

Jones, Sam, 76, 157

Jordan, Clarence, 140

Journal of Presbyterian History, 202

Joyner, Charles, 181

Joy Unspeakable (film), 66

Judson, Adoniram, 95

Justification, 153

Kansas, 107

Kashruth laws, 84

Katallagete, 176, 192

Kehukee Association of North Carolina, 129

Kelsey, George D., 189

Kenan, Randall, 94

Kennedy, D. James, 42, 43

Kennedy, John F., 186, 189

Kentucky, 70, 72, 127, 129, 147, 174, 192; Hindu temples in, 29; "traveling church" in, 71; Church of Christ in, 126

Kerouac, Jack, 31

Kester, Howard "Buck," 57, 140

Key West, Fla., 86

King, Ed, 57

King, Martin Luther, Jr., 105, 140, 159, 179, **189–91**, 192; and civil rights movement, 33, 38, 54; influence of Gandhi on, 33; and liberation theology, 38; and Selma to Montgomery March, 42; and Montgomery Bus Boycott, 56; and Southern Christian Leadership Conference (SCLC), 56; folktale preaching style of, 68, 117; role in politics, 112; spirituality of, 146; education of, 189; pastorate of, 189; assassination of, 190; and March on Washington, 190; and Poor People's Campaign, 190

King, Martin Luther, Sr., 54

King, Mary, 142

Kirk, Harris, 99

Know-Nothing movement, 156

Koinonia farm (Ga.), 140

Korean Baptists, 64

Korean Presbyterians, 65

Kroger, Grace, 57

Kroger, Harry, 57

Ku Klux Klan, 136, 156, 159

Lafayette, Bernard, 56

Lake Junaluska (N.C.), 145, 177, 178, 210

Lakeland, Fla., 27

La Luz del Mundo, 88

Land, Richard, 78

Landmarkism, 77

Landmark Baptists, 126, 129, 130

Lanterns on the Levee (Percy), 185

Latino religion, xviii, **85–89**; anticlericalism, 85; and mestizos, 85; and Oblates of Mary Immaculate, 85, 86; pervasiveness of, 85; Cuban, 86; and practice

March on Washington, 190
Mardi Gras, 34, 138
Marshall, Molly, 163
Mars Hill College (Mars Hill, N.C.), 150
Martin Luther King Jr. Center for Non-
    violent Social Change (Atlanta, Ga.),
    191
Mary Doyle Trust, xv
Maryland: Anglican churches in, 24;
    Catholic slaves in, 35
Mason, Charles Harrison, 109
Mather, Cotton, 68
Mayes, Benjamin, 189
McCullers, Carson, 91
McGee brothers, 71
McGill, Ralph, 48
McGready, James, 188
McKelway, Alexander, 140, 159
McKendree, William, 171
Meade, William, 204
Megachurches, 27, 124, 157
Meher Baba Clinic (Myrtle Beach, S.C.),
    29
Memphis, Tenn., 29, 109, 110, 191
Memphis Sanitation Strike, 190
Mencken, H. L., 93, 171
Mennonites, 23, 64; as pacifists, 64;
    Virginia Mennonite Conference, 65;
    Western Conservative Mennonite Fel-
    lowship, 65; similarities to Amish, 65
Mercer, Jesse, 147
Meredith, James, 176
Merton, Owen, 191
Merton, Ruth Jenkins, 191
Merton, Thomas, **191–92**
Mestizos, 85
Methodist Church, xvii, 21, 22, 63, 66,
    71, 122, 126, 128, 153, 187; architecture
    of, 26; antislavery stance of, 35; Afri-
    can Methodist Episcopal Church, 37,
    169; African Methodist Episcopal Zion
    Church, 37, 169; black, 37, 59; Colored
    Methodist Episcopal Church, 37; Meth-
    odist Episcopal Church, South, 37,
    76, 108, 192–93; and Calvinism, 48;

and country churches, 50, 52; United
    Methodist Church, 58; in Kentucky,
    71; Republican Methodists, 72; His-
    panic, 88; in literature, 90; divisions
    of, 95; missionary work of, 96; and
    modernism, 98, 99; defense of slavery,
    111; Methodist Episcopal Church, 156;
    women missionaries, 161, 162; sacred
    places of, 210
Methodist Episcopal Church, 156, 170, 192
Methodist Episcopal Church, South, 37,
    108, 178, **192–93**
Methodist Hospital (Houston, Tex.), 158
Mexican Americans, 60
Mexican Revolution, 86
Miami, Fla., 61, 86, 87
Michaelsen, Robert S., 118
Middle Eastern religions, xii
Midway, Ga., 26
Midwives, 52
Millennial Harbinger, The, 174
Millennium, 94
Miller, Francis Pickens, 201
Miller, Perry, 164
Mills, Robert, 156
Missionary activities, xvii, 21; to Africa,
    37, **94–97**; American Missionary As-
    sociation, 37; black, 37; from north-
    ern churches, 37; of Baptists, 94; and
    nationalism, 94–95; and Native Ameri-
    cans, 94, 103; American Board of Com-
    missioners for Foreign Missions, 95,
    103; General Missionary Commission
    of the Baptist Denomination in the
    United States of America for Foreign
    Missions, 95; in China, 95, 96, 194–95;
    Peking Treaties of 1860, 95; during Civil
    War and Reconstruction, 96; Foreign
    Mission Board, 96; in India and Near
    East, 96; and Lottie Moon, 96, 194–
    95; and Self-Strengthening movement,
    96; Women's Missionary Union of the
    Southern Baptist Convention, 96; non-
    denominational, 97; and modernism,
    99; led by women, 161, 162

National Cathedral (Washington, D.C.), 187

National Child Labor Association, 159

National Civil Rights Museum (Memphis, Tenn.), 191

National Council of Churches, 39, 97, 175, 176, 202

National Day of Prayer and Remembrance, 187

National Religious Broadcasters, 42

National Training School for Women and Girls (Washington, D.C.), 140

Nationalism, 95

Nation of Islam, 60, 80

Native American religion, xviii, **100–104**; after Indian removal, 72, 103; belief system, 100; importance of dreams in, 100; morality, 100; spiritual values, 100; architecture of, 101; and daily life, 101; and earthen mounds, 101; festivals, 101; as holistically associated with daily life, 101; and corn, 101, 102; of Mississippian society (900–1550 C.E.), 101; sacred sites of, 101; and Catholicism, 102; after contact with Europeans, 102; of Cherokees, 102, 103; of Choctaws, 102, 103; of Creeks, 102, 103; and disease, 102; of post-Mississippian groups, 102; and violence, 102; and Cherokee New Testament, 103; and intermarriage, 103; during Jim Crow, 103; modification of traditional practices of, 103; and Protestant missionaries, 103; revitalization of, 104

Native Son (Wright), 93

Natural theology, 154

Nature and Destiny of Man, The (Niebuhr), 47

Near East Relief, 178

Neo-Catholicism, 184

Neoevangelicalism, 77

Neomedievalism, 184

New Age Directory, 105

New Age religion, xviii, **104–6**; American Institute of Holistic Theology, 105;

among Baby Boomers, 104; lack of organization in, 104; beliefs and practices of, 105; and Eastern religion, 105; in Florida, 105; New Age Directory, 105; on Internet, 105; opposition to, 105; southern leaders of, 105; and Wicca, 105

New England Standing Order, 127

New Orleans, La., 29, 59, 169; Chinese Presbyterians in, 64; church architecture of, 157

New Religious Right, 58, 77, 113, 124, 183, 186, 195

New Seeds of Contemplation (Merton), 191

New Testament Christianity, 22

New York, N.Y., 38, 75, 169

Niagara, N.Y., 74

Niagara Bible Conference, 74

Nicene Creed, 44

Niebuhr, Reinhold, 47

Niebuhr, Richard, 193

Nixon, Richard, 186

"Noon Wine" (Porter), 92

Norris, J. Frank, 74, 77

North Carolina, 74, 80, 99, 105, 127, 129, 131, 187, 189, 210; Buddhists in, 31, 61; Highland Scot settlers in, 62; Moravians in, 63, 197; Quakers in, 64; Waldensians in, 64; Montagnard refugees in, 65; and Billy Graham's crusades, 68; Latinos in, 87, 88; camps and retreats in, 177

North Carolina Yearly Meeting of the Religious Society of Friends, 64

Northfield conferences, 75

Novel reading, 147

Nuns, Buddhist, 29, 32

Oblates of Mary Immaculate, 85, 86

Ocean Grove retreat (N.J.), 177

O'Connor, Flannery, 90, 91, 137, 172, 185, 191; and the Devil, 91; as Roman Catholic writer, 91, 137; and religion, **199–200**

O'Kelley, James, 171

Oklahoma, 29, 75, 107

Old Fashioned Revival Hour, 183

Cause, 112; and prohibition, 112; and segregation, 112; and separation of church and state, 112; of southern denominations, 112; Christian Coalition, 113, 124; and election of Ronald Reagan, 42, 78, 113; and Jews, 113; and George W. Bush, 113; and New Religious Right, 113, 124; views on social issues, 113, 114; and religious diversity, 114

Polk, Leonidas, 204

Poor Peoples' Campaign, 190

Pornography, 196

Porter, Katherine Anne, 91, 92, 137

Poteat, William Louis, 100

Preachers, black, 35, 93, **114–18**, 172; and call-and-response, 59, 60, 116; in literature, 92, 117; during Great Awakening, 114; intensity of, 115; musical experience of, 115; preaching style of, 115; education of, 116; folkloric influence on, 116; influence on black entertainers, 117; influence on white preachers, 117

Preachers, white, **118–21**, 172; as authority figures, 118; stereotypes of, 118; traveling, 118; education of, 119; power of, 119; image in literature, 120; as defenders of community, 120; influence in community affairs of, 120; as regional spokesman, 120; respect for, 120; women, 121

Predestination, 21, 45

Presbyterian Church, xvii, 21, 22, 46, 62, 63, 66, 74, 75, 122, 126, 187, 218; and Transylvania Presbytery, 22; architecture of, 26; seminaries of, 47; and Calvinism, 47–49, 152; and country churches, 50, 52; Southern Presbyterian Church in the United States (PCUS), 64, 75; Chinese Presbyterians, 65; Korean, 65; Presbyterian Church in the United States, 65, 99, 200–202; on colonial frontier, 70; and Disciples of Christ, 71; and Great Awakening, 70; in Kentucky frontier, 71; as leader in the Great Revival, 71; and Shakers,

71; in Tennessee, 71; Hispanic, 88; divisions of, 95; and modernism, 98; antievolution, 99; defense of slavery, 112; and theological orthodoxy, 155; Presbyterian Church in America, 155; women's missions, 161; and ordination of women, 163; Presbyterian Church of the Confederate States of America, 200, 218; United Presbyterian Church in the United States of America, 200; *Westminster Confession of Faith*, 201; *Book of Church Order*, 201; Declaration of Faith, 201; seminaries of, 202; sacred places, 210

Presbyterian Church in America, 155

Presbyterian Church in the United States (Presbyterian Church of the Confederate State of America), 64, 99, 163, **200–202**, 218

Presbyterian Outlook, 202

Presbyterian School of Christian Education (Richmond, Va.), 202

Presbyterian Survey, 202

Presbyterian Theological Seminary (Columbia, S.C.), 218

Pressler, Paul, 78

Primitive (Antimission) Baptists, 21, 22, 50, 72, 126, 128, 129, 155; Jacksonian ideals of, 51, 129; black members, 129; a capella signing style of, 129; National Primitive Baptist Convention of the U.S.A., 129; *Sign of the Times*, 129

Princeton Theological Seminary (N.J.), 47, 178

Prize fighting, 147, 149

Program for Research Tools and Reference Works of the National Endowment for the Humanities, xv

Progressive National Baptist Convention, 198

Prohibition, 112, 159, 179, **203–4**

Protestant Episcopal Church (Episcopal Church), 23, 62, 63, 66, 111, 122, 176, **204–6**; in Kentucky frontier, 71; Hispanic, 88; theological orthodoxy of,

152, 153; women clergy of, 163; church camps of, 178; Protestant Episcopal Church in the Confederate States, 205; black membership of, 205; and Freedman's Commission, 205; black colleges and universities of, 205; ordination of women and gays, 206; sacred places of, 210

Protestant Episcopal Church in the Confederate States, 205

Protestantism, xvii, 21, 44, 62, **121–25**; televised, 40, 125; and politics, 111–14, 124; distinctiveness of, 121; diversity of, 121; origins in revival movement, 121, 122; population of, 121; and assurance of salvation, 122, 123; during slavery and segregation, 122, 123; importance of conversion experience in, 122; preaching style of, 122; social responsibility of, 122; worship style of, 122; black, 123, 124; wartime, 123; white, 123, 124; in late twentieth century, 124; in megachurches, 124; musical tradition of, 124; secularization of, 124; theological orthodoxy of, 152; urban, 156

Providence (Campbell), 176

PTL (Praise the Lord) network, 41, 184

Purcell, John, 174

Puritans, 126, 164

Quakers, 62, 126; Monthly Meetings of, 64; in North Carolina, 64; practices of, 64; in frontier, 70, 71; English, 212

Race and the Renewal of the Church (Campbell), 176

Radio programs, religious, 40

Rainbow Coalition, 140

Raleigh, N.C., 65, 74, 81

Ramadan, 81

Randolph, Lucy Mason, 57

Randolph-Macon College (Ashland, Va.), 98, 178

Ransom, Theophilus, 128

Ravenscroft, John, 152

Ravenscroft, Stark, 204

Reagan, Ronald, 42, 78, 183

Rebirth, 154

Reconstruction, 37

Reed, John Shelton, 58, 90, 91, 172

Reed, Ralph, 142

Reformed Protestantism, 44, 62

Reformer, 128

Regent University (Virginia Beach, Va.), 180

Regular Baptists, 22, 70, 127, 128, 214

Religion and the American People (Thomas), 171

Religious Herald, 151

Religious Heritage Foundation, 188

Religious publications, 158

Religious Right, 78

Republican Methodists, 72

Republican Party, xii, 78, 111, 113, 124

Requiem for a Nun (Faulkner), 185

Restorationist Christianity, **126–32**; Baptist (Primitive and Landmark), 126, 128, 129, 130; Christian, 126, 127, 128; Church of Christ, 126, 128, 131; Holiness and Pentecostal, 126, 130, 131; influences of, 126; major movements of, 126; Mormon, 126; rejection of liturgy, 126; roots in British Protestantism, 126; in southern frontier, 126, 127; and antimissionism, 128; opposition to eastern churches, 128; pacifism of, 128; Assemblies of God, 131

Revels, Hiram R., 37

Revivalism, 74, 94, **132–34**, 154; during Great Awakening, 132, 133; during Second Awakening, 132, 133; and revival meetings, 132; and Arminianism, 133; of Billy Graham, 133; of Dwight Moody and Billy Sunday, 133; individual-based, 133, 134; hymns of, 134

Revivals, 35, 49, 62, 92, 119, 121, 132, 166

Revolutionary War, 26, 70

Rhodes College (Memphis, Tenn.), 29

Rice, David, 71

Rice, John Holt, 120

St. Michael's Episcopal Church (Charleston, S.C.), 24, 157

St. Paul Normal and Industrial School (Lawrenceville, Va.), 205

St. Philip's Episcopal Church (Charleston, S.C.), 24

St. Richard's Catholic Church (Jackson, Miss.), 27

Salem, N.C., 63

Salem, Va., 74

Salem Academy and College (Winston-Salem, N.C.), 197

Salvation on Sand Mountain (Covington), 94

Salzbergers, 62

San Antonio, Tex., 24, 151

Sanctification, 45, 153

Sanctuary (Faulkner), 92

San Jose mission (San Antonio, Tex.), 24

Sankey, Ira, 75

Santeria, 35, 60, 87, 114

Satanism, 105

Savannah, Ga., 62, 210

Scaife, Marvin F., 63

Schaeffer, Francis, 78, 79

Scholastic theology, 46, 47

Schools: Catholic, 38, 85, 87, 137, 138, 159; Christian academy, 58; Lutheran, 64; evolution taught in, 75, 99, 112; public, 75; fundamentalist, 79; Muslim, 80; Jewish, 84; prayer in, 124, 196; in urban areas, 158; private, 196; Moravian, 197

Schuller, Robert, 43

Schutt, Jane

Scofield, Cyrus I., 74, 75

Scofield Reference Bible, 75

Scofield School of the Bible (New York, N.Y.), 75

Scofield's Oral Extension department, 75

Scopes Trial, 76, 99

Scott, Walter, 173

Scottish Common Sense philosophy, 47, 154, 174

Second Baptist Church (Houston, Tex.), 158

Second Baptist Church (Richmond, Va.), 151

Second Great Awakening, 21, 84, 132, 187

Sectarianism, 50, 66

Secularization, 16, 124, 138

Segregation, 112, 138, 159

Self-Strengthening movement, 96

Selma, Ala., 42

Selma Lutheran Academy and College (Ala.), 64

Semi Tough (film), 106

Senses, the, 11–13

Separate Baptists, 21, 70, 127, 187, 214

Sephardic Jews, 81, 82, 156

September 11 terrorist attacks, 29, 34, 187

Serpent handling, 59, **211–12**; and Mark 16:18, 211; and bites, 211

700 Club (television program), 43, 180

Seven Storey Mountain, The (Merton), 191

Seventh-day Adventists, 156

Sewanee, Tenn., 204, 205, 210

Sewanee Review, 191

Seymour, William, 107

Shakers (United Society of Believers in Christ's Second Appearing), 71, 72, **212–14**

Shalem Spiritual Development Group (Washington, D.C.), 146

Shambhala Meditation Center (Asheville, N.C.), 29

Shaped note singing, 50, 66, 129

Sheen, Fulton, 40

Sherill, Lewis, 202

Sherrod, Charles, 56

Shi'a Islam, 80

Shield, T. T., 76

Shorter Catechism, The, 47

Shortridge, James R., 171

Shrine of Our Lady of Charity (Fla.), 87

Shrine of Our Lady of San Juan del Valle (Tex.), 86, 87

Shuttlesworth, Fred, 54, 140, 159

Sightler, Harold, 77

Sign of Jonas, The (Merton), 191

Sign of the Times, 129

Texas, 76, 105, 129, 147; Catholic churches in, 24; Sikhs in, 33; Tejano Catholics, 85; Pentecostals in, 107

Texas Baptists Committed, 216

Theodosia Ernest (Cooper), 130

Theological orthodoxy, 97, **152–55**; for Catholics, 152; disputes of, 152; for Protestants, 152; and Biblical interpretation, 152–53; and acceptance of salvation, 153; orthopraxy, 153; and sacraments, 153; and interpretation of Scripture, 154; as viewed by clergy, 154; diversity of, 155; and divisions of denominations, 155

Theravada (Buddhist), 31, 32

Thomas, John L., 171

Thomas Road Baptist Church (Lynchburg, Va.), 76, 183, 184, 195

Thompson, E. T., 202

Thompson, Ernest Trice, 99, 201

Thorncrown Chapel (Eureka Springs, Ark.), 27

Thornwell, James Henley, 47, 201, **218**

Tibetan Buddhism, 31

Tikkun Conference of Jewish intellectuals, 144

Tilly, Dorothy, 140

Tomlinson, Ambrose J., 23, 131, 109

Torrey, Reuben A., 74

Tougaloo College (Jackson, Miss.), 57

Town, The (Faulkner), 49

Toy, Crawford Howell, 98

Transylvania Presbytery, 22

Trinity Broadcasting Network, 41

Trinity Center (Winston-Salem, N.C.), 146

Trinity United Methodist Church (Durham, N.C.), 26

Truett Seminary (Baylor University), 145

Truman, Harry, 140

Tulane University (New Orleans, La.), xiii

Turner, Henry McNeal, 37, 140, 142, 169

Turretin, Francis, 47, 152

Tuskegee Institute (Ala.) 27

Twain, Mark, 91

Tweedie, Stephen W., 172

Twelve Step programs, 144

Two Black Churches (Ferris), 66

Two Seed in the Spirit Baptists, 59, 72

"Two-work" Pentecostals, 109

Union Gospel Tabernacle (Nashville, Tenn.), 157

Union Theological Seminary (Richmond, Va.), 47, 56, 57, 99, 202

Unitarians, 156, 210

Unitas Fratrum (Moravians), 63, 197

United Baptists, 21, 22

United Church of Christ, 56

United Methodist Church, 58, 163

United Society of Believers in Christ's Second Appearing (Shakers), 71, 72, **212–14**

United States Catholic Miscellany, 182

Unity of Brethren (Unitas Fratrum, Moravians), 63, 197

University of Arkansas (Fayetteville), 188

University of Berlin (Germany), 98

University of Massachusetts (Amherst), 189

University of Mississippi (Oxford), 175

University of North Carolina (Chapel Hill), 150

University of South Carolina (Columbia), 181; sand mandala, 32

University of Tennessee (Knoxville), 150

University of Texas (Austin), 140

University of the South (Sewanee, Tenn.), 204, 205, 210

University of Virginia (Charlottesville), xiii, 31

Urban religion, xviii, **155–60**; diversity of, 155; and African Americans, 156, 158, 159; and architecture of urban churches, 156, 157; of Catholic Church, 156; of Jewish community, 156; impact of immigration on, 156; and Northern migration, 156; post–World War II, 156; of Protestants, 156; and beautification of churches, 157; benevolent activities of,

158; and hospitals in urban areas, 158;
and megachurches, 158; and schools,
158; activism of urban whites, 159; and
community reform, 159; during the civil
rights movement, 159; social activism
of, 159
Utopian settlements, 212

Vacation Bible school, 66
Vajrayana centers, 31
Valdese Presbyterian Church (Valdese,
N.C.), 64
Valentine, Foy, 140
Valentine, Lila Meade, 159
Vanderbilt Agrarians, 181, 184
Vanderbilt Divinity School (Nashville,
Tenn.), 56
Vanderbilt School of Religion (Nashville,
Tenn.), 57
Vanderbilt University (Nashville, Tenn.),
98, 99, 142, 193
"Vanishing South," xi
Vatican II, 136, 137
Vedic Center (Greenville, S.C.), 30
Venkatesvara, 30
Vick, G. Beauchamp, 76
Violent Bear It Away, The (O'Connor), 200
Vipassana, 31
Virginia, 70, 105, 127; Anglican churches
in, 24; Mennonite settlers in, 64; Sepa-
rate Baptists in, 70; cockfighting in,
148
Virginia Anti-Saloon League, 178, 179
Virginia Mennonite Conference, 64
Virginia Polytechnic Institute and State
University (Blacksburg, Va.), xiii
Vishnu, 30
Vivian, C. T., 54
Von Zinsendorf, Count Nicholas, 63
Voodoo, 35, 60, 161
Voorhees College (Denmark, S.C.), 205
Voting Rights Act of 1965, 190

Wake Forest College (Wake Forest, N.C.),
99, 175

Wake Forest University Divinity School
(Winston-Salem, N.C.), 145
Waldensians, 63, 64; rejection of Old
World practices, 64
Waldo, Peter, 63
Walker, Alice, 93, 105
Walker, John, 174
Walker, Wyatt, T., 54
Wallace, George, 185
Warith Deen Muhammad High School
(Atlanta, Ga.), 80
Warren, Robert Penn, 91
Washington, D.C., 169, 195
Washington, James M., 199
Way of Faith, The, 109
Wesley, John, 23, 68, 130, 146, 170
Wesleyan Holiness movement, 107, 212
West, Don, 57
Western Conservative Mennonite Confer-
ence, 64
Westminster Confession of Faith, 152, 201,
218
West Point, Miss., 74
West Virginia, 29; Hindu temples in, 29
White, William, 169
Whitefield, George, 63
"White trash," xii
Whitsitt, William, 98
Who Speaks for the South? (Dabbs), 181
Wicca, 61, 105
Wilcox, James, 94
Williams, Claude, 57
Williams, Peter, 169
Williamson, Marianne, 105
Wilmington, N.C., 62, 96
Wilmore, Ky., 150
Wilson, Woodrow (Presbyterian layman),
201
Winchell, Alexander, 98
Winston-Salem State University (N.C.),
169
Wise Blood (O'Connor), 172, 200
Wofford College (Spartanburg, S.C.), 98
Wold Center (Nashville, Tenn.), 199
Women, xiii, 113, **160–63**; clergy, 121; and